MW00436020

To: _____

From: _____

Date: _____

IN THE
SHELTER
OF THE
MOST
HIGH

CHRIS JOHNSEN
& NANCY TAYLOR

CHRISTIAN ART PUBLISHERS

Published by Christian Art Publishers
PO Box 1599, Vereeniging, 1930, RSA

© 2020
First edition 2020

Designed by Christian Art Publishers
Cover designed by Christian Art Publishers

Images used under license from Shutterstock.com

Set in 12 on 15 pt Palatino LT Std by Christian Art Publishers

Printed in China

ISBN 978-1-4321-3247-7 (LuxLeather)
ISBN 978-1-4321-3404-4 (Hardcover)

HE WILL
cover you with his
FEATHERS.
HE WILL
shelter you
with his
WINGS.
HIS FAITHFUL
promises
ARE YOUR
armor and
PROTECTION.

Psalm 91:4

Introduction

In a story Jesus told, two men had the same goal: to build a house. One of them, the wise man, built his house on the rock. The other built his on the sand. When a storm hit, with torrents and floodwaters and strong winds, only one of the houses was able to withstand it—the one built on bedrock. In this story, both men had the same goal, they used similar building materials, and they faced the same hardships. The difference in whether their houses stood or collapsed was in the foundation, what they were building on.

The meaning of this parable is explicitly stated—if we are wise, we will listen to Jesus' teaching and follow it. In other words, we will build our lives on God's promises. We will put our confidence in the solid and secure foundation of what God has said in His Word rather than in the shifting winds of circumstance or public opinion. When we do this, we will stand firm in any storm.

If you think about it, people of faith are really people of the promise. God's promises are not trite afterthoughts to our faith, they are the basis of it. Trusting God is believing that God will keep His word. Our job as believers is to learn, meditate on, and proclaim what God has said He will do. It is our prayer that this devotional will help you deepen your understanding of and faith in God's promises.

The first type of promise we encounter in the Bible is the covenant. This is God's unbreakable commitment, first uttered in the Garden of Eden, then confirmed through Abraham and his descendants, that God will make a way for us to be with Him. The whole Bible fleshes out what this means, but in a nutshell, it is God promising sinful humankind that regardless of their rebellion, He will make for Himself a people, give them a homeland, and live with them in joy and blessing. At first this seemed to be all about the Jewish nation settling in the Promised Land, but eventually it became clear that the promise is really about people from all nations who put their faith in Jesus and will one day live under God's perfect rule in the new heavens and the new earth.

For those who have placed themselves under God's rule, there are even more promises—the great and precious promises that apply to every difficulty we face in life. These are the statements we can cling to even when everyone around us is falling away.

- Are you concerned about the future? God promises to be your refuge and strength (Psalm 46:1-3).
- Are you facing a health crisis? God promises to be your healer (Malachi 4:2).
- Anxious? God promises His peace (Isaiah 26:3).
- Lonely? God is always near (Psalm 16:8, 11).
- Rejected? God loves you with a steadfast love (Psalm 27:10).
- Worried about your children? God promises to be their refuge (Proverbs 14:26).

The best thing about God's promises is that they are secure and steadfast. No matter how we may feel, no matter how things may appear, no matter what storm clouds are gathering on the horizon, these things are true. We can take them at face value and live as if they are settled fact because the everlasting, unchanging, and all-powerful God has said them, and what He says, He does. Now that's something you can build a life on!

JANUARY

HOW KIND

the **LORD** is!
HOW GOOD HE IS!
SO MERCIFUL,
this God of ours!

PSALM 116:5

The Promise of Creation

God created human beings in his own image. In the image of God
he created them; male and female he created them.

—*Genesis 1:27*

God's very first action—the creation of the heavens and the earth and everything in them—was full of promise. Everything was created in perfect beauty and balance, innocent and unstained by sin. Everything God made was good, and human beings were best of all, the pinnacle of creation.

Indeed, creation wasn't "very good" until God put in it a reflection of Himself: humanity. What a promise that is for us—we have the imprint of God Himself built into our DNA. Our very existence proclaims His glory. You are a beautiful, beloved, and valuable creation of Almighty God. You matter.

God blessed humanity, enduing us with the power to succeed and prosper. He gave us a place of honor and authority over creation and promised the ability to succeed in that task. In fact, every time God blesses people in Scripture He also promises to be faithful to continue to bless and to enable us to carry out the task before us. Thus God's first promise is to maintain His connection to the creatures He loves and to continue to bless what He has made. We can trust that He is near, and He will help us to accomplish all His purposes for us.

What are mere mortals that you should think about them, human beings
that you should care for them? Yet you made them only a little lower
than God and crowned them with glory and honor. You gave them charge
of everything you made, putting all things under their authority.

—*Psalm 8:4-6*

The Blessing of Companionship

*This explains why a man leaves his father and mother and
is joined to his wife, and the two are united into one.*
—*Genesis 2:24*

God had created a perfect world and blessed Adam with meaningful work and the promise of His faithful involvement, but He wasn't done with the blessing yet. Adam needed a suitable companion, and so God gave him a wife, someone who was equally an image-bearer of God and could understand and help him. In this blessing was a promise—the promise of companionship and relationship. Human beings would not have to be alone, even when they created a separation between themselves and God through sin.

When Adam saw his bride, he burst into a poem of joyful praise: "At last I have a suitable companion!" Eve's identity as woman would serve as a continual reminder that she was taken out of "man," and the term "man" would always be a part of "woman." She was made from him and for him, and he needed her; therefore they should belong to each other and lovingly serve one another.

The blessing of companionship is one we should not take for granted. God is offering us enjoyment, comfort, and an opportunity to understand Him better through the people around us. And He is giving us the chance to reflect His glory to them as well.

Two people are better off than one, for they can help each other succeed.
—*Ecclesiastes 4:9*

*Each man must love his wife as he loves himself,
and the wife must respect her husband.*
—*Ephesians 5:33*

His Victory Is Ours

*And I will cause hostility between you and the woman,
and between your offspring and her offspring. He will
strike your head, and you will strike his heel.*

—Genesis 3:15

While many of the Bible's promises are comforting and full of hope, some of the Bible's promises are not good news at all—and this is one of them. There would be consequences to the sin Adam and Eve had committed. Now rather than a life of fellowship and joy, they would experience one of hardship and strife. Life would be a constant battle between good and evil, right and wrong. Sin cannot go unpunished because God is just.

Yet even here, even in the curse that put us all in bondage to sin and death, there is a promise and a hope. The Promised One would stamp out evil and put an end to the curse of sin and death. No sooner was the sentence for their crime passed down than the promise of gospel pardon was proclaimed. Specifically, here God promises an Incarnation (the offspring of the woman), the suffering and death of this Promised One, and His ultimate victory over Satan.

When we embrace Jesus as the promise fulfiller, we experience this victory over sin and death. His victory is ours! Even if it looks like we are losing the battle and evil has the upper hand, we are on the winning side. The battle is won. We are no longer cursed, but rather declared righteous. And this promise was made right from the beginning!

The God of peace will soon crush Satan under your feet.

—Romans 16:20

Enter the Boat

*Look! I am about to cover the earth with a flood that will destroy
every living thing that breathes. Everything on earth will die.
But I will confirm my covenant with you. So enter the boat—
you and your wife and your sons and their wives.*

—Genesis 6:18

Just a few generations after Adam and Eve, the world had become so evil that God was sorry He had made it (Genesis 6:6). So God decided to destroy His creation with a flood. The great judge over all the earth was going to rise up against evil. But He would not wipe them all out. God made a covenant promise to the one man who still feared Him, Noah, to preserve him and his family. In God's justice, there is great mercy—covenant blessing and enduring promises to preserve and rescue those who are His.

Noah's story reminds us that God rescues and redeems not based on our deserving, for none of us can measure up to His perfect standard, but because of His loving promises. For the sake of His glory, His character, and His name—things which can never fail or change, God sets His covenant love on us and keeps us in His care.

Our job, like Noah's, is to get in the boat. To put our faith in who God is and what He has said He will do. To act as if His promises are as good as done because we trust that He is the kind of God who does what He says. If we do that, we will be safely held in His everlasting arms.

*I am confirming my covenant with you. Never again will floodwaters kill
all living creatures; never again will a flood destroy the earth. . . . This rainbow
is the sign of the covenant I am confirming with all the creatures on earth.*

—Genesis 9:11, 17

A Promise for the Nations

I will make you into a great nation. I will bless you and make you famous, and you will be a blessing to others. I will bless those who bless you and curse those who treat you with contempt. All the families on earth will be blessed through you.
—*Genesis 12:2-3*

These verses make up the famous Abrahamic covenant, the promise made to Abram that is ultimately fulfilled in Christ, the one through whom we are saved. This is God's promise to make for Himself a people from every tribe and tongue and nation who will live under His rule and blessing.

In chapters 1–11 of Genesis God uttered the curse five times. Here, in Genesis 12, he blesses Abram five times, overriding the curse. It is as if God is overflowing with love for His people, and this despite the fact that humankind had become so evil that God had essentially wiped them out and started over. God makes His promises dependent on His own name and character, not our obedience or effort. In other words, He is going to undo the curse with or without us. Though we sin, God blesses. No matter what we do, God sustains those who are His.

This amazing truth isn't something we should keep to ourselves. God's promise is for all nations. Every people group, every tribe, every race is blessed through Abram's line. Jesus came to save all people, and in Him there is no distinction. All of us are equally deserving of the curse and equally recipients of the blessing if we will receive it.

There is no longer Jew or Gentile, slave or free, male and female. For you are all one in Christ Jesus.
—*Galatians 3:28*

And Abram Believed the Lord

The LORD spoke to Abram in a vision and said to him, "Do not be afraid, Abram, for I will protect you, and your reward will be great." . . . And Abram believed the LORD, and the LORD counted him as righteous because of his faith.

—*Genesis 15:1, 6*

Abram believed God's promises and stepped out in faith, leaving his homeland and his people. In a sense, he gave up every logical means to make a name and a secure future for himself and trusted that God would make a name for him. He put his future completely in God's hands.

Here we find Abram some time later, and God not only repeats His promises, but also ratifies them with a formal covenant ceremony. Nothing has changed in Abram's outward circumstances. He still has no heir, let alone descendants as numerous as the stars. Short of a miracle, that can never happen because now he is too old to have a child. He and his wife, Sarai, still have no homeland. They have endured famine and lived in Egypt as foreigners (Genesis 12:10). He has experienced family discord (Genesis 13) and war (Genesis 14). Yet Abram believes. He trusts that God will protect him and give him a great reward.

This is how we find eternal life and covenant blessing too—in forsaking our own security and human support to place our faith in God alone. In stepping out into an unknown future holding the hand of our known God. In trusting God's character and promises even when our circumstances suggest that our faith is misplaced. And like Abram discovered, when we give up all for Him, we gain far more in return.

It was by faith that Abraham obeyed when God called him to leave home and go to another land that God would give him as his inheritance. He went without knowing where he was going.

—*Hebrews 11:8*

Is Anything Too Hard for the Lord?

*Is anything too hard for the LORD? I will return
about this time next year, and Sarah will have a son.*

—*Genesis 18:14*

The Lord had come all the way from heaven with two angels to give Abraham and Sarah some incredible news—at that same time next year, Sarah would give birth to the promised son. Sarah laughed. How could such a thing happen to two elderly people? Her laughter was marked with doubt; she questioned God's ability to fulfill His promise. But rather than chasten her for her unbelief, God simply asked a rhetorical question—is anything too hard for God?

It's a question we should ask ourselves when we wonder if God will keep His word. *Is anything too hard for the Lord?* Of course not! So then surely He can do this thing—answer our prayer, remove this obstacle, heal our pain, bring faith where there is none.

Do you ever have moments of doubt, or even seasons of doubt? Listen to the words of the Lord: "Is anything too hard for Me?" The One who created the mountains, who set the stars in place and calls them by name, who commands the armies of heaven, and who turns the hearts of kings can surely do anything. And one thing He always does is keep His promises. Trust and rest in God's limitless power that is working to redeem and restore what is broken and lost, just as He promised.

*Now all glory to God, who is able, through his mighty power at work
within us, to accomplish infinitely more than we might ask or think.*

—*Ephesians 3:20*

Yahweh-Yireh: The Lord Will Provide

Abraham named the place Yahweh-Yireh (which means "the Lord will provide"). To this day, people still use that name as a proverb: "On the mountain of the Lord it will be provided."
—*Genesis 22:14*

As we trust God for our daily needs, we often seek answers ahead of time. We want to know how, when, and where He will provide. It's hard to trust that God will provide when we don't see it yet. But God provides mercy and grace "when we need it most" (Hebrews 4:16), not before we need it. Often it seems like God waits until the last minute, as if He wants to test our faith. We can trust that He will meet our needs at the right time, and in the right place. God's provision is done in God's way, not ours.

God is our provider. The very best thing God provides for us is the same thing He provided for Abraham and Isaac on the mountain—a sacrifice. For Abraham, God provided a sacrificial animal so he wouldn't have to kill his only son, the child of the promise. For us, He provided the eternal Lamb of God, Jesus Himself, the only Son of God who was the Promised One. His sacrificial death cleanses us from sin and gives us eternal life.

This God who has provided us with salvation also provides us with everything we need for today. He has promised to! As Romans 8:32 puts it, "Since he did not spare even his own Son but gave him up for us all, won't he also give us everything else?" Whatever your need is today, trust Yahweh-Yireh, God the provider, to meet it.

This same God who takes care of me will supply all your needs from his glorious riches, which have been given to us in Christ Jesus.
—*Philippians 4:19*

God Intended This for Good

The LORD was with Joseph in the prison and showed him his faithful love.
—Genesis 39:21

Joseph was Abraham's great-grandson, a direct heir of God's covenant promises. And yet, his life was unusually difficult. He was abused and then sold into slavery by his own brothers. He was falsely accused of adultery and languished in prison for many years. After interpreting some dreams, he thought he would be released—but instead he was betrayed and left in prison. Had God forgotten him? Had God forgotten His promises? Of course not!

One day many years later Joseph was reunited with his brothers and had the opportunity to save not only them, but many other people from starvation during a drought. Was he bitter and angry at the way he had been mistreated? Did he take the opportunity to pay people back for the way they had abused him? No, because Joseph saw God's hand in it all. He said, "God intended this for good." Even the slavery. Even the abuse. Even the betrayal. Even the suffering. God used it all.

Whatever your story, whatever you are facing today, look for God in it. He's there, working for your good just as He did for Joseph. Trust the God who keeps His promises to orchestrate the symphony of your life for your good and His glory, because He has promised it.

And we know that God causes everything to work together for the good
of those who love God and are called according to his purpose for them.
—Romans 8:28

We Are Part of God's Promise

The scepter will not depart from Judah, nor the ruler's
staff from his descendants, until the coming of the one to
whom it belongs, the one whom all nations will honor.

—*Genesis 49:10*

At first glance this may seem like an obscure promise. But in the unfolding narrative of God's promises, this is a turning point. The promise of a deliverer made in the Garden, and reiterated to Abraham, is now given a specific family line. Jacob prophesies that it is through the line of Judah that the promised King will come. This promise was first fulfilled in the dynasty of David, but ultimately it is Jesus, the Davidic King who will reign forever.

Now let's pause here for a moment and notice whom this promise is made to. Judah is not the one we would expect. He was not the firstborn, and he did not have a terribly good track record. Among other things, he slept with his son's wife because he thought she was a prostitute. And then when her sin was discovered he nearly burned her at the stake, taking no ownership of his part in the matter until she proved that her baby was his. This is who God chose to receive the promise?

Yes! And we receive it as well when we trust in Jesus for salvation. No matter how terrible our sins—pride or lust or murder or the worst thing we have ever done—God forgives us and places His covenant love on us the moment we repent and believe. We are part of God's promise.

One of the twenty-four elders said to me, "Stop weeping! Look,
the Lion of the tribe of Judah, the heir to David's throne, has won
the victory. He is worthy to open the scroll and its seven seals."

—*Revelation 5:5*

I Will Be Your God

Therefore, say to the people of Israel: "I am the LORD. I will free you
from your oppression and will rescue you from your slavery in Egypt.
I will redeem you with a powerful arm and great acts of judgment.
I will claim you as my own people, and I will be your God. . . . I will
bring you into the land I swore to give to Abraham, Isaac, and Jacob.
I will give it to you as your very own possession. I am the LORD!"

—Exodus 6:6-8

The story of these verses actually begins several chapters earlier, in Exodus 2:24, where it says, "God heard their groaning, and he remembered his covenant promise to Abraham, Isaac, and Jacob." You see, all of God's actions hinge on this overarching covenant promise, to make for Himself a people, give them a land, and live among them. When God's people cry out in desperation, He remembers His promises and responds by rescuing them.

Notice in these verses that the rescue is all about God: God's power, God's initiative, God's acts of redemption. He does it not because the people are deserving—what a hope that gives us, for none of us deserves His salvation— but rather for His own name's sake. Because He is the Lord and He has made this promise, He will carry it out. His reputation is at stake.

This day, with all of its struggles, cry out to God. He hears your groaning. Tell Him how desperate your situation is. And then listen to Him speak His covenant love over you. He will save you. What you are powerless to do, He will do. What you are undeserving of, He will give. What you most need, He will gladly provide.

I, the LORD, am your Savior and your Redeemer, the Mighty One of Israel.

—Isaiah 60:16

Great Wonders

Who is like you among the gods, O LORD—glorious in holiness, awesome in splendor, performing great wonders? . . . The LORD will reign forever and ever!

—*Exodus 15:11, 18*

These verses are part of the song of praise that Moses sang after the Lord had rescued the Israelites from the Egyptians. God had parted the Red Sea and allowed His people to walk through on dry land. Then He caused the sea to roar back into place over the Egyptian soldiers and chariots that were chasing them. It was a mighty miracle, a great wonder that showed God's awesome power and glorious holiness.

Moses commemorated God's powerful salvation so that the people would remember what God had done for them. Their future trust in God would be dependent on their ability to remember His faithfulness in the past. It is so easy to forget God's mighty deliverance when we are faced with a new problem, and that is why we must work at remembering who God is—glorious in holiness, awesome in splendor—and the great wonders He has done.

The same God who parted the Red Sea is working in your life too. He is still glorious in holiness, awesome in splendor, and performing great wonders. Truly there is no one else like Him. Don't look at the mighty sea before you or the armies chasing you. Look instead to this God of the promise and trust that He will bring you through.

No one is holy like the LORD! There is no one besides you; there is no Rock like our God.

—*1 Samuel 2:2*

A Long, Full Life

Honor your father and mother. Then you will live a long,
full life in the land the LORD your God is giving you.
—*Exodus 20:12*

This is one of the few commandments that is quoted by both Jesus and Paul (Matthew 15:4; Ephesians 6:1-3). It is also one of the few commands with a promise attached to it—if we honor our father and mother, we will live a long, full life. To *honor* means to treat with respect and deference. It requires humility, for in order to honor we must recognize our own limitations and choose to count others as more important than ourselves.

It's easy for the relationship between parents and children to become strained. Every parent fails, and their failures affect their children in sometimes painful ways. Honoring your parents means celebrating the things they got right and forgiving them for the ways they failed. It means finding ways to empathize with the struggles they faced and letting go of bitterness.

This command is actually about more than just expressing love and respect to our parents. Honoring those whom God has placed in authority over us, starting with our parents, is a way of honoring God Himself. It is an expression of trust that He will take care of us, either through the work of our parents and others in authority or in spite of it. When we live in a posture of trusting God, we experience His peace and blessing that can heal any hurt we may have.

Don't be selfish. . . . Be humble, thinking of others as better than yourselves.
—*Philippians 2:3*

God Is with Us

*I will meet with you and speak with you. I will meet the people
of Israel . . . in the place made holy by my glorious presence.*
—*Exodus 29:42-43*

God gave very specific instructions for worship. The Israelites were to build a Tabernacle and instruments of worship that would remind them of God's holiness and of the covenant commitments they had made to worship Him alone. In the midst of the detailed building plans lies this beautiful promise. Notice all the things God will do—He will meet with us, speak with us, show us His glorious holiness, consecrate us, and best of all, live among us and be our God!

Like so many of God's promises, these are ultimately fulfilled in Jesus Christ, Emmanuel, *God with us* who "tabernacled among us" (see John 1:14). He is the Word who set aside His glory to put on human flesh, and then paid the penalty for our sin so we could be made holy and one day dwell with Him in eternal glory. Until that day, God gives us His presence through the Holy Spirit. The great and glorious God chooses to draw near to us and indwell us. We have become His temple. He is with us in our joys and in our sorrows. In our triumphs and our failures. In our loving devotion and even our sinful rebellion. All of our days, now and through eternity, God is with us just as He was with Israel.

*So the Word became human and made his home among us.
He was full of unfailing love and faithfulness. And we have
seen his glory, the glory of the Father's one and only Son.*
—*John 1:14*

*I heard a loud shout from the throne, saying, "Look,
God's home is now among his people! He will live with them,
and they will be his people. God himself will be with them."*
—*Revelation 21:3*

Compassion and Mercy for Generations

*The LORD passed in front of Moses, calling out, "Yahweh!
The LORD! The God of compassion and mercy! I am slow to anger
and filled with unfailing love and faithfulness. I lavish unfailing
love to a thousand generations. . . . But I do not excuse the guilty.
I lay the sins of the parents upon their children and grandchildren."*
—*Exodus 34:6-7*

God had appeared to Moses before (Exodus 3; 13–14; 19–20; 24), and each of those times it was with a visual display of His glory. This time God showed His invisible qualities—compassion, mercy, patience, unfailing love, faithfulness, forgiveness . . . and judgment. These promises of God's character are repeated throughout Scripture. If you want to know what God is like, this sums it up.

At first glance, God's judgment to multiple generations seems contradictory to His mercy, forbearance, and love. But notice that His love is for a thousand generations, while the judgment is only for three or four. In addition, His judgment is only for the guilty. It is reversed as soon as we repent and receive the blood of Christ shed on our behalf for the forgiveness of sins. Actually, God's words quoted above are both a merciful warning that our sin affects those who come after us and an invitation to turn back to the God of unfailing love who is slow to anger and abounding in love and faithfulness.

How should we respond to this revelation of God's character? Moses himself offers a good example. In the next verse, he bows his head, worships, and asks forgiveness for the sins of his people. Won't you repent and take refuge in the God of mercy, unfailing love, and forgiveness? He longs to pour out His blessing on you and the generations who come after you.

How kind the LORD is! How good he is! So merciful, this God of ours!
—*Psalm 116:5*

God's Power on Display

The LORD replied, "Listen, I am making a covenant with you in the presence of all your people. I will perform miracles that have never been performed anywhere in all the earth or in any nation. And all the people around you will see the power of the LORD—the awesome power I will display for you."
—Exodus 34:10

God here reminds Moses of His covenant promises that Israel will live under His rule and blessing in the land He will bring them to. Then He adds in a new detail—this will involve spectacular miracles that will demonstrate His power. Isn't that a great promise? God will do things in the lives of His people that will make unbelievers say, "The God they worship has awesome power!"

In our individual lives, this display of God's power often doesn't come in the package we expect. Often it comes through struggle, suffering, and doubt. The road is not always easy. That's because God's power shines most brightly through our weaknesses, not our strengths. It is only when we come to the end of ourselves that we rely fully on God. Paul wrote, "That's why I take pleasure in my weaknesses, and in the insults, hardships, persecutions, and troubles that I suffer for Christ. For when I am weak, then I am strong" (2 Corinthians 12:10).

When you are discouraged, weak, and weary, turn to God in expectation that He will do great things. That is the moment when God can show up in great power. God works best when we are at our worst.

Each time he said, "My grace is all you need. My power works best in weakness." So now I am glad to boast about my weaknesses, so that the power of Christ can work through me.
—2 Corinthians 12:9

His Death in Your Place

Lay your hand on the animal's head, and the LORD will accept its death in your place to purify you, making you right with him.

—*Leviticus 1:4*

The sacrifices outlined in Leviticus were designed to show God's people that the penalty for sin against a holy God is death. Because God is just, the price for sin must be paid, and there is no other way to be made right with God than the shedding of blood. Leviticus 17:11 says, "I have given you the blood on the altar to purify you, making you right with the LORD. It is the blood, given in exchange for a life, that makes purification possible." Similarly, the book of Hebrews says "without the shedding of blood, there is no forgiveness" (9:22).

But God is also merciful. Jesus shed His own blood as the final, once-for-all sacrifice for sin. There is no more need for animal sacrifice or the daily atoning for sin, nor do we have to die for our own sin. It was all placed on Jesus at the Cross. "It is finished," He cried, and so it was. Those who accept His sacrifice on their behalf are no longer under the curse, but under God's blessing. We are no longer unrighteous, unloved, and bound by sin. In Christ we are declared righteous, beloved, and free. What love! What grace! What a promise!

Christ suffered for our sins once for all time. He never sinned, but he died for sinners to bring you safely home to God. He suffered physical death, but he was raised to life in the Spirit.

—*1 Peter 3:18*

Abundant Life

If you obey my decrees and my regulations,
you will find life through them. I am the LORD.

—*Leviticus 18:5*

A common misconception is that Christians are dour killjoys, out to spoil everyone's fun with their rules and legalistic law-keeping. Nothing could be further from the truth. Those who know the truth should be the most joy-filled and gracious people of all, for that is the kind of God we serve. Indeed, the laws of God are designed to bring life, not death—blessing, not curses.

The word "living" in the Old Testament refers to life enjoyed under God's pleasure (Deuteronomy 4:1; 8:1). Those who love God bring Him joy.

In the New Testament, Paul used this verse to demonstrate that keeping the whole law of God would bring life, but since none of us can keep God's law perfectly, we rely on Jesus' death and resurrection to bring us the life promised in this verse (Romans 10:5; Galatians 3:12). The application is clear: 1) living God's way brings a natural blessing because He created the natural order and knows how life works best, and 2) we can only find true and eternal life through Christ.

He is the one who kept the law perfectly, and when we join ourselves with Him by faith we have life abundant now and eternally.

So now there is no condemnation for those who belong to Christ Jesus.
And because you belong to him, the power of the life-giving Spirit
has freed you from the power of sin that leads to death.

—*Romans 8:1-2*

My purpose is to give them a rich and satisfying life.

—*John 10:10*

Walk with Your Heads Held High

I will walk among you; I will be your God, and you will be my people.
—*Leviticus 26:12*

This section of Leviticus outlines all the blessings of obedience (Leviticus 26:1-13). The Israelites would enjoy abundant rain in season, fruitfulness, peace, and security if they obeyed. These were visible expressions of God's presence among them—things that would happen if they lived as God's people, obeying His commands.

God reminds them not only of the blessing of living under His rule, but also His past care for them. Because He had rescued them from slavery according to His promise, they could trust that He would keep all His covenant promises.

For us, these promises have a more general application. Christians have been freed from slavery to sin. We walk with our heads held high because of who we are in Christ and the freedom we have in Him. And we enjoy God's presence and peace when we walk with Him in faith.

God's blessings abound in the lives of His people. That does not necessarily mean that we will always have a life of outward prosperity, but our inner life will be rich and satisfying far beyond any material blessings when we walk by faith in God's promises. We will enjoy a life of spiritual fruitfulness that is of eternal value.

I am the LORD your God, who brought you out of the land of Egypt so you would no longer be their slaves. I broke the yoke of slavery from your neck so you can walk with your heads held high.
—*Leviticus 26:13*

God's Smile

*May the L*ORD *bless you and protect you. May the L*ORD
*smile on you and be gracious to you. May the L*ORD
show you his favor and give you his peace.

—Numbers 6:24-26

This well-known and well-loved blessing, with its simple but remarkably comprehensive wording, reminds us of the source of all blessing: Yahweh. The Lord is the One who protects us, for without Him we could not even draw a breath. The Lord is the One who looks on us with love and goodness, for He is the giver of all good gifts. The Lord is the One who gives us grace and peace, for until He saved us, we were His enemies.

When the Bible talks about God's favor, it means His special attention. Isn't it amazing to think that God looks down on you with a smile on His face? He is intimately involved in your life, down to the number of hairs on your head. He knows everything about you and everything you need, better than you do yourself. And not only does He know it, He will take care of it with His unlimited power and boundless love. Those who love God enjoy His blessing, protection, grace, and peace in every moment from before they are born until they go to be with Him.

That's a promise that can get you through anything! Let God speak this blessing over you today.

*I am leaving you with a gift—peace of mind and heart. And the peace
I give is a gift the world cannot give. So don't be troubled or afraid.*

—John 14:27

His Arm Is Not Too Weak to Save

Then the Lord said to Moses, "Has my arm lost its power?
Now you will see whether or not my word comes true!"

—Numbers 11:23

The people of God were complaining, saying that they were better off in Egypt as slaves than with God taking care of them in the wilderness, despite the fact that He gave them bread from heaven each morning. They weren't content with God's provision. So God told Moses He would give them the meat they so desperately wanted in abundance—so much that they would come to hate it. It was a fitting discipline for their rebellion.

Moses looked around and saw that God's threat was impossible to carry out . . . at least in human terms. And then he had the audacity to question God, saying that there wasn't enough meat even among the flocks and herds to feed all of the people. God responded to his argument with a rhetorical question: Have I lost my power? The obvious answer—the only possible answer—is of course not! That could never happen!

The God who led the Israelites out of slavery in Egypt and parted the Red Sea is alive and well. His arm is as powerful as ever, able to do anything and everything that is in His perfect plan. You don't need to worry that the thing you are asking for is too hard for Him. God will answer your prayers in a way that maximizes your good and His glory. But in the meantime, take the lesson of the Israelites to heart and be grateful for the provision He has given you today.

Listen! The Lord's arm is not too weak to save you,
nor is his ear too deaf to hear you call.

—Isaiah 59:1

Keeping Our Eyes on Jesus

Then the LORD told him, "Make a replica of a poisonous snake and attach it to a pole. All who are bitten will live if they simply look at it!"
—Numbers 21:8

This is sort of an odd episode in Israel's history, but it pointed to an enormous promise. The short story is this: When the Israelites complained about the way God was leading them, God sent poisonous snakes as a punishment for their rebellion. Then they repented of their sin, and God provided salvation in the form of a bronze snake on a pole. Those who looked to it in faith were healed. The bronze snake in and of itself held no healing power. Rather, it was the act of putting their faith in God that saved them.

Jesus interpreted this Old Testament event as a type of foreshadowing that pointed to His own death on the cross: "As Moses lifted up the bronze snake on a pole in the wilderness, so the Son of Man must be lifted up, so that everyone who believes in him will have eternal life" (John 3:14-15). The fact that Jesus referenced this event means that it was an important story for us to remember.

Do you look to Jesus in faith? Do you have faith not just that He will save you from hell, but also that He will save you this day from your sin and selfishness? Do you have faith in His power to help you with all of today's trials and temptations? Take your eyes off of your problems and look to Jesus in faith. He alone has the power to heal and save.

Let us run with endurance the race God has set before us. We do this by keeping our eyes on Jesus, the champion who initiates and perfects our faith. Because of the joy awaiting him, he endured the cross, disregarding its shame. Now he is seated in the place of honor beside God's throne.
—Hebrews 12:1-2

God Never Changes

*God is not a man, so he does not lie. He is not human, so he
does not change his mind. Has he ever spoken and failed to act?
Has he ever promised and not carried it through?*

—*Numbers 23:19*

Wicked King Balak had summoned the prophet Balaam to utter a curse against God's people, but Balaam found himself unable to do it. That's because of this truth: God is not human like us. He can't be manipulated or maneuvered. He can't be controlled or limited or cajoled. He is not fickle with His affections or His plans. Sometimes that is a frustration to us because we'd like to bargain with God and get our way. But what a merciful thing it is that God is not like us.

You can always depend on God, because He cannot lie. He does not change His mind based on whims or emotions. He always keeps His promises. People may fail you, but God never will. When people deceive you, He is always true. God will always do what is right and just and good—and best of all, because He's God, He knows how to balance all those things in perfect harmony. He will never let you down, because to do so would go against His very nature.

Rejoice in God's unchangeable God-ness. When everything around you seems to be giving way, when unwelcome changes and transitions force you to find a new normal, rest in the God who can never lie or change His mind or fail you.

*So God has given both his promise and his oath. These two
things are unchangeable because it is impossible for God
to lie. Therefore, we who have fled to him for refuge can have
great confidence as we hold to the hope that lies before us.*

—*Hebrews 6:18*

Remembering God's Faithfulness

The LORD your God is going ahead of you.
He will fight for you, just as you saw him do in Egypt.
—*Deuteronomy 1:30*

As we journey through life, it's helpful to occasionally look back and take stock of where we've been. In the Old Testament, God's people made memorials to commemorate God's faithful care. That's really what this verse is, in verbal form. Moses was reciting Israel's history to give the Israelites courage to take the Promised Land.

God promised to go ahead of them, but they didn't just have to blindly believe it—they had a whole lifetime of history on which to base their faith. God fought for them in Egypt, He cared for them all through the wilderness with a father's tender care, and He brought them to the land He promised them. They could confidently enter the Promised Land because they could trust God to be with them.

Whatever challenge lies before you, God is already there. He knows the future and He is already preparing you for it. How can you know this is true? Just look back at your life and see God's faithful care for you. Remember the quiet waters He led you to. Remember all the little love notes He sent—answered prayers, joy-filled days, and the peace of His presence. Then press on into the future with confidence, knowing God holds all things in His powerful hand.

He will cover you with his feathers. He will shelter you with
his wings. His faithful promises are your armor and protection.
—*Psalm 91:4*

Search for the Lord and for His Strength

You will search again for the LORD your God. And if you search
for him with all your heart and soul, you will find him.
—*Deuteronomy 4:29*

The Israelites would one day reject God, and as a consequence be scattered into exile among the nations. This promise was something for them to hang on to in those dark days. God knew how they would chase after and worship other gods, how they would reject His covenant love. But He promised that even from that pit of sin they would reach out to God, and they would find God as soon as they sought Him with their heart and soul.

St. Augustine said that our hearts are restless until they find rest in God, and our life experience tells us that's true. People who don't know God are constantly searching for meaning, love, and peace—whether they realize it or not. For a time they may think they have found those things, but in the end, apart from God there is no true and lasting peace and no perfect love.

That's why this promise is so important: God is near, and if we search for Him, we will find Him. The truth is, He is looking for us! As soon as we cry out with a sincere heart, God enfolds us in His loving arms. The minute we realize we are lost, God finds us.

Keep on asking, and you will receive what you ask for. Keep on
seeking, and you will find. Keep on knocking, and the door will be
opened to you. For everyone who asks, receives. Everyone who
seeks, finds. And to everyone who knocks, the door will be opened.
—*Matthew 7:7-8*

Unconditional Promises

For the LORD your God is a merciful God; he will not abandon you or destroy you or forget the solemn covenant he made with your ancestors.
—*Deuteronomy 4:31*

God's memory is an interesting thing. Somehow He forgets our sin (Isaiah 43:25; Psalm 103:12), but He does not forget His promises, even when we forget Him. Even in His remembering God shows His love.

The terms of the covenant between God and His people were that they would keep God's laws and He would be their God. In keeping with covenant customs of the day, if the people failed to keep their end of the bargain, God was released from His. Except that's not how God set up His covenant. When He sealed His promises to Abraham and his descendants, God ratified the terms while Abraham slept (Genesis 15). The meaning was clear—God's covenant promises were unconditional. He would keep His end of the bargain even if Israel failed in theirs, which of course they did.

This is why God can say with utter assurance that He will not abandon His people or forget His promises. Whatever you have done, whatever you will do to let God down or outright rebel against Him, if you are a child of God then you will be kept until the end. He will never leave you, never abandon you, never forget all the precious promises He has made to you in His Word.

The LORD will not reject his people; he will not abandon his special possession.
—*Psalm 94:14*

Lavish, Unfailing Love

*Understand, therefore, that the LORD your God is indeed God. He is
the faithful God who keeps his covenant for a thousand generations and
lavishes his unfailing love on those who love him and obey his commands.*
—*Deuteronomy 7:9*

It's hard to wrap your mind around what a thousand generations means in numeric terms. If each generation is 40 years, then this is 40,000 years. According to the biblical account human history has only spanned 150–200 generations. So this is really an unending promise. God promises to lavish unfailing love on His children into eternity.

How can we know this is true? Because God is God. He does not change. He is holy and loving in His very essence. God cannot do anything other than be faithful and loving toward those who are His. And He isn't stingy with His affection. He doesn't hold back for fear that His love will not be returned (for He knows it can't be returned in equal measure), nor does He dole it out in proportion to our obedience. Rather, He delights to lavish it on us. God is overflowing with love and pours it over us like a refreshing rain from heaven. We can't even contain it all.

Who is this promise for? It is for everyone who loves God. Do you long for more of Jesus in your life? Do you praise God for who He is and rejoice over His holiness and goodness? Then this promise is for you. To unending generations, God will pour out His love on you like a tidal wave. Get ready to drink it in!

*May you have the power to understand, as all God's people should,
how wide, how long, how high, and how deep his love is. May you
experience the love of Christ, though it is too great to understand fully.*
—*Ephesians 3:18-19*

Living by Every Word of God

*Yes, he humbled you by letting you go hungry and then feeding you
with manna, a food previously unknown to you and your ancestors.
He did it to teach you that people do not live by bread alone; rather,
we live by every word that comes from the mouth of the LORD.*

—Deuteronomy 8:3

Sometimes it feels like what is happening in our lives must be God's plan B. It doesn't feel like a blessing when we lose our job or experience debilitating illness. How can this be part of God showing goodness to us? How could He be leading us if we find ourselves in the wilderness, without the daily necessities of life?

But with God there is no plan B. He planned all the circumstances of our lives from before we were born, and they are indeed good. This verse explains how. God sometimes lets us go hungry before He meets our need so that we will learn what is truly important. God's good plan for us is that we learn to prioritize the things that last forever over the things that are of value only in this life. He makes us hungry so that we will feast on Him.

This is another promise that finds its ultimate fulfillment in Christ. He declared, "I am the bread of life. Whoever comes to me will never be hungry again" (John 6:35). Just as God fed the Israelites with manna from heaven each day, Jesus nourishes our souls with Himself. He satisfies and fills us with His presence by the Holy Spirit and through His Word as we read it each day.

*Your ancestors ate manna in the wilderness, but they all died. Anyone
who eats the bread from heaven, however, will never die. I am the living
bread that came down from heaven. Anyone who eats this bread will live
forever; and this bread, which I will offer so the world may live, is my flesh.*

—John 6:49-51

Generous Living

*Give generously to the poor, not grudgingly, for the LORD your
God will bless you in everything you do. There will always be some
in the land who are poor. That is why I am commanding you to
share freely with the poor and with other Israelites in need.*

—*Deuteronomy 15:10-11*

The command to give generously is put in the context of two promises. The second is one of practicality: In a fallen world, there will always be poverty. Greed, inequality, and oppression are an unavoidable reality of human society because of sin. Therefore, as Christians, it is our duty to give generously and joyfully because we know that everything we have is a gift from our heavenly Father, on loan to us while we are on earth. We have nothing that did not originally come from Him, and we can take nothing with us when we depart this life. Therefore, we have an obligation to love our neighbors by meeting their needs in practical ways.

But there is another promise here that gives us further motivation for generous giving. Simply put, our generosity toward others unleashes God's generosity toward us. When we bless others, we receive a blessing in return. Elsewhere, God urges us to test this promise (Malachi 3:10). I have never met a believer who regrets giving generously, but I have met plenty who wish they had given more. What are you waiting for? Test God and see if He won't give you far more blessing in return for the ways you bless those in need.

The generous will prosper; those who refresh others will themselves be refreshed.

—*Proverbs 11:25*

Whom Do You Trust?

Do not be afraid as you go out to fight your enemies today!
Do not lose heart or panic or tremble before them.
For the LORD your God is going with you! He will fight for you
against your enemies, and he will give you victory!
—Deuteronomy 20:3-4

It's easy for us to fall into a pattern of thinking that it all depends on us. We've got work to do—important work that God has given us—and we want to do it with the excellence that befits our glorious King of kings. The problem is, we often work so hard at doing our best that we forget God's part in it. If we are doing His work, then it's His battle. And if what we're doing is not His work then it's not a battle worth fighting.

The Israelites had to be reminded of this over and over again. The daily battles to take the Promised Land took everything they had. How easy it was to forget the reason behind it all: They were taking the land that God had already promised them. It was their land. All they had to do was let God work through them, and it would be theirs.

Where is your trust? Are you trusting in your healthy habits or self-help strategies to get you through the day, or are you trusting in the energy and wisdom that God provides? If you've been working in your own strength, chances are that you're exhausted. You know you just aren't up to the task. If that's how you're feeling, maybe it's time to let God fight this battle.

The LORD himself will fight for you. Just stay calm.
—Exodus 14:14

God's Delight

*The LORD your God will then make you successful in everything
you do. . . . The LORD your God will delight in you if you obey his voice
and keep the commands and decrees written in this Book of Instruction,
and if you turn to the LORD your God with all your heart and soul.*
—Deuteronomy 30:9-10

The promise of success, fruitfulness, and prosperity in Deuteronomy 30:9 hinges on the condition of verse 10. If you obey God and love Him with your heart and soul, then He will delight to give you these good gifts. By implication, the reverse is true as well: If you do not obey and love Him, you have no part in God's covenant blessings.

How easy it is for us to subscribe to a version of cheap grace. We expect God to bless us even if we do not strive to live for Him. But life doesn't work that way. Our devotion to God is proof that we belong to Him, and belonging to Him is a condition of being part of His covenant family. If you are not a child of God, then the promises of God's blessing do not apply to you.

But if you are His child by faith in Jesus Christ, then you are God's delight. Do you live in this promise? Do you sense God's pleasure in you and trust that whatever comes, even hardship, is a blessing from the hand of God designed for your ultimate good?

*God will generously provide all you need. Then you will always
have everything you need and plenty left over to share with others.*
—2 Corinthians 9:8

FEBRUARY

MY SHEEP

LISTEN

TO MY VOICE;

I KNOW THEM,

AND THEY

FOLLOW ME.

JOHN 10:27

Our Rock and Fortress

He is the Rock; his deeds are perfect. Everything he does is just and fair.
He is a faithful God who does no wrong; how just and upright he is!
—Deuteronomy 32:4

Rocks are steady. Dependable. Strong. Immovable. Something we can lean on when we feel unstable. Rocks are the things we build our homes on if we want them to be strong, and God is the Rock we build our lives on if we want to be able to withstand the storms of life. When everything else gives way, He is still there, faithfully loving us.

The fact that God is a Rock is what enables Him to promise that He is perfect, just, fair, faithful, and upright. The unchangeable steadfastness of our holy God means that we can trust that He will always do what is right. He cannot fail or act unjustly.

What a mercy the perfect justice of God is! He has declared what is right and what is wrong, and it will always be so. He has promised to do what is right, and He always will. When we are betrayed or slandered or oppressed, we can entrust ourselves to the God who does no wrong. When we see injustice, we can bring our case to God, the one who judges thoughts and motives and who always does what is just and fair. In every circumstance, we can take refuge in the Rock of our salvation.

The LORD is my rock, my fortress, and my savior;
my God is my rock, in whom I find protection. He is my shield,
the power that saves me, and my place of safety.
—Psalm 18:2

Everlasting Arms

The eternal God is your refuge, and his everlasting arms are under you.
—Deuteronomy 33:27

Children feel utterly secure and safe when they are in the arms of their parents. They sense innately that nothing can harm them as long as they are enfolded in the loving embrace of Mom or Dad. That's because they know without a doubt that their parents will do whatever it takes to care for them. Even if a storm is howling, even if things are in chaos, one touch from a parent brings peace.

God holds us like that, every minute of every day. The old hymn says, "Leaning on the everlasting arms, safe and secure from all alarms." There is no threat we need to fear, no danger to our eternal security, no catastrophe that will harm us because God's everlasting arms hold us fast. Even if the worst happens, His strong arms are still there beneath us. We are held, and we can relax into His embrace. It's a picture of perfect peace.

As we go forward by faith, God holds us up. This is why we can be confident to take risks. If we sense that God has called us to something, we can step out in faith and know that He's holding us. And no matter what happens—even if we fail or we get it all wrong—He won't let go. His arms are everlasting and His embrace is eternal.

I hold you by your right hand—I, the LORD your God.
And I say to you, "Don't be afraid. I am here to help you."
—Isaiah 41:13

Be Strong and Courageous

*Be careful to obey all the instructions Moses gave you. Do not deviate
from them, turning either to the right or to the left. Then you will be
successful in everything you do. Study this Book of Instruction continually.
Meditate on it day and night so you will be sure to obey everything written
in it. Only then will you prosper and succeed in all you do. This is my
command—be strong and courageous! Do not be afraid or discouraged.
For the LORD your God is with you wherever you go.*

—Joshua 1:7-9

These are the Lord's words to Joshua as he took up the mantle of leadership
from Moses. He would lead God's people into the Land of Promise. It was a
daunting task, especially since the last time they had stood at this spot they had
failed to trust God's promises, and as a result had been forced to wait forty years
while that faithless generation died. Into this tense moment God spoke—Be
strong and courageous! Which was really shorthand for *trust Me.*

God's promise to help Joshua succeed in the task before him was based on
Joshua knowing, meditating on, and obeying God's words. If he wholeheartedly
followed after God, he would be successful in everything he did. However,
God's promise at the end of these verses is not conditional—*do not be afraid or
discouraged, because I am with you.* Even if Joshua failed to keep God's Word and
failed in the task before him, God would still be with him.

If we devote ourselves to God's Word—knowing it and doing it—then we will
succeed. Our hearts will be attuned to God's will and He will help us accomplish
it. But even when we fail to follow Him as we ought, God is still with us. Let these
amazing promises keep you from fear and discouragement today.

Commit your actions to the LORD, and your plans will succeed.

—Proverbs 16:3

Rest on Every Side

The LORD gave them rest on every side, just as he had solemnly promised their ancestors. None of their enemies could stand against them, for the LORD helped them conquer all their enemies. Not a single one of all the good promises the LORD had given to the family of Israel was left unfulfilled; everything he had spoken came true.

—Joshua 21:44-45

These verses are proof that God keeps His promises. Not some of the time, not every now and then, but every time. None of the bold, impossible promises that God had given to Abraham and his descendants had failed or been left unfulfilled. Everything He spoke, He did. They had rest not just from their enemies, but the deep soul rest that comes from knowing that God is trustworthy.

If you read the rest of Joshua, you will see that the Israelites did not completely take over the land. Through laziness or fear or some combination of the two, they left some of that task undone. They lived in the land, but because they failed to finish the work God had given them, they missed out on all that they could have had. Their unfaithfulness does not negate the fact that God had kept His promises, but it did have consequences.

Isn't that so often true for us, as well? How often do we miss all that God has for us because we quit too soon? Whatever promises you are believing by faith today, don't give up. Are you looking for healing? For restoration of a broken relationship? For freedom from addiction? Keep on believing and obeying God's Word—don't give up. God will follow through, you just need to keep trusting.

The Lord isn't really being slow about his promise, as some people think. No, he is being patient for your sake. He does not want anyone to be destroyed, but wants everyone to repent.

—2 Peter 3:9

Redemption

May the Lord, the God of Israel, under whose wings you have come to take refuge, reward you fully for what you have done.

—*Ruth 2:12*

After the dark chapter of the Judges, when everyone was doing right in his own eyes and it sometimes appeared that God had forgotten His promises, the book of Ruth is a refreshing story of love and restoration. Not everything was dark; God was still present, still providing for His people, still working out His plan to save His people.

At its heart, Ruth is a reminder that God is still working His redemptive purposes even through loss and heartache. Naomi returned to Israel empty, having endured the deaths of her husband and sons. She then experienced not only the faithful love of her daughter-in-law, who was "better than seven sons" (Ruth 4:15), but also the birth of a grandson who would carry on the family name. God restored her joy and used her to bring hope to the world. Two generations later, King David would arrive through this family line to fulfill the promise of a mighty nation. Many generations after that, King Jesus would fulfill the promise once and for all.

No matter how dark your present circumstances may seem, God is at work in unlikely ways. He provided a redeemer for the Moabitess Ruth, and through her line He provided the Redeemer for us all. He is at work redeeming your losses as well, for your good and His glory.

He gave his life to free us from every kind of sin, to cleanse us, and to make us his very own people, totally committed to doing good deeds.

—*Titus 2:14*

He Will Protect His Faithful Ones

The LORD gives both death and life. . . . The LORD makes some poor and others rich. . . . For all the earth is the LORD's, and he has set the world in order. He will protect his faithful ones, but the wicked will disappear in darkness.

—*1 Samuel 2:6-9*

These verses are part of Hannah's song, the praise poem of a woman who was barren but received the child God had promised her. When she dedicated her beloved son to the Lord's service, she overflowed with praise for His sovereign goodness. Worship is the natural result of experiencing God's faithfulness.

These verses use a poetic technique called *merism*, in which two opposites are used to express the totality of everything between them. God controls death and life—and by extension, every day in between. He makes people poor or rich—and everything in between. Verse 8 offers the summary: All the earth is the Lord's, and He has set the world in order. Everything happens according to His sovereign will.

This context is important for the promise found in verse 9. God, the One who controls everything, protects His people and judges evil. He is working things out according to His perfect will. We cannot thwart His plans or stand against them, and neither can our enemies. Everything that happens to us in this life is undergirded by the truth that justice will be done and God will be glorified.

Let that promise give you comfort today when you feel afraid or are angered by injustice. God gives death and life, poverty and riches, and in the end every part of His sovereign will works together for the protection of His people and the eventual defeat of evil.

He never takes his eyes off the innocent, but he sets them on thrones with kings and exalts them forever.

—*Job 36:7*

God Cannot Lie

He who is the Glory of Israel will not lie, nor will he change
his mind, for he is not human that he should change his mind!
—1 Samuel 15:29

Lies destroy trust, ruin relationships, abolish integrity, and darken the soul. They also connect you with the devil, who is the father of lies: "He has always hated the truth, because there is no truth in him. When he lies, it is consistent with his character; for he is a liar and the father of lies" (John 8:44). By contrast, God is the God of truth. He will never lie.

In 1 Samuel 15 we learn of the devastating consequences of a lie in the life of King Saul. God had told Him to destroy the enemy completely, but Saul kept back the best of the plunder and then lied about it. Saul did what was right in his own eyes, and as a result God's presence departed from him and his kingdom started to fall apart.

In this context comes the promise of 1 Samuel 15:29 that God is faithful to His word. The book of Numbers reiterates, "God is not a man, so he does not lie. He is not human, so he does not change his mind. Has he ever spoken and failed to act? Has he ever promised and not carried it through?" (Numbers 23:19). Truth is consistent with the character of God. Every word He speaks, every promise He makes, will prove to be true. Be assured that God's promises are irrevocable and cannot be reversed. They are our shield in days of trouble.

This truth gives them confidence that they have eternal life, which
God—who does not lie—promised them before the world began.
—Titus 1:2

Heart Vision

But the LORD said to Samuel, "Don't judge by his appearance or height,
for I have rejected him. The LORD doesn't see things the way you see them.
People judge by outward appearance, but the LORD looks at the heart."
—1 Samuel 16:7

Being truly seen and known is both wonderful and terrifying. On the one hand, we long for people to love us for who we are. When someone sees us stripped bare and accepts us anyway, that is a true gift. Viewing us at our worst and continuing to love us—that is unconditional love.

At the same time, it's a lot easier when we can hide a little bit. We like to keep back the worst bits of ourselves and secret away our pet sins. If someone sees us for who we truly are, it forces us to strive to be a little better, and we don't always want that kind of challenge.

God sees our innermost selves—beyond all the hiding, even deeper than we can see—and yet He loves us still. He looks at our heart in all of its sinfulness, and He says, "Come to me, all of you who are weary and carry heavy burdens, and I will give you rest" (Matthew 11:28). He gently peels back every layer that we allow Him to and helps us become the people we were made to be. He restores us and then keeps us to the end, even when we shrink back or falter. What a gift it is that God sees us and knows our hearts, for it enables us to be fully, completely, and unconditionally loved.

O LORD, you have examined my heart and know everything about me.
—Psalm 139:1

Light for the Darkness

*O Lord, you are my lamp. The Lord lights up my darkness.
In your strength I can crush an army; with my God I can scale any
wall. God's way is perfect. All the Lord's promises prove true.*
—2 Samuel 22:29-31

David's life was constantly in danger, but the Lord kept him alive and provided all he needed. Part of the way God did that was by empowering David to face the enemy without fear. God showed him the right path and made his arms strong enough to bend a bow of bronze and shoot arrows with great power. David said, "The Lord is my light and my salvation—so why should I be afraid? The Lord is my fortress, protecting me from danger, so why should I tremble?" (Psalm 27:1).

But God's promise doesn't end there. The next verse says God does everything perfectly. His promises are dependable, fixed in the heavens from eternity past to eternity future. Nothing happens to us outside of His will, and He is the One who directs our steps.

What makes you feel like the darkness is pressing in? The unknown future? The injustices you hear about in the news or see in your own life? A mysterious shadow that has fallen over your soul? Whatever your darkness, know that God is light, and He will light up your darkness. Let the One whose ways are perfect and who keeps every one of His promises shine the light of His presence in your heart, empower you to face the darkness without fear, and bring you His peace.

The light shines in the darkness, and the darkness can never extinguish it.
—John 1:5

Open My Eyes, That I May See

"Don't be afraid!" Elisha told him. "For there are more on our side than on theirs!" Then Elisha prayed, "O LORD, open his eyes and let him see!" The LORD opened the young man's eyes, and when he looked up, he saw that the hillside around Elisha was filled with horses and chariots of fire.
—2 Kings 6:16-17

Spiritual blindness can corrupt our eyes and influence the decisions even of godly people. But when Gods opens our eyes and gives us a glimpse of who He is, our view of the world changes completely.

The Lord's prophets were outnumbered and outmaneuvered. There was no hope left—except the hope they had in God's promises, and that was more than enough. What Elisha knew is that appearance is not always reality. The truth was that they weren't outnumbered after all; the armies of heaven were on their side. Sometimes what we most need is eyes to see the unseen.

With undeserved oppression and suffering around us, and sometimes even in our own lives, our view can be obstructed. What we really need in those moments of defeat is eyes to see the reality of our situation. The truth is, there are more on our side than on theirs. The Lord of Heaven's Armies is fighting the forces of darkness. Almighty God is for us. Therefore, we have nothing to fear.

Ask God to show you the chariots of fire that surround you. Ask for a glimpse of the angels that are camped around you, and then do the work before you with the courage that befits someone who is surrounded by the armies of heaven.

The angel of the LORD encamps around those who fear him, and delivers them.
—Psalm 34:7, ESV

Decided Long Ago

But have you not heard? I decided this long ago. Long ago
I planned it, and now I am making it happen. . . . [You] will
put roots down in your own soil and will grow up and flourish.
—*2 Kings 19:25, 30*

The impact of bad news about our health, finances, or safety can pull us into a pit of darkness and leave us in a cloud of depression. Fear is paralyzing. The day King Hezekiah received the message that Judah would be attacked by the Assyrian army he tore his clothes, fell on his knees, and cried out to the Lord, "Today is a day of trouble, insults, and disgrace" (2 Kings 19:3). Maybe you sometimes feel that way, and you wonder if God has a plan behind it all.

That's why I love this promise: God says He had everything planned from long ago. From this side of eternity sometimes it seems like life is all chaos and consternation. But God has a plan, and He's working it out. What is that plan? For His people to put down roots, grow up, and flourish. Elsewhere we are told to root ourselves in the love of God (Ephesians 3:17), and that if we do so we will never fail to yield fruit in season (Psalm 1:3).

The things that are happening to you right now, whether they bring you joy or sorrow, are all part of a master plan to help you grow in faith and be fruitful in ministry. You can rest in God's care and enjoy the journey because He has a plan, and unlike us, there are no unexpected events that will derail His plan.

Blessed are those who trust in the LORD and have made the LORD
their hope and confidence. They are like trees planted along
a riverbank, with roots that reach deep into the water. Such trees
are not bothered by the heat or worried by long months of drought.
Their leaves stay green, and they never stop producing fruit.
—*Jeremiah 17:7-8*

Don't Be Afraid or Discouraged

And now the Lord has fulfilled the promise he made. . . . I have built
this Temple to honor the name of the Lord, the God of Israel.
—*2 Chronicles 6:10*

King Solomon offered this prayer of praise at the dedication of the Temple. God had fulfilled His promise, as David had said He would when he told Solomon, "Be strong and courageous, and do the work. Don't be afraid or discouraged, for the Lord God, my God, is with you. He will not fail you or forsake you. He will see to it that all the work related to the Temple of the Lord is finished correctly" (1 Chronicles 28:20).

Solomon had done his part in getting this task done—he had been strong and courageous and done the work. But the results really depended not on his power, but on God's—and God had fulfilled His promise. God's covenant promises are a mysterious combination of His work and ours. He guarantees them, He makes them come to pass, and they cannot fail. They depend on God, not on us. But He invites us into the work. He honors us with meaningful, purposeful tasks that require courage and commitment on our part.

It is so inspiring and joyful to be a part of God's work. What is the task before you today that will further His Kingdom? Tackle it with courage, hard work, and gratitude that the results are in God's hands.

In the same way, let your good deeds shine out for all
to see, so that everyone will praise your heavenly Father.
—*Matthew 5:16*

For God is working in you, giving you the desire
and the power to do what pleases him.
—*Philippians 2:13*

Repentance and Restoration

*If my people who are called by my name will humble themselves and
pray and seek my face and turn from their wicked ways, I will hear
from heaven and will forgive their sins and restore their land.*

—2 Chronicles 7:14

This promise of forgiveness and restoration is a call to humility. The list of things that God's people do—humble themselves, pray, seek God's face, and turn from wickedness—are all aspects of repentance. Note the progression here: First we realize our status as sinful creatures, then we bring our sins to God, then we seek God wholeheartedly, and finally we choose to turn away from sin. If we stop at a prayer of repentance—or, worse, at feelings of guilt and shame—we haven't gone as far as we ought in humble repentance. We're cheating ourselves out of the full forgiveness and restoration God promises.

When we heed God's call to repentance, He hears. His heart posture toward us is one of loving forgiveness and restoration, and all we have to do to receive this loving response is humbly repent.

How often do you follow these steps of repentance? If you're not experiencing the forgiveness and restoration of God in your life, perhaps a place to start is by heeding the call of this verse and fully seeking God's forgiveness. Don't shortchange the process. God is reaching out to you, poised to offer you forgiveness and restoration the moment you truly repent.

*Seek the LORD while you can find him. Call on him now while
he is near. . . . Turn to our God, for he will forgive generously.*

—Isaiah 55:6-7

Lord, Hear My Prayer!

If you return to me and obey my commands and live by them,
then even if you are exiled to the ends of the earth, I will bring you back to the place I
have chosen for my name to be honored.

—*Nehemiah 1:9*

Jerusalem, the capital of God's chosen people whose name means "foundation of peace," lay in ruins. The people were exiles and slaves in a foreign land. It seemed that God had not only abandoned His people, but also rejected them. And they deserved it, since they had first rejected Him.

But one man, Nehemiah, still had faith. He knew that God would not forget His promises, and so he called on God to remember. In Nehemiah 1, he first reminded God of His character as the One who keeps His covenant of unfailing love (verse 5). Then he confessed the sins of the people, acknowledging that it was their own fault they were in this situation (verses 6-7). Finally he reminded God of His specific promise—even if the people were unfaithful and were scattered among the nations, the moment they repented He would forgive and restore. We know from the rest of the book of Nehemiah that God responded to Nehemiah's prayer and was faithful to return the people to their homeland.

This is a helpful model of prayer for us. When we are in a hopeless situation, the wise thing to do is to turn to Almighty God and ask for help. Like Nehemiah, we can call on God's character and promises, reminding ourselves of what kind of God He is and of His care for us. And then we can repent, which releases an outpouring of God's compassionate love.

Remember, O Lord, your compassion and unfailing
love, which you have shown from long ages past.

—*Psalm 25:6*

The Joy of the Lord Is Your Strength

And Nehemiah continued, ". . . Don't be dejected
and sad, for the joy of the LORD is your strength!"

—*Nehemiah 8:10*

Nehemiah urged the Israelites to stop weeping over their sin and rejoice in the fact that they understood God's Word and had responded to it. Once we have turned to Jesus, the time for shame and guilt is over and the day of holy joy has come. That joy will give us strength to keep on following Him.

Looking at Jesus and meditating on all He has done for us and all He has in store for us naturally makes us joyful. Indeed, when we realize that we are forgiven and freed from the curse of sin, how can we be anything but joyful? What a relief it is to be known and loved and made a child of the King of kings. The longer we know Him and the closer we walk with Him, the more joyful we will be.

If your life is characterized by guilt and gloom, take these words of Nehemiah to heart. As believers we do not need to be dejected and sad, for God's promised joy gives us strength—strength to obey, strength to overcome adversity, strength to keep on fighting the good fight of the faith. Even in days of grief, joy over God's promises can give us strength to keep walking by faith.

For the Kingdom of God is not a matter of what we eat or drink,
but of living a life of goodness and peace and joy in the Holy Spirit.

—*Romans 14:17*

For Such a Time as This

*If you keep quiet at a time like this, deliverance and relief for the Jews
will arise from some other place, but you and your relatives will die.
Who knows if perhaps you were made queen for just such a time as this?*

—*Esther 4:14*

The Jews were facing extermination under King Xerxes, and their only hope lay with a beautiful young woman who was his queen. The problem was, this particular king had a history of turning on his wives with little provocation, and the fact that Queen Esther had not disclosed her nationality and now had the audacity to question his judgment was surely more provocation than he needed to be angry with her.

Fortunately, Esther's relative Mordecai had not lost sight of God's promise. He emphasized the fact that Esther being in the palace was not an accident, for she had "come to royal position for such a time as this." He knew that God would rescue His people, and he was willing to bet his beloved niece's life on it. The question wasn't whether the people would be saved—that was assured because God had promised it. The question was whether Esther would have enough courage and faith to be an instrument in God's hands.

What is your "for such a time as this"? What unique position has God put you in? What unique talent or opportunity lies before you? If God is calling you to act, take courage in the fact that He will work His good purposes for you and in the world, and then step out, trusting that He will do it. Don't miss your moment to be part of God's redemptive plan.

*Trust in the LORD with all your heart; do not depend on
your own understanding. Seek his will in all you do,
and he will show you which path to take.*

—*Proverbs 3:5-6*

Our Advocate on High

Even now my witness is in heaven. My advocate is there on high.
—*Job 16:19*

Job's entire life had fallen apart in a way that we can hardly imagine, and his friends' only reaction was to wonder what he had done to deserve it. Their view was that because God is just, He gives us what we deserve. If Job was suffering, he needed to figure out what sin he had failed to repent of and make things right.

But Job knew better. He trusted the character and goodness of God, and so he threw himself on God's mercy. Though he didn't understand the whys and hows of his suffering, he fully trusted that God was Advocate as well as Judge, and had faith that one day he would be vindicated.

If Job, who lived many years before Jesus, trusted God to advocate for him, how much more can we trust Him? Unlike Job, we know that "Christ Jesus died for us and was raised to life for us, and he is sitting in the place of honor at God's right hand, pleading for us" (Romans 8:34). Jesus stands in the gap for us, ensuring our place as a beloved, righteous child of God and bringing our daily needs before our loving heavenly Father.

Whether your life is in shambles like Job's was or is going pretty well, your only hope is to entrust yourself to Jesus, the Advocate on high. He is the only one who can reconcile you to God and bring you true peace that can get you through good days and bad.

There is one God and one Mediator who can reconcile
God and humanity—the man Christ Jesus.

—*1 Timothy 2:5*

My Redeemer Lives

But as for me, I know that my Redeemer lives, and he will stand upon the earth at last.
—*Job 19:25*

What words of faith these are from the lips of Job, many generations before Jesus the Redeemer came to save us. He trusted that there would come a Savior who would right all wrongs. He had faith that there is life after death and was overwhelmed by the hope of what he would one day see.

We know the truth of Job's words because we know about Jesus. He is the Redeemer, the One who will one day return to judge and rule over the new heavens and the new earth. And we know about the eternal life He promises, that after our body decays we will live on, seeing Jesus face-to-face.

Job faced his suffering armed with this hope, and it is enough to get us through our suffering as well. When we watch our bodies fail, we know that we will one day put on immortal flesh and live with Jesus. When we are weighed down by the injustices around us, we can trust in the Redeemer who will stand on the earth on the last day and judge the nations. When we are overwhelmed by the cares and struggles of life, we can arm ourselves with the knowledge that we are kept safe for all eternity by our gracious Redeemer.

For your Creator will be your husband; the LORD
of Heaven's Armies is his name! He is your Redeemer,
the Holy One of Israel, the God of all the earth.

—*Isaiah 54:5*

When He Tests Me

But he knows where I am going. And when he tests me, I will come out as pure as gold.
—*Job 23:10*

When dark days block our view of God, it is comforting to think that God knows all about our situation. He sees our struggle, He bottles our tears, and best of all He knows what's next. His view is not blocked by our circumstances, His view of the future is crystal clear. What a comfort it is to tell ourselves, "He knows where I am going."

Job was convinced that when God tested him, he would be vindicated. At first glance that feels a bit arrogant to us. Who would so boldly dare God to test them and confidently state that they will be declared innocent?

But those who belong to Jesus can claim this promise as their own. When we enter the refiner's fire, God burns away the dross and nothing but the pure mettle of faith remains. He makes us shine with His glorious light. We are declared innocent not because of what we have done, but because of what Jesus has done for us. This day, with all of its ups and downs, its hopeful expectations and jarring realities, remind yourself that God knows where you're going and is purifying you so that you can stand mature and complete in Him.

I have refined you, but not as silver is refined. Rather,
I have refined you in the furnace of suffering.

—*Isaiah 48:10*

His Deeds Are Perfect

I know that you can do anything, and no one can stop you.

—Job 42:2

The ESV translates this verse "no purpose of yours can be thwarted." God always does exactly what He intends to do. The joy of this promise is not just that God is all-powerful, but that everything He does is in line with His holy and loving character. All the things God chooses to do are exactly perfect, with no deviation or disappointment or change of plans. He does what He wants, and everything He wants is loving and good.

Job didn't come by this kind of faith easily. He had argued and railed against God for allowing him to suffer so deeply. He fully expressed his deep disappointment with God. But then God put him in his place, reminding him of the vast gulf between humanity and God, and Job realized that he had spoken out of turn: "I was talking about things I knew nothing about" (Job 42:3).

There is a place for us to express our grief and doubt to God. He welcomes our honesty, because after all He knows what is in our hearts. But after all of that we should end up just where Job did, realizing that God is God and we are not, and submitting to His will because we trust that He loves us and is perfectly good. Have you reached that point of joyful surrender? If not, start the conversation and ask God to help you get there.

He is the Rock; his deeds are perfect. Everything he does is just and fair.
He is a faithful God who does no wrong; how just and upright he is!
—Deuteronomy 32:4

Two Ways and Two Destinies

They are like trees planted along the riverbank, bearing fruit each season. Their leaves never wither, and they prosper in all they do.
—*Psalm 1:3*

Psalm 1 is built around the concept of two ways to live, and they end in two very different destinies. If we follow the wrong counsel, then we will stand with the wrong companions and finally sit with the wrong crowd. The "sinners" described in this psalm are people who are willfully and persistently evil, who make light of God's laws and ridicule what is sacred. They laugh at holy things and disobey the Lord for entertainment, and following them leads to destruction.

By contrast, those who "delight in the law of the LORD, meditating on it day and night" (Psalm 1:2) enjoy lives of blessing. Delighting in God's Word means to enjoy, think about, and pursue it. It is a settled way of life oriented toward God. Remember God's advice to Joshua: "Study this Book of Instruction continually. Meditate on it day and night so you will be sure to obey everything written in it. Only then will you prosper and succeed in all you do" (Joshua 1:8). The way we treat the Bible is the way we treat Jesus Christ, for the Bible is His Word to us.

God blesses us that we might be a blessing to others. We should be like trees planted along riverbanks, alive, fruitful, beautiful, and enduring, with a hidden root system that draws deep nourishment from God's Word. If we live this way, we will bear fruit as God's love flows in and through us.

The Holy Spirit produces this kind of fruit in our lives: love, joy, peace, patience, kindness, goodness, faithfulness, gentleness, and self-control.
—*Galatians 5:22-23*

Look to the Lord

You can be sure of this: The LORD set apart the godly
for himself. The LORD will answer when I call to him.

—*Psalm 4:3*

David needed God's help. His people turned against him and made Absalom king, which seemed like an end to God's promises. Though he had done nothing wrong, everything had been taken away from him. David brought all his frustrations and questions to God: "Answer me," he demanded (Psalm 4:1).

In that desperate moment of prayer David was reminded of the truth, the only thing he could be sure of: The Lord would answer him because he belonged to God. And with God's reassurance came a sense of calm. David was no longer angry (Psalm 4:4) but rather offered a sacrifice of thanksgiving and trusted God (Psalm 4:5). In the end, he found that he had more joy in his struggle than if his circumstances had been perfect, because he found that God's peace was better than anything else (Psalm 4:6-8).

When you find yourself in desperate circumstances, when all you can do is cry out to God, "answer me," remind yourself of these truths. The Lord has set you apart, and He will answer you. Let go of your anger and choose gratitude. Trust that God is working His purposes. When you do, you will experience God's peace and abundant joy, just like David did.

I love the LORD because he hears my voice and my prayer for mercy.
Because he bends down to listen, I will pray as long as I have breath!

—*Psalm 116:1-2*

A Place of Safety

The LORD is a shelter for the oppressed, a refuge in times
of trouble. Those who know your name trust in you, for you,
O LORD, do not abandon those who search for you.

—*Psalm 9:9-10*

Psalm 9 centers around the theme of God as judge, the one who rights wrongs and rules the world with justice and fairness. Specifically in this psalm, that means He deals with people according to where they put their trust. Anyone who takes refuge in Him is saved. If we know Him through personal experience and earnestly search for Him, we are kept safe in His care. By contrast, those who love evil and oppress others will be caught in their own snares (Psalm 9:16).

There is a temptation from our limited human knowledge to question God's judgments. We want Him to be a refuge for everyone. We don't like it that not everyone will be saved. But the choice lies with us: Are we tucking ourselves under His wings, trusting Him to take care of us, or are we pridefully thinking that we can take care of ourselves and rejecting His judgments?

We can't trust a God we don't know. That's why it's so important to search for Him, to get to know His character by reading the Bible and praying. Then we will have deep faith that everything God does is perfect and all His ways are right. He deals with us not as we deserve, but in mercy forgives all who come to Him for refuge. He is our place of safety forever.

The LORD is good, a strong refuge when trouble comes.
He is close to those who trust in him.

—*Nahum 1:7*

The Lord Loves Justice

For the righteous LORD loves justice. The virtuous will see his face.
—*Psalm 11:7*

In so many parts of society, law and order have collapsed. Society is built on truth, and when truth is questioned or denied, the foundations shake. What we need to remember is that God sometimes shakes things up to bring us back to true worship, and no matter what, we can trust Him.

Here is God's promise: He will, in the end, bring justice. It's not often on our timetable or in the way we expect, but God does work justice. He is on His throne, He sees into every heart, and we can trust that He will do what is right.

This side of eternity, we don't always see justice win the day. Some days it feels like goodness and righteousness are on the losing side. But we can be assured that in the end, our just God will carry out His perfect will. And that assurance enables us to rest in His sovereign choice. Sometimes He chooses to allow evil to prevail for a time. Sometimes justice is done. But either way, the Lord who loves justice is on His throne, and He rules in righteousness. One day we will see His face, and in the meantime we can trust His loving care.

He loves whatever is just and good; the
unfailing love of the LORD fills the earth.

—*Psalm 33:5*

My Cup of Blessing

LORD, you alone are my inheritance, my cup of blessing.
You guard all that is mine. The land you have given me
is a pleasant land. What a wonderful inheritance!

—*Psalm 16:5-6*

In the biblical era, land was more than an asset—it was the very means of survival. Passing property from one generation to the next through an inheritance ensured that one's descendants would be able to grow food and feed livestock. To the Israelites it even had a spiritual component, since God's covenant promises included a land where He would dwell with them. This was especially true for the author of this psalm, King David, for the promises to the nation would come through his family.

How surprising it was, then, that David declared his most treasured inheritance was not his land or dynasty, but God Himself. He chose to put his hope not in what God had promised to give him—not in the blessing—but in God. His relationship with God was what gave him security and delight. It was his most treasured possession.

In the New Testament we are told that we are co-heirs with Christ, destined to inherit the glory that has been His from eternity to eternity. We have been given the greatest treasure of all, Christ Himself, and with Him eternal life that begins even now. The pleasures of this world pale in comparison with the fullness of joy we find in His presence. What a treasure we have inherited! Let's hold loosely the temporary blessings so we can treasure Him above all else.

And since we are his children, we are his heirs. In fact,
together with Christ we are heirs of God's glory. But if we
are to share his glory, we must also share his suffering.

—*Romans 8:17*

God's Perfect Way

God's way is perfect. All the LORD's promises prove true.
He is a shield for all who look to him for protection.

—*Psalm 18:30*

This psalm depicts God as the mighty warrior who miraculously saves His people. It celebrates His powerful protection in days of uncertainty and danger. Whether the danger comes from the shaking of the earth or the thundering footsteps and false accusations of human enemies, even the very cords of death cannot pull God's people away from His care.

The summary statement comes in this verse, where we are told that God's way is perfect and He keeps His promises. He is a shield for His people because nothing happens outside His loving control. We can run to Him for protection knowing that He has the ability to keep us safe. The rest of the psalm outlines all the ways God helps us—He makes us as surefooted as a deer so we can stand on mountain heights and trains us for battle. It is through His power that we are able to overcome, all because His way is perfect and His promises prove true.

How can we gain access to this protection and deliverance? By asking. Our loving heavenly Father is poised to help us. He knows what we need even before we ask, and He is eager to help. The moment we reach out to Him, He reaches down to help us and deliver us from whatever danger is threatening us. Praise God for His perfect, loving care!

You saw me before I was born. Every day of my life was recorded in your
book. Every moment was laid out before a single day had passed.
How precious are your thoughts about me, O God.
They cannot be numbered!

—*Psalm 139:16-17*

The Lord Our Shepherd

Surely your goodness and unfailing love will pursue me all the days of my life,and I will live in the house of the Lord forever.

—*Psalm 23:6*

Sheep are helpless creatures who are unable to survive very long without the constant care of a shepherd. They lack good vision and are easily frightened, especially where it's dark. Sometimes they get so worked up about an imagined danger that they literally worry themselves to death. The shepherd meets the needs of these helpless creatures, giving them water, food, rest, safety from danger, and direction. Only the presence of their shepherd can calm them.

David was a shepherd by profession, and he knew that he needed to trust God, his Shepherd. Only the Lord could renew his strength and meet all his needs for rest, guidance, and protection in dark valleys. God was the one who would seek him when he wandered from the right path and bind up his wounds. And God's protection and provision would carry him even through difficult times.

The valley of darkness represents any difficult experience of life that makes us afraid, including death. In the dark valley, God walks before us and beside us, leading the way and calming our fears. He will carry us through all the highs and lows of life, and the closer we stay to our Shepherd, the safer we are and the more peace will fill our hearts.

Do not be afraid, for I have ransomed you. I have called you by name; you are mine. When you go through deep waters, I will be with you. When you go through rivers of difficulty, you will not drown. When you walk through the fire of oppression, you will not be burned up; the flames will not consume you.

—*Isaiah 43:1-2*

The Lord Will Hold Me Close

Even if my father and mother abandon me, the LORD will hold me close.
—*Psalm 27:10*

There is nothing like a mother's love. It is at once tender and fierce, gentle and stern. She will do anything for her child, even die. Indeed, the process of mothering is a process of dying to self. A father's love is likewise steadfast and dependable. Or at least, that is how God created it.

But sin has marred our closest relationships, including the parent-child relationship. Sometimes those who should be our greatest support cause the greatest hurt. Yet even if the worst happens, even if our parents abandon us, God is there. He holds us close and loves us with a love deeper and higher and longer and wider than even the most loving parent.

Whatever your relationship with your parents, whether it is full of loving support or bitter rejection, God is the perfect parent for you. He will never let you down, never disappoint you, never abandon you. He knows you like the most attentive parent. He cares for your needs. He holds you close when you are brokenhearted and encourages you when you are disheartened. Imagine the most perfect parent, the one who can balance every aspect of love and discipline to help a child grow—God is all that and more. Whatever your need, whatever you hurt, even when everyone abandons you, your heavenly Father holds you close.

The LORD is like a father to his children, tender
and compassionate to those who fear him.

—*Psalm 103:13*

Can a mother forget her nursing child? Can she feel
no love for the child she has borne? But even if
that were possible I would not forget you!

—*Isaiah 49:15*

Joy Comes with the Morning

For his anger lasts only a moment, but his favor lasts a lifetime!
Weeping may last through the night, but joy comes with the morning.
—*Psalm 30:5*

There is a common misconception that God is angry with us, ready to pounce on us for our sins. People think of Him as a judge and forget that He is also a merciful father. This verse promises us that though God is sometimes moved to righteous anger, it is for but a moment. He is angry about sin and evil, but He is not perpetually angry with us. By contrast, His favor is for a lifetime. His default posture toward humanity is forgiveness and love, not anger and judgment. He is eager to show us mercy and love.

This difference in time and span also applies to our sorrows. This life is full of trials and sorrows—Jesus promised that it would be (John 16:33). But because He has overcome the evil one, there is eternal joy in store. Weeping is only for a night, and then comes everlasting satisfaction at God's right hand.

Your sorrows may seem long. The days may stretch out in a progression of heartache and disappointment and pain. But God promises joy. There is joy now when we find our satisfaction in Him, and joy everlasting when Christ returns to claim those who are His. Take courage in the fact that the good days will far outlast the bad.

The LORD passed in front of Moses, calling out, "Yahweh!
The LORD! The God of compassion and mercy! I am slow
to anger and filled with unfailing love and faithfulness."
—*Exodus 34:6*

God will

GENEROUSLY

PROVIDE

all you need.
Then you will always have
EVERYTHING YOU NEED
& plenty left over
to share with others.

2 CORINTHIANS 9:8

The Shadow of the Almighty

You are my hiding place; you protect me from trouble. You surround me with songs of victory.

—*Psalm 32:7*

As you think back on your life, where have you felt the most safe? When was a moment that you felt totally secure, like no harm would befall you? Perhaps it was in your father's arms, or in a cozy room. David found that secure place in God. He called Him a hiding place, the One to whom he could go and feel utterly safe. When he was near to the Lord, he could even hear God singing victory songs over him. He heard an almost audible echo of God's powerful care for him.

The interesting thing is that this psalm starts out with David in a place of utter despair over his sin. His guilt weighed so heavily on him that he felt the physical effects of it. His bones wasted away and he felt God's hand pressing down on him.

How did David turn it around? He confessed. He laid bare his sin and guilt, told God all about it, and received forgiveness. In that instant, God became a hiding place rather than a heavy hand. And that is how we can find our safe place in God as well. If you're longing for God to be your hiding place and to hear His victory song in your life, confess your sin. When you do that, you will be surrounded by His steadfast love and find yourself shouting for joy.

The LORD is a shelter for the oppressed, a refuge in times of trouble.

—*Psalm 9:9*

Guided along the Best Pathway

*The LORD says, "I will guide you along the best pathway
for your life. I will advise you and watch over you."*
—*Psalm 32:8*

Christians spend a lot of time worrying about finding God's will. They long to do what is right, and they know that God's will is best. The problem is, they are a little worried they won't be able to figure out what His will is. There is a common misconception that God is trying to hide it from us, as if it's a mystery we need to solve.

God doesn't hide His will from us. But He often shows us only the next step. He wants us to follow and trust Him, and the best way to build our trust and keep us close to Him is to show us only as much as we need to take the next step. Besides, if we knew where the path was leading, we might get scared and not want to take it.

The promise of God is that we will have grace and provision for each day, not for years into the future. You can trust that He will reveal to you just what you need in order to do the next right thing if you're looking for it. The key is to stay close to Him. Listen to His voice and watch for His leading, and you are sure to find it. He will lead you on the best paths, those that lead to life, eternal joy, and kingdom impact.

We can make our plans, but the LORD determines our steps.
—*Proverbs 16:9*

*The LORD will guide you continually, giving you water when
you are dry and restoring your strength. You will be like
a well-watered garden, like an ever-flowing spring.*
—*Isaiah 58:11*

True, Just, and Good

For the word of the LORD holds true, and we can trust everything he does.
He loves whatever is just and good; the unfailing love of the LORD fills the earth.
—*Psalm 33:4-5*

These verses communicate an important truth about God: He is good and holy in His being and essence. Everything He has revealed, both in nature and in the written Word of God, is true, good, and just. Everything He has commanded is exactly as it should be. Therefore, we should trustingly obey. It is not ours to second-guess what God has said or apply our human wisdom to rationalize weakening or changing it.

This has implications for our theology of suffering. Since God's Word is true, and He loves justice and goodness, we can know that He created all things well—as stated in the next two verses of this psalm. That means that the problems and suffering in the world are the fault of sin, not of God. Let's put the blame where it lies, with Satan and the evil he has introduced into the world, as well as the sin in every human heart.

Perhaps most important of all, the promise that the earth is full of God's steadfast love reminds us to look for His gracious presence all around us. There is goodness and justice filling the earth, we just need to look for it. Rather than fretting over what's wrong in the world, choose to focus on the evidence all around that God loves you and be grateful for His merciful care of His creation. The very rocks and trees cry out that He is God—listen to them!

Look at the birds. They don't plant or harvest or store
food in barns, for your heavenly Father feeds them.
And aren't you far more valuable to him than they are?
—*Matthew 6:26*

Surrounded by Angels

For the angel of the LORD is a guard; he surrounds and defends all who fear him. Taste and see that the LORD is good. Oh, the joys of those who take refuge in him!
—Psalm 34:7-8

Do you ever sense that you are in danger? Perhaps it is danger from evil people who seek to do you harm, but more likely the danger you face is spiritual in nature. Satan and his demons want to see you fail in your spiritual journey. They want you to fall away from God to the point where you think you can't be forgiven and lose faith that He can save you.

What a comfort it is to read that God's angels set up camp around you. Every moment of every day, you are surrounded by heavenly beings who are protecting you from harm, both spiritual and physical. The next time you sense that you are in danger, call on God for help and know that it is already there!

Of course, that doesn't mean that nothing bad can happen to you. That's where the promise of verse 8 comes in. God is good, and you can find joy by taking refuge in Him. Even if your circumstances are bad, God is still good and still in charge. Rest in the knowledge that He is taking care of you, and nothing can happen to you that hasn't been filtered through His loving hands. He is with you in the pain, and you can turn to Him for comfort and rest in the midst of it.

How great is the goodness you have stored up for those who fear you. You lavish it on those who come to you for protection, blessing them before the watching world.
—Psalm 31:19

Delight in the Lord

Take delight in the LORD, and he will give you your heart's desires.
—*Psalm 37:4*

When we encounter a verse like this, there is a temptation to embrace only the phrase "he will give you your heart's desires" and ignore the condition of that promise: "Take delight in the LORD." This isn't a health-and-wealth, prosperity gospel promise. Rather, this is a promise about the blessing of devotion. We must first delight ourselves in the Lord. On a practical level that means spending time with Him in Bible study and prayer. It is gazing at Christ with such a single-minded purpose that our number one priority is His glory, His name being honored among the nations, His will being done.

When we get that part right, then our heart's desires will be satisfied because our heart's desires will be the same as God's will. You see, when we pray for God's glory to be made known, we know that He will do it because that's what He does. When we pray for His will to be done, we can be assured that He is already answering that prayer because that's who He is.

Where is your delight? Is it in the pleasures and comforts of this world, or in the eternal God? Is it in the treasures that moth and rust will destroy, or in the precious Savior?

Wherever your treasure is, there the desires of your heart will also be.
—*Luke 12:34*

Be Still

Be still, and know that I am God! I will be honored
by every nation. I will be honored throughout the world.

—*Psalm 46:10*

Stillness and quiet gets a little harder with each passing year. The rush and bustle of daily life sweeps us along, and it's hard to stop and listen for God's voice. Quieting our souls requires discipline and effort. Yet stillness is what we need in order to reorient ourselves to God's limitless power. He is God and we are not, and we need to quiet our hearts in order to realize that.

Quietness does more than recalibrate our own lives—it also makes God's name be honored in the lives of those around us. As they see our peace they will be encouraged to slow down and look up as well. When they see the joy we have in knowing and worshiping God, they will want to participate in the life of faith we have.

When was the last time you were still before the Lord? No cell phones, no list of all the things you want God to do for you, just quietness and listening. The silence of acknowledging God's mighty power. The deep soul knowing of who He is. Take some time today to find that soul quiet, and then watch for how God will use your peace to make His name honored among the nations.

Acknowledge that the LORD is God! He made us, and we are his. We are his
people, the sheep of his pasture.

—*Psalm 100:3*

The Joy of Your Presence

*But as for me, God will redeem my life. He will
snatch me from the power of the grave.*

—Psalm 49:15

The psalmist's assurance of God's redemptive power is in contrast to the hopelessness of those who don't know the Lord. They will die and then rot in the grave (Psalm 49:14), "but as for me," God will save me from death. God's people have the assurance of eternal life, while those who make themselves His enemies are assured eternal death.

The psalmist utters this promise as he looks around at the success of the wealthy and the trials of the godly. In this life it seems like nice guys finish last. We are tempted to envy worldly success and all the pleasures it brings. But when those who have rejected God reach the end of their lives, they have received all the reward they are going to get. By contrast, for those who love God, life is just beginning when they die, and they will receive an eternal reward that cannot be taken away.

What is really being held up in this psalm is the wisdom of living the life of faith. In the eyes of the world it is foolish to store up treasures in heaven rather than on earth, but in the end that is the only wise way to live. Invest in eternity and you'll never regret it. That is the way of everlasting joy.

*My sheep listen to my voice; I know them, and they follow me. I give them
eternal life, and they will never perish. No one can snatch them away from me.*

—John 10:27-28

Faithful and Just

The sacrifice you desire is a broken spirit. You will
not reject a broken and repentant heart, O God.

—*Psalm 51:17*

World religions all center around humanity trying to appease or earn favor with a reluctant deity. They are attempts to manipulate a god through sacrifice or good works.

The true God of heaven and earth is eager to forgive. He reaches down to us in love and sacrifices Himself to save us. It is the opposite of every other world religion. And it all hinges on this promise: God will never reject a repentant sinner. We don't have to earn an audience with Him or perform certain rituals before He will accept us. He doesn't want sacrifices; all He wants is a repentant heart. He accepts us as we are, broken and sinful and desperately aware of our need. All He asks is that we acknowledge our unworthiness. When we do that, He accepts us once and for all eternity.

Do you realize how radical this is? What good news it is? God wants us—all of us—just as we are. We don't need to try to impress Him. We don't need to clean ourselves up. Just come to Him with your broken and repentant heart, and He will heal you from the inside out. He will transform your heart of stone into a heart of flesh that pleases Him. All you have to do is repent.

If we confess our sins to him, he is faithful and just to
forgive us our sins and to cleanse us from all wickedness.

—*1 John 1:9*

Cast Your Burdens on the Lord

Give your burdens to the LORD, and he will take care of you.
He will not permit the godly to slip and fall.

—*Psalm 55:22*

Negative thoughts and emotional stress are like a backpack that feels manageable at the beginning of the day but becomes heavier and heavier as the hours wear on, and by the end of the day it is an unbearable burden. Whether our burdens are sins or heartaches, they work the same way. We may not notice them at first, but the longer we carry them the more they weigh us down.

There is a solution: Give them to God. He will take care of you, either by removing the burden or helping you to bear it. The verse doesn't specify what type of burden, which means that it includes any type of burden. Whatever is bothering you, God cares. That's because His main concern isn't the problem, which He has completely under control, but your heart and soul. If it's bothering you, it's bothering Him because He cares for you.

There's another promise here as well: God won't let you fall. The burden may feel like a crushing load. You may be hopeless and despairing. There may be no human way for your problem to be solved. But God has you safely in His hand. You may struggle, but you won't fall because your safety rests not on your own ability but on God's, and He never fails.

Then Jesus said, "Come to me, all of you who are weary
and carry heavy burdens, and I will give you rest. Take my
yoke upon you. Let me teach you, because I am humble
and gentle at heart, and you will find rest for your souls.
For my yoke is easy to bear, and the burden I give you is light."

—*Matthew 11:28-30*

Father to the Fatherless

Father to the fatherless, defender of widows—this is God, whose dwelling is holy.
—*Psalm 68:5*

The lasting effects of fatherlessness are well documented. When that bond is severed there are very real and often devastating consequences. But God promises that He will stand in the gap. Where there is no earthly father, He will provide all that is needed. When earthly fathers disappoint, He will stand by with His perfect father-love.

This promise is really a guarantee that God will meet our emotional needs. When we feel unloved, He offers His steadfast love. When we feel defenseless, He promises to defend. When we are abandoned, He is with us. Whatever your need, whatever is lacking in the love you have received, God will make it up.

You have a role in this process, though. God offers His limitless resources, but we have to reach up to take them. Enter His holy dwelling and receive His love. Ask for Him to come to your defense. God will not force Himself on you, but rather responds in love the moment you come to Him. Won't you reach up in faith to take hold of what God is holding out to you in love? Won't you receive His fatherly care? God is ready to pour out His love in your heart the moment you ask for it.

He ensures that orphans and widows receive justice. He shows love to the foreigners living among you and gives them food and clothing.
—*Deuteronomy 10:18*

Praise Him!

*Praise the LORD; praise God our savior! For each day
he carries us in his arms. Our God is a God who
saves! The Sovereign LORD rescues us from death.*

—*Psalm 68:19-20*

A good editor will tell you not to use too many exclamation points in your writing. It can be distracting and lessen the impact. But here they just seem to be necessary. Praise God, He carries us in His arms like a shepherd carries his precious lamb! He saves us from death through His own death on the cross! How can you say either of those things without an exclamation point?

Have you thought recently about how exciting, how unbelievable, how awesome it is that God carries us in His arms? How amazing it is that He rescues us from death? Praise the Lord indeed!

Spend some time today meditating on the aspects of your salvation that have become so familiar you take them for granted. The gospel is the best news possible—Jesus died in our place. We who were God's enemies have been made His friends. God is our heavenly Father and we are His beloved children. These simple facts, which perhaps we have known since we were children, are cause for celebration and worship. Listen to them as if for the first time and praise Him with exclamation points!

*He will feed his flock like a shepherd. He will carry
the lambs in his arms, holding them close to his heart.
He will gently lead the mother sheep with their young.*

—*Isaiah 40:11*

Held Secure

*My health may fail, and my spirit may grow weak, but
God remains the strength of my heart; he is mine forever.*

—*Psalm 73:26*

What is your greatest fear, that thought that keeps you up at night with anxiety about the what-ifs? One thing most of us fear is failing health. There is a sense that if we can keep our physical, mental, and spiritual health we can face almost anything else that life might send our way. And the reverse is true as well—when our bodies fail, everything becomes more difficult.

The psalmist assures us that even if we lose both our physical and emotional health, we will still be okay because we belong to God. He will provide strength of heart, the emotional stamina to face any setback with hope and courage. Ultimately, nothing can harm us because we are eternally secure in His embrace. Even if we die, we will go to be with Him in a place that is better than anything this world can offer.

Once you realize that nothing can snatch you away from God's love, you realize that you don't have anything to fear. Even if the worst happens, God holds you fast. When everything else falls away, He is there. He is with you in every moment and every circumstance, even failing health and emotional despair. That's a promise that can help you sleep soundly at night.

In peace I will lie down and sleep, for you alone, O LORD, will keep me safe.

—*Psalm 4:8*

Every Good Thing

The LORD will withhold no good thing from those who do what is right.
—*Psalm 84:11*

Sometimes when things aren't going our way we think that God is holding out on us. We beg and plead and bargain with Him, as if He were a stingy taskmaster. But God isn't like that at all. He doesn't hold back from blessing us.

God, the almighty Creator who can do all things, has promised that if something is good for us, we will have it. He is our loving heavenly Father, and He knows what is best for us. Our responsibility is to do what is right. Jesus said, "Seek the Kingdom of God above all else, and live righteously, and he will give you everything you need" (Matthew 6:33).

Of course, God doesn't always define good like we do. Or rather, we don't always define good like God does—because after all, He is the standard of good. But that just further proves the point: God is good, He can do anything, and He has promised that He will give us everything good. We can rest in that. Everything that happens to us is for our ultimate spiritual good, which means that He sometimes withholds something that appears good from our earthly, temporal perspective and sometimes allows something that seems very bad to us. Through the ups and downs we can cling to this: God won't withhold anything good from us.

We know that God causes everything to work together
for the good of those who love God and are called
according to his purpose for them. For God knew his people
in advance, and he chose them to become like his Son.
—*Romans 8:28-29*

Resting in the Shadow

*Those who live in the shelter of the Most High
will find rest in the shadow of the Almighty.*

—*Psalm 91:1*

In the desert world of the Bible, shade from the hot sun was often a matter of life and death. If a person found themselves out in the hot sun and couldn't find shelter, they were in trouble. That's the kind of shelter the psalmist had in mind in this verse. Tuck yourself under the shelter of God's presence. Rest under the shade of His wings. And let yourself be at peace, for all is well in the deepest sense of the word and for all eternity.

The rest promised in this verse is more than physical rest, though of course we need that kind of rest too. The rest we find in God's shadow is soul rest. It is that peaceful feeling that all is well. It is the kind of live-in-the-moment relaxation that says we don't need to be anxious for the future. It is finding joy and peace even in the midst of difficult circumstances and busy days.

Take a break from worry and stress and anxiety. Find peace by taking shelter under the shadow of God's presence. The soul rest of a deep relationship with God will make it possible for you to live the public life of peace and rest.

*Don't worry about anything; instead, pray about
everything. Tell God what you need, and thank him for all
he has done. Then you will experience God's peace, which
exceeds anything we can understand. His peace will guard
your hearts and minds as you live in Christ Jesus.*

—*Philippians 4:6-7*

Sheltered by His Wings

He will cover you with his feathers. He will shelter you with his wings. His faithful promises are your armor and protection.

—Psalm 91:4

This verse continues the theme of Psalm 91:1 in yesterday's reading, God's protection, but with the added imagery of God as a mother hen. We are invited to tuck ourselves under His wing, cozy up next to His heart, and be sheltered from the storms of life. We can slow down our breathing as we listen to the steady beat of His heart. And we can stay there in warm, cozy peace for as long as we need to. He is our soft landing place, our secure home.

There is a second type of protection mentioned in this verse that is even stronger than feathers. God's promises are like armor, shielding us from the attacks of both human and supernatural enemies. They are the solid ground beneath our feet, the anchor to cling to in every storm, and the bulwark that never fails. God is our strong guard.

Whether what you need today is a warm embrace or steel armor, God is the One you need. He is shelter and protector from every danger. His promises will keep you safe. Forsake every other source of security and let Him be your comfort and shelter. Hide under His covering, for He is ever faithful and sure.

Have mercy on me, O God, have mercy! I look to you for protection. I will hide beneath the shadow of your wings until the danger passes by.

—Psalm 57:1

Angels: Agents of God's Protection

For he will order his angels to protect you wherever you go.

—Psalm 91:11

Angels are created spiritual beings who have existed since before the world. They are not omniscient or all-powerful, but they are spiritual beings, not bound by physical laws, who have the powers that God chooses to give them. These are the agents of God's protection, and we are assigned not one "guardian angel," but a whole host of them to keep us safe. Note that the protection comes from God, not angels. They work at His command.

When Satan quoted this verse to tempt Jesus to cast Himself from the roof of the Temple, Jesus refused on the grounds that it is not right to put God to the test (Luke 4:9-12). We are not to take foolish risks or test whether God's angels will protect us. But whenever you feel threatened—or even when you don't realize that you are in danger—you can take courage in the fact that you are surrounded by an army of angels.

Angels are not sent to protect us because God is absent or asleep on the job or unable to do it Himself—He is always with us and His power is what saves us. But it is nice to know that God cares about us enough to send heavenly messengers to help us. The Lord of Heaven's Armies summons His majestic messengers to protect us. That's how important we are to Him!

And I saw another angel flying through the sky, carrying the eternal Good News to proclaim to the people who belong to this world—to every nation, tribe, language, and people.

—Revelation 14:6

As Far as the East Is from the West

He has removed our sins as far from us as the east is from the west.
—Psalm 103:12

The primary way we experience God's love is forgiveness. God doesn't just say, "It's okay," when we confess our sins. He doesn't give us a few chances and then give up on us. He doesn't say "I'll forgive you if . . ." And He doesn't pretend to forgive and then throw our failures back in our face the next time we hurt Him. God takes the sins away. He removes them so far they can never be recovered. He expunges them from our record and remembers them no more.

It's easy for Christians to lose their wonder at God's forgiveness. We become so accustomed to being forgiven that we take it for granted. But it is an amazing thing. The holy God of the universe, the One who created us and is worthy of all praise, chooses to forgive even though our sin grieves Him, even though it is a rejection of His love and an affront to His holiness.

Spend some time in confession, acknowledging your sin fully, and then receive the extravagant forgiveness of God. Thank Him for this magnificent expression of love that came at such great cost, the precious blood of Jesus. And then walk forward in freedom, unbound by your sin because it has been removed from you.

I—yes, I alone—will blot out your sins for my
own sake and will never think of them again.

—Isaiah 43:25

Faithful to Every Generation

Your eternal word, O Lord, stands firm in heaven. Your faithfulness extends to every generation, as enduring as the earth you created.

—*Psalm 119:89-90*

The Word of God is born in eternity, rooted in history, and speaks to every generation that will listen. It is founded forever and will endure forever. As Jesus said, "Heaven and earth will disappear, but my words will never disappear" (Matthew 24:35). If you build your life on the Word of God, you will experience His faithfulness, which is firm through every change.

In the changes and seasons of life, God's Word is the thing that is firmly fixed. It is our true north, our anchor, our foundation stone. We can depend on it in a way that is unique in all of life because it is the only thing that will never fail. God's Word is where His faithful love is revealed, and it will endure to the end of time.

Whatever you are facing, whether you have the support and love of others or are facing it alone, God is faithful. You can cling to His Word and His promises, for even when everything else fails you, He will not. He who promised will be faithful to love you and care for you to the end. His Word is as enduring as the earth He created.

It is the same with my word. I send it out, and it always produces fruit. It will accomplish all I want it to, and it will prosper everywhere I send it.

—*Isaiah 55:11*

The Lord Stands beside You

The LORD himself watches over you! The LORD stands beside you as your protective shade. The sun will not harm you by day, nor the moon at night.

—*Psalm 121:5-6*

There is no greater feeling than to know that someone is watching out for us. We love to know that we are being looked after and protected, that someone is paying attention to everything that is happening to us in order to keep us safe and provide for our needs. We all long for that kind of safety and security.

Better yet is having someone beside us, standing by us through thick and thin, in good times and bad, and being on our side. This is the type of person who has our back, who will pick up the slack if we are weary or disabled, and who will stand up for us when injustice or false accusations are lobbed against us.

Best of all is to have God Himself as our watchkeeper who stands beside us. No evil can befall us, no danger overwhelm us, no calamity overtake us, because God is on our side. Day and night and every moment in between, He is watching over us, meeting our needs with His mercy and keeping us from the clutches of the evil one. The Lord Himself, Creator of all and King of the universe is our protector.

They will neither hunger nor thirst. The searing sun will not reach them anymore. For the LORD in his mercy will lead them; he will lead them beside cool waters.

—*Isaiah 49:10*

Now and Forever

The LORD keeps watch over you as you come and go, both now and forever.
—Psalm 121:8

The word *keep* used in this psalm carries with it the connotation of being hedged in by thorn bushes. It is the image of a landowner creating a natural fence around his property to keep his livestock in and any dangerous predators out. The Lord watches over His children by setting a protective hedge around us. Nothing can get in without His consent, and we cannot escape His care through our own rebellion.

God sets a protective barrier between us and the dangers of the world, including spiritual dangers. We are hemmed in on every side by His watchful concern. Isn't it a comfort to know that God has hedged us in—and hedged in our loved ones who know Him?

Whatever difficulties you face in your comings and goings during your journey on earth, know that you are in a safe place. God is with you and God surrounds you. The trials and sorrows of life are being carefully monitored by your loving heavenly Father. He will use every one for your good and His glory, and anything that can't be redeemed in that way He will not allow. You are surrounded by His gracious and loving care, today and always.

He will not let you stumble; the one who watches over you will not slumber.
—Psalm 121:3

The Promise of God's Name

Your promises are backed by all the honor of your name. As soon
as I pray, you answer me; you encourage me by giving me strength.
—*Psalm 138:2-3*

The names of God present who He is; they are inseparable from His character. God is the Almighty (El Elyon), eternal God (Yahweh), the all-sufficient God who is adequate for every situation (Jehovah), the covenant-making God who is faithful to His promises (Elohim), and our heavenly Father (Abba). Because His holy name is connected with His actions, we can count on every one of His promises coming true.

In Psalm 138, David worshiped God with all his heart (verse 1) for the steadfast certainty of His promises to humankind. Specifically here he had in mind the promise God made to establish David's kingdom (2 Samuel 7:12-16). But more generally this refers to all of God's promises. Everything He has said, He will do, because His perfect reputation is at stake.

How could David be so certain that God would keep His word? Personal experience—his prayers were answered and his spirit was strengthened as he prayed. God is not silent, unmoving, or unseeing like other gods. Rather, He listens, He responds, and He truly sees us, in a way that no human being ever could. Have you cried out to God like David did? When you do, you will learn firsthand that you can trust all His promises. He is the ultimate promise keeper.

Listen to my prayer for mercy as I cry out to you
for help, as I lift my hands toward your holy sanctuary.
—*Psalm 28:2*

God's Will

The LORD will work out his plans for my life—for your faithful love,
O LORD, endures forever. Don't abandon me, for you made me.

—Psalm 138:8

We spend a lot of time and energy planning our lives. Whether it is setting five- or ten-year goals or making plans with a friend for lunch, we have a lot of ideas about how our lives should go. But life can be confusing, and sometimes it's hard to know what we should do. Wouldn't it be nice if someone could give us a calendar with the right path for our lives marked out?

We'll never get that elusive calendar, but we do have a perfect life planner. He not only knows which way we should go, but also has the power to help us find the right path. God is working, even in the murky circumstances of your humdrum life, to bring you to the right path.

Your job in all of this is to follow the Guide. When God gives you a direction, do it. When He tells you to wait where you are, have patience and wait with faith and joy. When He changes course with a sudden storm, trust Him to pilot you through it. In all these things, your Creator and Lord is working out His plans for your life. Everything that happens to you is part of His faithful lovingkindness.

God . . . will fulfill his purpose for me.

—Psalm 57:2

God Knows Everything about You

You go before me and follow me. You place your hand of blessing on my head.
—Psalm 139:5

The Lord knows everything about us—what is going on in our lives, what we are thinking, and every word we will ever say. All that we are, everywhere we go, and anything we do is known by God from eternity past. Nothing is hidden from His sight, not even the things we can't see about ourselves. This indeed is amazing knowledge (Psalm 139:6)!

What a promise it is, then, that this God who knows us so intimately hems us in with faithful love. His plans for you are not arbitrary. They are not one-size-fits-all or hastily made. They are not impulsive, not a reaction to something that is happening.

Rather, God's plans for you are made with you in mind. They are tailored to your personality (which God made, after all!), your temperament, your needs, and in many cases even your wants. They are for your best—a best which only the perfect and all-knowing God can dream up. And they are also for the world, plans made so that you will leave a you-sized mark on the world for God's glory. Go forward today knowing that God is before you, behind you, and beside you to help you.

Nothing in all creation is hidden from God. Everything is naked and exposed before his eyes, and he is the one to whom we are accountable.
—Hebrews 4:13

Help for the Fallen

The Lord helps the fallen and lifts those bent beneath their loads.
The eyes of all look to you in hope; you give them their food as they need it.
—Psalm 145:14-15

Some seasons just weigh us down. Whether it is the very obvious and well-defined burden of a health crisis, job loss, or natural disaster—or the more ambiguous weight of mental distress or spiritual doubt, life often seems to beat us down. Just when we conquer one problem, another one comes at us. We can identify with the psalmist who was bent beneath his load.

The Christian's hope lies in the fact that God helps the downtrodden. He is the victorious, conquering King—but also a gentle Shepherd. A bruised reed He will not break. When we are at our weakest, when we have nowhere left to turn except toward Him, that is when He lifts us up. He removes our burden and helps us walk again. He shows His strength in our weakness.

Whatever food you need right now, whether it is a dose of encouragement or literal food for the table, look to God in hope. He sees that you are bent beneath your load, and He will provide just what you need, right when you need it, so that you can walk straight. When you are weak, He will make you strong.

He will not crush the weakest reed or put out a flickering
candle. Finally he will cause justice to be victorious.
—Matthew 12:20

Eyes to See

The Lord opens the eyes of the blind.

—*Psalm 146:8*

This psalm praises God for the many ways He cares for the vulnerable—He gives justice to the oppressed, provides food for the hungry, sets prisoners free, lifts up the bowed down, and upholds the cause of widows and orphans. Tucked into the list is this promise: God is the sight-giver, the One who gives both physical and spiritual vision. He who made the eye brings light to it.

There are so many things we can be blind to. It's easy to have a blind spot regarding our sin, an area where we just don't see the log in our eye that is so obvious to those around us while we point out the splinters in others. Or we can be blind to the goodness of God, His grace and blessing that is poured out on us even in—or especially in—the midst of trials. We can be blind to truth, unable to wade through the relativistic messages of culture to uncover the eternal truths of salvation. Perhaps most of all, we can be blind to the right path to take, the way God is leading us.

God is the One who can open our eyes, whatever the nature of our blindness. Ask Him to reveal to you the truth about Himself, the truth about yourself and your sin, the truth about where you need to go next. And then look for His leading in His Word and in your life.

Open my eyes to see the wonderful truths in your instructions.

—*Psalm 119:18*

Wounded Hearts

He heals the brokenhearted and bandages their wounds.
—Psalm 147:3

God's prophetic word had proved true yet again. Through the prophet Jeremiah, He had predicted the captivity and release of the Jews. Their sins had been forgiven, but their hearts and emotions were shattered by the hardships they had endured in Babylon, the loved ones they had lost in the invasion, and the devastated land and ruined houses that lay before them.

What they needed was healing for their broken hearts, and God could provide it. He knows us better than we know ourselves and knows all the factors that have gone into our heartaches. And He desires to heal our hearts; He cares about our broken hearts no matter what caused the wounding.

Is your heart sad today? Beaten down and on life support? God sees, He knows, and He cares. He is even this moment tenderly bandaging your wounds and healing you from the inside out so that you can be fully restored. It will take time. You may have to respond to His care in ways that are challenging for you. But take courage; the skillful hands of the master Healer are at work. He took your wounds upon Himself and died to redeem every painful scar caused by the fall. Give Him your heart and He will heal it.

He was pierced for our rebellion, crushed for our sins. He was beaten so we could be whole. He was whipped so we could be healed.
—Isaiah 53:5

O LORD, if you heal me, I will be truly healed; if you save me, I will be truly saved. My praises are for you alone!
—Jeremiah 17:14

The Fear of the Lord Is True Wisdom

For the LORD grants wisdom! From his mouth come knowledge and understanding.
—Proverbs 2:6

Obtaining spiritual wisdom is not a once-a-week hobby, it is the daily discipline of a lifetime. It will require time and energy to dig deep into Scripture, for that is where true wisdom is found. We can only understand the world and how to live in it by acknowledging the Creator and bowing before Him in worship.

The final authority for how to live well is the wisdom God gives us through His Word. It is a treasure trove of common sense. There we learn how to love God and love our neighbor. We learn the specifics of who God is and what He wants us to do. Best of all, we learn the gospel story that saves us.

Do you sometimes feel confused about all the messages the world tries to give you? Do you wonder who is right or what you should do? Go to the source of wisdom. He has promised to give wisdom in abundance to everyone who asks. Go to His Word, which is so rich and deep that you will never plumb its depths or exhaust its riches. And then do the next wise thing before you—once you've done that, God will show you the next thing, and the next. He will guide you as you follow Him step-by-step.

If you need wisdom, ask our generous God, and he
will give it to you. He will not rebuke you for asking.

—James 1:5

God Determines Our Course

Trust in the LORD with all your heart; do not depend on your own understanding. Seek his will in all you do, and he will show you which path to take.

—**Proverbs 3:5-6**

God's promise to show us which path to take is built on a condition—obedience. When we seek God's will rather than choosing our own path, we will find the best way of all, for obeying God adds joy to our lives and life to our days. There are three practical steps to obedience outlined in these verses.

First, we are told that we need to trust God with all our hearts. Is He your beloved? Do you think about Him first thing in the morning and last thing at night? Do you sometimes overflow with worship and devotion? Do you do what He says?

Next, we are told that we need to stop depending on our own ideas. Let go of what you think you know and truly ask God to reveal His truth. Let go of your agenda and resolve to obey God.

Finally, we need to seek God's will in everything. We can't pick and choose which areas to obey, which commands make sense to our modern ears. We need to seek His will in everything—in our entertainment choices, our eating habits, our career path, our family life. Then, when all these things are lined up, the promise: God will show you which path to take.

Commit everything you do to the LORD. Trust him, and he will help you.

—**Psalm 37:5**

Overflowing with Blessing

*Honor the LORD with your wealth and with the best part
of everything you produce. Then he will fill your barns
with grain, and your vats will overflow with good wine.*

—*Proverbs 3:9-10*

Tithes and offerings are not "payment" for God's blessings; rather, they are evidence of our faith and obedience. As Jesus said, "Wherever your treasure is, there the desires of your heart will also be" (Matthew 6:21). If we aren't willing to give faithfully to the Lord, we don't really trust Him.

But how many of us can say we do well with verse 9—honoring the Lord with our wealth and giving Him the best, not the leftovers, of everything we have? When the bank account is running low, do we still give God the first portion, perhaps the top ten percent, of our income? Do we give Him the best we have of our time, talent, and treasure, or what remains after we've spent first on ourselves and our family?

What can you do this month to help your budget and calendar reflect your priority of giving God your best and your first? Is it a rearrangement of your day so you spend time with Him while you are freshest? Is it a reallocation of funds so you are sure not to shortchange God even if it means going without a few luxuries? Give God your first and best, and see if He doesn't fulfill His promise to overflow your life with blessing.

*Give your gifts in private, and your Father,
who sees everything, will reward you.*

—*Matthew 6:4*

A Peaceful Harvest of Right Living

My child, don't reject the LORD's discipline, and don't be upset when he corrects you. For the LORD corrects those he loves, just as a father corrects a child in whom he delights.
—Proverbs 3:11-12

Good parents discipline their children. They do it for their own good, to keep the children safe and help them grow up to be kind, successful adults. In fact, children are happiest when they have boundaries and know where they are. So when God disciplines us, He is treating us as His own children. That is why we are told to consider it a joy to experience God's correction (James 1:2).

God's discipline is always carried out perfectly. It may be painful and unpleasant in the moment, but it is always right, always fair, always done in love. And, of course, always done for our good. Nothing God does is ever wasted.

These verses give a warning—it is possible for us to reject God's discipline. When we do that, we are also rejecting His love. We are allowing our sin to create a lasting separation between us and God rather than allowing God to remove the barriers that keep us from experiencing the full impact of His love. And we are refusing to submit to God's pruning, which He does to help us be fruitful and prevent us from being thrown into the fire (John 15). Have you submitted to God's discipline? He promises to discipline the ones He loves—won't you let Him show you His love?

No discipline is enjoyable while it is happening— it's painful! But afterward there will be a peaceful harvest of right living for those who are trained in this way.
—Hebrews 12:11

Trusting in the Lord

The LORD is your security. He will keep your foot from being caught in a trap.
—*Proverbs 3:26*

What makes you feel secure? Is it a full bank account? A steady income? A good doctor's report? A relationship? A safe and cozy home in a good neighborhood? Friends who stick by you through thick and thin?

Those are all wonderful blessings from God, but when it comes right down to it, they can't keep you safe. True security is found in God alone. When He is on your side, you cannot be moved. When He is leading you, you won't fall into a trap. He is the One who holds everything in His hands and sustains the universe with a word. Therefore, true and lasting security is found in trusting Him to guide your steps.

Those who find their security in God don't have anything to fear even when all earthly supports are taken away. They know that God has them in His grip and will carry them safely through this life and into an assured eternity with Him. There is no threat, no disaster, no bad news, no calamity that can take you outside of His tender, loving embrace. Whatever you fear today, release that worry into God's care. He is your eternal security.

Don't be afraid, for I am with you. Don't be discouraged,
for I am your God. I will strengthen you and help you.
I will hold you up with my victorious right hand.

—*Isaiah 41:10*

APRIL

The
eternal **GOD**
IS YOUR REFUGE,
AND HIS
everlasting
arms
ARE UNDER YOU.

DEUTERONOMY 33:27

Wisdom for a Lifetime

Fear of the LORD is the foundation of wisdom.
Knowledge of the Holy One results in good judgment.
Wisdom will multiply your days and add years to your life.
—*Proverbs 9:10-11*

The promise in verse 11 isn't necessarily long life in human terms, but prolonged life. In the short term, making wise choices in daily life will lead to better health and greater satisfaction during the years God gives you on earth. Wisdom is learning to balance life, to have healthy habits. In the long term, the promise is that a life lived in fear of the Lord leads to eternal life—salvation in Jesus.

But what is fear of the Lord? What is the secret to becoming wise and gaining good judgment? An old-fashioned word for it might be reverence or awe. In practical terms, it means calibrating all of life toward God. It is recognizing our dependence on Him and responding to His goodness by serving, loving, and obeying Him.

There is no way to rightly understand life without recognizing its Creator and sustainer. How easily we forget that all we are and all we have are gifts from Him. How quick we are to take credit for things that are undeserved graces from above. Today, bow in humble recognition that God is the Holy One and acknowledge that you have grieved Him with your sin. Give Him the honor He deserves, and see how your life will abound with wisdom and delight as a result.

Fear of the LORD lengthens one's life, but the years of the wicked are cut short.
—*Proverbs 10:27*

A Refuge for Your Children

Those who fear the LORD are secure; he will be
a refuge for their children. Fear of the LORD is a life-giving
fountain; it offers escape from the snares of death.
—Proverbs 14:26-27

The moment you become a parent, your priorities are upended. You live no longer for yourself, but for a tiny, helpless infant who depends on you for everything. You prioritize their welfare and happiness above your own, and no matter how old they are, you don't really feel settled unless you know they are safe.

Do you want refuge and security for yourself and your children? Fear the Lord. Order your life around His priorities and everything else will fall into place. When you truly recognize His supreme power, you will know that as long as you are His, you are safe. As the apostle Paul said, "If God is for us, who can ever be against us? Since he did not spare even his own Son but gave him up for us all, won't he also give us everything else?" (Romans 8:31-32).

Having faith in the God who is all-powerful, all-good, and all-loving is indeed a fountain of life. As long as you know in the core of your being that you are His and He is yours, you need not fear anything else, either for yourself or your children. You have escaped the snares of death through Jesus, and He will also give you everything else.

If you make the LORD your refuge, if you make the Most High your
shelter, no evil will conquer you; no plague will come near your
home. For he will order his angels to protect you wherever you go.
—Psalm 91:9-11

Humility before Honor

Fear of the LORD teaches wisdom; humility precedes honor.
—*Proverbs 15:33*

Humility is an overlooked virtue these days. You probably won't see it on any secular list of character traits to work toward, certainly not as often as you might see courage or kindness. But for the Christian, it is key. In fact, humility is a prerequisite for every promise and blessing of God.

Until we humble ourselves, we cannot approach God at all, for it is humility that acknowledges that He is the Almighty Maker of heaven and earth, and we are His creatures. We must bow our hearts in worship and awe in order to come to Him. This isn't false humility, it isn't done in public, and no one will praise us for it. True humility is recognizing in the quiet of our hearts who we are before God, and asking Him to have mercy on us.

When we bow in reverence before God, all the blessings of the Christian life are opened up to us. The moment we humble ourselves, asking for God's forgiveness and salvation, we get all of God's rich blessings poured out: life abundant, now and forever. Sharing in the inheritance of Christ our brother. Being one of God's own dear children. That is rich honor indeed.

So humble yourselves under the mighty power of God,
and at the right time he will lift you up in honor.
—*1 Peter 5:6*

Commitment

Commit your actions to the LORD, and your plans will succeed.
—*Proverbs 16:3*

What a great promise for life—our plans will succeed. Who wouldn't want that? But there is that pesky condition attached: *If* we commit our actions to the Lord, then our plans will succeed.

It's important to note verse 1 of this chapter—"We can make our own plans, but the LORD gives the right answer"—and also verse 4, which states that God has made everything "for his own purposes." God is sovereign over all things. We can make our goals and work our plans, but ultimately God has the final say over what will happen. Our success is totally dependent on His will, for without His help we cannot even take a breath, let alone succeed in anything.

So what does it mean to commit our actions to the Lord? The root word actually means "roll." In other words, we are to roll our burdens and our plans onto God. Put the ball in His court. Resolve to submit to His will and leave the results up to Him. When we do that, our plans will succeed because our plans become God's plans—or rather, His plans become ours. The best part is, when we choose to want what He wants, every minute of every day, we will always be satisfied with the outcome. What do you need to roll over to God today?

*Give your burdens to the LORD, and he will take care
of you. He will not permit the godly to slip and fall.*
—*Psalm 55:22*

Unshakable

The name of the LORD is a strong fortress; the godly run to him and are safe.
—*Proverbs 18:10*

When a crisis hits, we discover where our confidence truly is. When faced with a crippling medical diagnosis, do we first turn to the Internet for information and statistics—or do we pray? When faced with the loss of a job, do we first shoot an email to all our friends asking for leads—or do we pray? When faced with betrayal, do we first find a friend to confide in—or do we pray?

All too often we turn to everyone and everything else first, and come to God as a last resort when none of those things have helped. It is wise to do research and to get support from our friends. God has given us those resources and we should use them. But that shouldn't be our first stop if we truly believe that God is a strong fortress. If we truly trust Him, if we truly believe that God is who He says He is, we will run to Him in moments of crisis. We will pray and read Scripture before we call a friend.

Trust in your strong fortress and run to Him for safety, in good times and bad. Make Him your first call rather than your last.

He alone is my rock and my salvation,
my fortress where I will not be shaken.

—*Psalm 62:6*

Fear of the Lord

Fear of the LORD leads to life, bringing security and protection from harm.
—Proverbs 19:23

If you haven't noticed, the fear of the Lord is a big theme in both Psalms and Proverbs. This verse is a concise summary of the Bible's teaching on the fear of the Lord. At its most basic, fearing the Lord is rightly ordering our lives according to reality. The truth is, God is the holy Creator and Lord of all, and we are very sinful and fallen creatures who deserve His wrath for our rebellion against Him. The only sensible way to live in the light of those two truths is to reverently bow before God and make Him our Lord and King.

What does fearing the Lord look like? It is acknowledging God in every area of life. Repenting of our sin. Choosing to submit to God's laws. Making decisions based on what will bring glory to Him. Forsaking our own desires when they go against God's best for us.

When we live in this way, we will be secure and protected because we will be living under the umbrella of God's blessing. That doesn't mean nothing bad will happen to us, but it does mean that the bad things that happen to us will be filtered through His protective covering. They will be for our eternal good. Best of all, it means that in our moments of sorrow we have the strong and steady presence of our faithful God.

The LORD watches over those who fear him,
those who rely on his unfailing love.

—Psalm 33:18

Divine Appointments

No human wisdom or understanding or plan can stand against the LORD.
—*Proverbs 21:30*

This promise has two sides—on the one hand, it is a recognition that God's ways prevail. Since He is all-wise, all-knowing, and all-good, that is a glorious promise to cling to. When we aren't sure what the best path is, God promises to do the right thing for us. When we are threatened by people who are trying to harm us, we can take comfort in knowing that their plans will not prevail unless they are part of God's sovereign will.

On the other hand, there's a warning here too. We should never suppose that we know the future. We can make our plans, but God may choose to do something else. The most prayerfully thought-out proposal, made with the best of intentions, may be thwarted in the end. All our plans should be loosely held and joyfully submitted to God's sovereign will.

Perhaps the best test for whether we are acknowledging God's sovereignty is how we react when our plans don't work out. Do the upsets in our daily schedule derail us, making us frustrated and even angry? Or are we open to God's interruptions and do we see them as divine appointments? God has the final word on how our days will go and how our lives will go—and what a blessed thing that is!

You can make many plans, but the LORD's purpose will prevail.
—*Proverbs 19:21*

Confession and Repentance

*People who conceal their sins will not prosper, but if they
confess and turn from them, they will receive mercy.*

—*Proverbs 28:13*

Sometimes it's helpful to turn a verse on its head to get at the real issue. The promise? Mercy—compassion and forbearance from a holy God no matter how heinous our sin. The prerequisite? Confession and repentance. We can't access God's mercy until we've acknowledged that what we did was an affront to His holiness and also determined in our hearts to turn away from our sin.

The warning? Concealing our sin just won't work. On the one hand, usually our sin finds us out. God won't let us wallow in our misery; He will in His mercy bring our sin to light so we can find forgiveness. On the other hand, sin has a way of weighing on us so that even if it isn't discovered, it eats us from the inside out until we simply must confess it. The psalmist described it as his bones wasting away (Psalm 32). Again, this is God's mercy to us. Sin is so destructive and God loves us so much that He keeps after us until we release it.

When was the last time you spent significant time confessing your sin? Do it today. It is so freeing, and you won't experience the depths of God's forgiveness and love until you do.

*But if we confess our sins to him, he is faithful and just to
forgive us our sins and to cleanse us from all wickedness.*

—*1 John 1:9*

A Dangerous Trap

Fearing people is a dangerous trap, but trusting the LORD means safety.
—Proverbs 29:25

Any recovering people pleaser can tell you that fearing people is a dangerous trap. It leads you to make bad decisions based on poor criteria, often with disastrous results. In the end, it leaves you feeling insecure and unsatisfied at best, and in the worst-case scenario possibly even in trouble with the law.

This verse sets out the alternative: trusting the Lord. It's not a dichotomy we often think about, but when it comes right down to it, we are either trusting God or we are trusting in other people, either fearing the judgment of God or fearing the judgment of people. Jesus told His disciples, "Don't be afraid of those who want to kill your body; they cannot touch your soul. Fear only God, who can destroy both soul and body in hell" (Matthew 10:28).

When you fear God over people, you are safe because you are held tightly in His grasp. People may betray you, they may make your earthly life miserable, but no ultimate harm can befall you if you trust in Jesus. He will keep you safe, and afterward take you to glory. Choose the safety of fearing God and you will discover freedom from the fear of mere humans.

So we can say with confidence, "The LORD is my helper,
so I will have no fear. What can mere people do to me?"
—Hebrews 13:6

Beautiful in Its Time

Yet God has made everything beautiful for its own time. He has planted eternity in the human heart, but even so, people cannot see the whole scope of God's work from beginning to end.
—*Ecclesiastes 3:11*

God's timing is so often a veiled mystery to us. We can't see that there is anything good in our circumstances. This side of heaven there is rarely an explanation for the trials of life, though we can always see God at work through them if we look for it. But in God's eyes, in the scope of eternity, there is beauty even in the pain.

The place we see this most vividly illustrated is at the Cross. In the moment when Jesus hung there, betrayed and beaten and seemingly defeated, there was nothing but darkness. But God knew—that was His greatest triumph! It was the beautiful joining of all His promises, the perfect meeting of justice and mercy when Jesus took our sin, our pain, our curse and paid the price once and for all.

Our longing to see things worked out in justice is one aspect of the eternity God has placed in our hearts. The only logical explanation for our longing for beauty and perfection is that it exists somewhere—in the presence of God. Nevertheless, the scope of God's work is hidden from us. While we wait to see the unfolding of His plan, we have to cling in hope to the promise that He will make everything beautiful, now and for eternity.

We know that God causes everything to work together for the good of those who love God and are called according to his purpose for them.
—*Romans 8:28*

God's Purpose

And I know that whatever God does is final. Nothing can be added
to it or taken from it. God's purpose is that people should fear him.
—*Ecclesiastes 3:14*

Sometimes it's refreshing to hear the truth in simple, straightforward terms. This is one of those verses that tells it like it is. The basic truth of life is that God calls the shots, and His overarching purpose is that people should fear Him.

So here's the question we should ask ourselves: Do I really believe that whatever God declares, will be? Do I believe it when the promise seems out of my grasp? When so many bad things have happened that I can't imagine how this could be part of God's good plan (Romans 8:28)? When I read the newspaper and am overwhelmed by the evil in the world? On dark nights, do I truly believe that God is in control?

And then the follow-up: If the purposeful plan God is working is that people should fear Him, am I working toward that goal too? Am I sharing the good news of salvation? Do I revere God in a way that speaks of His love, His goodness, and His power? Does my life proclaim His glory in a way that draws others to glorify Him too? These may be simple truths, but they have profound implications for our lives.

Only I can tell you the future before it even happens.
Everything I plan will come to pass, for I do whatever I wish.
—*Isaiah 46:10*

Let's Settle This

*"Come now, let's settle this," says the LORD. "Though your sins
are like scarlet, I will make them as white as snow. Though
they are red like crimson, I will make them as white as wool."*

—Isaiah 1:18

God's people had broken the covenant. In breaking God's law, they had severed the relationship by which they agreed to live under God's rule and He promised to bless them. They had rejected God's rule and His blessing, thereby removing themselves from God's presence and His promises. They had failed to keep the faith. What hope did they have now?

Imagine the pure joy of hearing God say in that moment, "Let's settle this. I'll take care of it. You made a mess of your life, you betrayed and rejected Me, but I will purify you and remove the stain from your life. What you have turned into a decaying, bloody mess I will cleanse into pure white, like new-fallen snow."

You don't have to imagine it—God does say that to you. He has personally paid the price to make you righteous. He longs to restore the relationship that has been broken. He offers you reentry into the life of His blessing—forgiveness, joy, and peace forever. What good news this is! All you must do is what is described in Isaiah 1:19-20: Turn from sin and obey God. Your account is settled the moment you turn away from sin and toward God.

*Purify me from my sins, and I will be clean;
wash me, and I will be whiter than snow.*

—Psalm 51:7

A Time of Peace

The LORD will mediate between nations and will settle international disputes.
—Isaiah 2:4

It's a fleeting dream equally touted by naive children, idealistic politicians, and beauty-pageant contestants: "I dream of world peace," they say. The cynic in each of us quietly scoffs. That will never happen! As long as the earth turns and seasons come and go, we will use swords, spears and other weapons to settle international disputes.

Except this settled time of world peace *will* happen because God has declared it to be so. The promise will be finally fulfilled when the Messiah returns. A few chapters later Isaiah describes a time when wolf and lamb will live together and "the earth will be filled with people who know the LORD" (Isaiah 11:6-10). In a sense, this promise is one we're still waiting for. It won't be complete until Jesus returns to rule over the new heavens and the new earth.

But there is also a sense in which this promise is for now. The occasion of this time of peace is when God's Word has gone into all the earth—something we have already seen, and continue to see. Jesus brings peace between humanity and God and on a human-to-human level. As we look forward to the final fulfillment of peace when He returns, let us also spread gospel peace to all those we come in contact with.

Everyone will live in peace and prosperity, enjoying their
own grapevines and fig trees, for there will be nothing
to fear. The LORD of Heaven's Armies has made this promise!
—Micah 4:4

Our Hiding Place

He will provide a canopy of cloud during the day and smoke and
flaming fire at night, covering the glorious land. It will be a shelter
from daytime heat and a hiding place from storms and rain.
—Isaiah 4:5-6

Isaiah 4 offers great hope for God's people. Even in the midst of judgment and exile, when the city is left like a "ravaged woman, huddled on the ground" (Isaiah 3:26), God is at work. There is beauty and glory as God lifts the shame and disgrace from His people (Isaiah 4:2). The promise here is for redemption, fruitfulness, cleansing, and relationship.

This promised blessing comes through the Messiah, the righteous Branch. He will cleanse His people and restore the relationship they once had with God. Just as God led them in the Exodus with a pillar of cloud by day and a pillar of fire at night, so He will once again lead them from slavery to freedom in Christ.

These are promises for everyone who is in Jesus. God is our canopy, our shelter from the scorching sun and torrential downpour. He guides our comings and goings with His protective hand. God is our guardian. Whatever storms you see on the horizon, whatever heat you are feeling from the circumstances of your life, God is there. He covers you with His beautiful and glorious presence, and nothing can take that away from you. You are hidden and safe in His care.

For he will conceal me there when troubles come; he will hide me
in his sanctuary. He will place me out of reach on a high rock.
—Psalm 27:5

God with Us

All right then, the Lord himself will give you the sign.
Look! The virgin will conceive a child! She will give birth to a son
and will call him Immanuel (which means "God is with us").

—Isaiah 7:14

I love the rendering here: "All right then"! God is responding to the questioning and doubting of the king. You want a sign? All right then, here it is: The virgin will conceive and give birth to Immanuel. Herein is His response to all of our doubts as well. You want a sign? All right then, God has already given it!

The Virgin Birth is the prophecy and fulfillment upon which every other promise in Scripture hinges. Without this historical event, we do not have a Savior who is both fully God and fully man. In short, we do not have a Savior at all. Jesus had to be both God and man in order to live a sinless life and die in our place. It's the only way the gospel could work.

Wrapped up in this promise of God becoming man is the assurance that God understands our weakness. He knows what it is like to be hungry, to thirst, to be unable to take another step. He knows what it is like to be tempted. He knows what it is to be betrayed and to suffer an agonizing death. This is what it means that God is Immanuel, God with us. He is with us in our humanity, and He did it so we can one day be with Him in glory if we place our trust in Him.

Mary asked the angel, "But how can this happen?
I am a virgin." The angel replied, "The Holy Spirit will
come upon you, and the power of the Most High will
overshadow you. So the baby to be born will be
holy, and he will be called the Son of God."

—Luke 1:34-35

God's Passionate Commitment

His government and its peace will never end. He will
rule with fairness and justice from the throne of his
ancestor David for all eternity. The passionate commitment
of the LORD of Heaven's Armies will make this happen!

—*Isaiah 9:7*

God has given us a perfect King whose reign is eternal. He came not with royal fanfare, but as one of us, born in humble circumstances and worshiped by the lowest members of society and the highest—shepherds and kings. This is our Lord and King.

The verse just before the one quoted above tells us what kind of King this will be. He is the Wonderful Counselor—one who makes wise plans that foil the wisdom of humankind. He is Mighty God, the Lord of Heaven's Armies who will conquer all His foes and break the curse of sin and death. He is our Everlasting Father—benevolent protector who tenderly cares for His people, like a father has compassion on his children. He is Prince of Peace, the One who will usher in a time of eternal, perfect peace that enters into every corner of heaven and earth. His peace even now dwells in our hearts through faith.

This King is more than able to rule with fairness and justice. His understanding is unfathomable, His power limitless, His love for you without end. Won't you trust Him with your life, with your triumphs and failures, with your joys and heartaches? His passionate commitment is to be all these things for you.

From his abundance we have all received one gracious blessing after another.

—*John 1:16*

Like a Root in Dry Ground

Out of the stump of David's family will grow a shoot—yes,
a new Branch bearing fruit from the old root.

—Isaiah 11:1

The family line of the Messiah was dried up, cut down with nothing left but a dead stump. Isaiah had prophesied their demise and exile. By the time this promise was fulfilled, not only was there no dynasty, there seemed to be no people of God, either. Certainly not the mighty nation God had promised. No line, no land, not even a word from God for 400 years.

God specializes in keeping His promises, in doing the impossible, in bringing life from death. The promise was not dead, it was merely waiting for the right time. Sure enough, just when things seemed their most hopeless, a new Branch sprouted from the old stump. Jesus the Messiah was born, fulfilling every prophecy of Scripture and every promise of God.

Are there things in your life that seem hopeless? Areas where you need God to breathe new life and redeem what seems like it's lost forever? Take heart. The Branch bears fruit. God can bring forth vibrant life even from something that appears to be dead. He is working His purposes, even now. And He loves to do the impossible to show His power. Pray for Him to touch what is dead and bring forth new life in His name. Then watch Him work!

All of us, like sheep, have strayed away. We have left God's paths
to follow our own. Yet the LORD laid on him the sins of us all.

—Isaiah 53:6

Everyone Will Know the Lord

*Nothing will hurt or destroy in all my holy
mountain, for as the waters fill the sea, so the earth
will be filled with people who know the Lord.*

—Isaiah 11:9

This passage describes what it will be like "in that day"—when Jesus returns to make all things right again. The wolf and lamb will live together. The leopard and goat, the calf and the lion, the cow and the bear, all will dwell together in harmony. It will be a new heaven and a new earth, a new order under the rule of the perfect and just King who rules forever.

It's like all the best fairy-tale happy endings rolled into one, only better. The curse of Genesis 3 is reversed once and for all. But Isaiah saved the best part for this verse—everyone will know the Lord. That is the key for how things can be so perfect in this new heaven and new earth.

There are two implications of this promise. One is that we have a great future to look forward to. This is the kind of hope that can keep us going on the hard days when everything that could go wrong, does. Even better, we can know the Lord and experience a bit of this even now. The closer we get to Jesus, the more we will experience His peace in our hearts, and the more it will spill over into our relationships with others so that they may know Him too.

*And the Lord will be king over all the earth. On that day
there will be one Lord—his name alone will be worshiped.*

—Zechariah 14:9

My Strength and My Song

God has come to save me. I will trust in him and not be afraid.
The LORD GOD is my strength and my song; he has given me victory.
—Isaiah 12:2

This chapter describes the joy God's people would experience when the Messiah appeared, the Redeemer and promise-fulfiller. It is the two-layered worship that believers of every age participate in as we meditate on God's promises.

First there is private praise as individual believers realize the great joy of God's anger being turned away and His comfort being given. What an amazing thing it is to realize "God has come to save *me*." He has given me victory. This great fountain of salvation is not just for others, not just for the corporate body of believers; it is for me. I am the object of God's affection.

There is also a corporate praise that takes place at the throne of the Messiah in the next four verses. His mighty deeds are for the nations, and His praise will be made known throughout the world. The Holy One of Israel lives among us; great is His name. This dual-pronged praise—private and public—should make up the fabric of our lives. We are to quietly thank God in our prayer closet for all that He does for us in our little corner and also to join with others in our home, in church, and around the world to make His mighty name known.

Sing to the LORD, for he has done wonderful things. Make known his
praise around the world. Let all the people of Jerusalem shout his
praise with joy! For great is the Holy One of Israel who lives among you.
—Isaiah 12:5-6

Our Anchor for Life

The LORD of Heaven's Armies has spoken—who can change
his plans? When his hand is raised, who can stop him?
—Isaiah 14:27

Isaiah has just prophesied the destruction of Babylon and Assyria, the great oppressors of God's people. In the eyes of the world, these great superpowers were invincible. How could the God of the insignificant and defeated nation of Israel declare their defeat so decisively?

From our vantage point the answer is simple: God said it, and so it would be. The author of Hebrews puts it this way: "So God has given both his promise and his oath. These two things are unchangeable because it is impossible for God to lie" (Hebrews 6:18). Only God has the power to predict the future because only God is all-powerful, all-wise, all-knowing. When He makes a promise, it is done. No one can thwart His plans or prevent Him from carrying out His holy will.

This is our anchor for life, our hope in the storm. The writer of Hebrews continues, "We who have fled to him for refuge can have great confidence as we hold to the hope that lies before us. This hope is a strong and trustworthy anchor for our souls. It leads us through the curtain into God's inner sanctuary" (Hebrews 16:18-19). Have you tied yourself, your hopes, and your desires to this anchor? He is the sure and strong refuge you can always depend on.

From eternity to eternity I am God. No one can snatch
anyone out of my hand. No one can undo what I have done.
—Isaiah 43:13

Peace of Mind and Heart

*You will keep in perfect peace all who trust
in you, all whose thoughts are fixed on you!*

—Isaiah 26:3

Who among us doesn't want peace? We seek peace and quiet from a busy day, peaceful surroundings at a favorite vacation spot, and peace from strife in our relationships. All those things are foretastes of what this verse talks about—perfect peace. This is the kind of lasting peace we can only find in a relationship with Jesus.

What does this perfect peace look like? The Hebrew word is *shalom*, and it implies completeness, favor, tranquility. It is a permanent and settled reality, not a fleeting emotion. There is absence of fear, for sure, but it is more than that. It is a deep wellness of soul, a sense that all is well that keeps us unaffected by the circumstances or storms swirling around us. It is calm that settles so deep into our identity that we are untroubled by troubling news.

This verse tells us how to find this perfect peace—by fixing our minds on Jesus. We must choose to turn our thoughts back to God's promises and put our hope there. It is an act of the will to avoid spiraling out into what-ifs or what-thens. This is what trust really is—fixing our mind on the Prince of Peace and being at rest in Him.

*I am leaving you with a gift—peace of mind and heart. And the peace
I give is a gift the world cannot give. So don't be troubled or afraid.*

—John 14:27

A Precious Cornerstone

Therefore, this is what the Sovereign LORD says:
"Look! I am placing a foundation stone in Jerusalem, a firm
and tested stone. It is a precious cornerstone that is safe to
build on. Whoever believes need never be shaken."

—Isaiah 28:16

There are a lot of things in this world that can shake us up: Bad news from the doctor. The loss of a loved one. A life-changing accident. The loss of a job or a home or a way of life. It's easy to feel vulnerable when these things happen, a little shaky and insecure. We wonder what might happen next, and we're not sure how to recalibrate our lives to the new reality. It can feel like we have nothing firm to depend on.

God's promise is that if we believe in Jesus, we need never be shaken. The worst might happen, there might be a whole long series of bad news, but we are anchored to the foundation stone with cords that cannot be broken. He is firm and tested and safe. The trials of life won't leave us vulnerable because we have built our lives on the solid cornerstone, and He never fails.

If you're feeling shaky today, entrust yourself to Jesus, the One who is faithful and tested and sure. He will never change, never leave you, and never let you down. It is safe to trust Him with everything you have and everything you are.

How joyful are those who fear the LORD. . . . They do not fear
bad news; they confidently trust the LORD to care for them.

—Psalm 112:1, 7

Rest for Restlessness

This is what the Sovereign LORD, the Holy One of Israel, says:
"Only in returning to me and resting in me will you be saved. In quietness
and confidence is your strength. But you would have none of it."

—Isaiah 30:15

There is something really sad about the end of this verse. Here God offers His people rest, quietness, confidence, and strength. He tells them they can stop trying so hard and just be with Him. He offers relationship and perfect peace. But they would have none of it.

Who in their right mind would reject such an offer? Well, I'm afraid all too often I do, and I bet you do too. I like to be independent and self-sufficient. I like to call the shots, to choose my own adventures, to do things my way. I want to set my goals and meet them. All too often I reject God's way of submission and quietness, preferring instead my loud blustering and constant striving to be more—to do more.

If that sounds familiar, maybe it's time to choose rest over restlessness. To just stop and be with Jesus instead of checking off a to-do list. Maybe it's time to let Him be your confidence rather than relying on yourself and your accomplishments. I don't know about you, but I don't want God to ever have to say of me, "But you would have none of it." I want to take the peace He offers.

Then Jesus said, "Come to me, all of you who are weary and carry heavy
burdens, and I will give you rest. Take my yoke upon you. Let me teach
you, because I am humble and gentle at heart, and you will find rest for
your souls. For my yoke is easy to bear, and the burden I give you is light."

—Matthew 11:28-30

Wait for His Help

So the LORD must wait for you to come to him so he can show you his love and compassion. For the LORD is a faithful God. Blessed are those who wait for his help.

—Isaiah 30:18

The image in this verse is so powerful. God is *waiting* for us to come to Him. The word could also be translated as "longing." It's a picture of God poised with hands outstretched, eager to pour out His love and compassion in our lives. There are echoes here of the image in Revelation of Christ knocking on the door of our hearts (3:20). He longs for connection and relationship. All we have to do is invite Him to be present with us, and He will be.

But there is another person waiting in this verse—us! When God pours out His love and compassion on us, all too often we then try to run ahead of Him. We get going in a direction and charge on ahead, usually without making sure that we are going at the pace God wants us to. Sometimes He changes direction and we are so far ahead that we don't even notice for a while.

But blessed are those who wait for God to help. Those who are patient with the process, allowing things to unfold in His timing. Walk in step with Him rather than running ahead. God wants to walk beside us in loving relationship—will we choose to walk with Him?

Wait patiently for the LORD. Be brave and courageous. Yes, wait patiently for the LORD.

—Psalm 27:14

Healing Light

*The moon will be as bright as the sun, and the sun will be seven times
brighter—like the light of seven days in one! So it will be when the
LORD begins to heal his people and cure the wounds he gave them.*

—*Isaiah 30:26*

The book of Isaiah has a good bit of doom and gloom in it as God judges the nations for their evil—including His own people. It is both sobering and comforting to learn that some of our wounds are given by God.

But as verses like this make clear, unlike the sorrows we experience that are caused by bumping up against fallen humans or as the consequence of sin, God wounds so that He can heal. God must judge sin and rebellion in keeping with His righteous character, but He does it so that He can have a relationship with us. And He Himself administers the cure.

The healing God promises in this verse hinges on light. This is the light of God's glory, His presence that was experienced in the wilderness on Mount Sinai and at the Cross of Christ and among His people today through the presence of the Holy Spirit. It is better and brighter than anything we could ever experience in the natural world. When God begins to heal His people and cure their wounds, it is with the brilliance of His presence shining in our hearts, illumining the truth and bringing the warmth of His healing touch.

*Look now; I myself am he! There is no other god but me!
I am the one who kills and gives life; I am the one who wounds
and heals; no one can be rescued from my powerful hand!*

—*Deuteronomy 32:39*

Quietness and Confidence Forever

This righteousness will bring peace. Yes, it will bring quietness and confidence forever.
—Isaiah 32:17

This chapter presents the future reality of what it will be like when the Messiah returns to rule the new heavens and the new earth. It promises justice, shelter, satisfaction, and relief from the weariness of life. Like so many other passages, there is a sense in which these things are already a reality since the first coming of Christ. But we will not experience the full force of these promises until Jesus returns.

Here is one promise that we can experience now—peace, quietness, and confidence. These things are a reality for those who are in Christ, who have received His righteousness. This is the kind of peace Jesus promised when He returned to heaven.

If you have ever seen a mature believer face devastating circumstances, you know a bit of what this verse means. There is a quiet confidence about them even when the worst happens. They are sad, but not panicked. Grieving, but not without hope. They have the quiet peace that comes from years of walking in the security of trusting God and finding Him faithful. Do you want more peace? Ask for more of God's presence and righteousness in your life and you can have it. The quietness and confidence we long for is found in Him and will last forever.

I am leaving you with a gift—peace of mind and heart. And the peace I give is a gift the world cannot give. So don't be troubled or afraid.
—John 14:27

A Sure Foundation

*In that day he will be your sure foundation, providing
a rich store of salvation, wisdom, and knowledge.
The fear of the LORD will be your treasure.*

—Isaiah 33:6

What do you treasure most in this life? What is the thing you would grab if your house was burning down and you had one minute to grab something? Obviously you would start with your loved ones, perhaps your pets, and then maybe a family heirloom that reminds you of your roots. Maybe even a favorite Bible.

This verse says that our greatest treasure is fear of the Lord. The way we reverence Him in our hearts and love Him is far more important and beautiful than anything else we value. Why? Because He is the only sure foundation, and He provides a rich store of salvation, wisdom, and knowledge. Put that way, it is a clear choice that our relationship with God is our greatest treasure.

How can you more highly prize the fear of the Lord in your life? Are you spending your time, talent, and treasure to deepen your relationship with Him? Do you look forward to your time with Him with the same excitement you have when going on a date with your new love or a dear friend? The fear of the Lord is indeed the greatest treasure we can ever possess—let's prioritize our relationship with God as the precious thing that it is.

*Fear of the LORD is a life-giving fountain;
it offers escape from the snares of death.*

—Proverbs 14:27

Eternal Word

The grass withers and the flowers fade, but the word of our God stands forever.
—*Isaiah 40:8*

The eternal permanence of God's word—what He has spoken and what He has willed as well as what is written in the Bible—is contrasted with the brevity of life. Flesh is like grass, and beauty fades like a flower, but God's purposeful plan for all things endures forever.

Have you been confronted recently with the transience of life? A young person is cut down in the prime of life. The mirror tells us we're not as young as we feel—or perhaps we feel older than we think we ought to as sickness overtakes our youth. These things all serve as helpful reminders of what really matters and what truly lasts.

God's Word is trustworthy and true because it outlasts the generations. Before there was life, God was. Long after this world perishes and is replaced, God will be. He is the same righteous, holy, and loving God through all time. What He has willed and what He has spoken is eternal. And that is why we can trust Him with our lives and our future and everything that happens to us. Building a life on the unchanging Word of God is the only sensible way to live.

I send [my word] out, and it always produces fruit. It will accomplish all I want it to, and it will prosper everywhere I send it.

—*Isaiah 55:11*

Running without Weariness

Those who trust in the LORD will find new strength. They will soar high on wings like eagles. They will run and not grow weary. They will walk and not faint.
—Isaiah 40:31

Experience tells us, and God's Word confirms, that youth is no guarantee of strength. All of us fall in exhaustion. None of us escapes the reality that life is tiring and we are but flesh.

The promise is that the everlasting God does not grow weary. He does not tire of our prayers. His energy to care for and love us is never exhausted. With unmeasurable depth, He understands us and our weakness, and better still He understands everything about our situation so He can do what is best. He comes to our aid, giving power when we are weak and strength when we are powerless.

Do you need new strength today? Are you in a place where you can't even remember what it's like to run without growing weary or walk without fainting? Then listen to these promises. Hear and understand—God, who is everlasting and unwearying, promises to help you with His limitless power and strength. You will soar like an eagle and run like a gazelle. You will have what it takes to put one foot in front of the other because God will give you His strength in place of your weakness. Turn to Him in your weariness and you will find that He is more than able to help.

He will not let you stumble; the one who watches over you will not slumber. Indeed, he who watches over Israel never slumbers or sleeps.
—Psalm 121:3-4

I Am with You

Don't be afraid, for I am with you. Don't be discouraged, for I am your God.
I will strengthen you and help you. I will hold you up with my victorious right hand.
—Isaiah 41:10

When life is at its worst, when we are devastated beyond what we can imagine or so discouraged we don't know if we can face another day, the thing we most want is the presence of someone who loves us. We want someone to come hold our hand and just be there, not trying to fix the unfixable or offer platitudes that can't touch our sorrow.

That's what God offers us in this verse. He doesn't tell us not to be afraid because everything is in His control, although that is true. He doesn't tell us how He is going to fix things. He just says, "I'm here. I understand the sorrow because I faced it too. I will sit here with you in the midst of it." Then, after offering Himself, God says, "I will help you. The strength you don't have, I will give you. The victory you can't imagine, I have already won at the Cross."

Aren't these amazing promises from a God who really understands us in our weakness? Whatever your heartache or fears are today, cling to the God who is with you in it. Let Him take your shaking hand in His and give you His peace.

I hold you by your right hand—I, the LORD your God.
And I say to you, "Don't be afraid. I am here to help you."
—Isaiah 41:13

MAY

COMMIT YOUR ACTIONS TO

the
LORD,
and your PLANS
will
SUCCEED.

PROVERBS 16:3

You Will Not Drown

The one who formed you says, "Do not be afraid, for I have ransomed you. I have called you by name; you are mine. When you go through deep waters, I will be with you. When you go through rivers of difficulty, you will not drown. When you walk through the fire of oppression, you will not be burned up; the flames will not consume you. For I am the LORD, your God, the Holy One of Israel, your Savior."

—Isaiah 43:1-3

These verses are reminiscent of Paul's declaration of God's unstoppable love in Romans 8:35, where he wrote, "Can anything ever separate us from Christ's love? Does it mean he no longer loves us if we have trouble or calamity, or are persecuted, or hungry, or destitute, or in danger, or threatened with death?" Then he answered his own question a few verses later—not even these things can separate us from God's love.

God's love is both proven and guaranteed by the fact that He ransomed us. Our faith in Christ makes us God's children, and based on that identity, God makes these bold promises.

Note that some bad things happen in these verses. There are deep waters, rivers of difficulty, and fires of oppression. These are things we wish would not happen to us, but God doesn't promise that they won't. What He does promise is His presence and protection in the midst of them. We will not be alone, we will not drown, we will not be consumed because God is our Savior. Ultimately, nothing can harm us, because we are His.

I am convinced that nothing can ever separate us from God's love. Neither death nor life, neither angels nor demons, neither our fears for today nor our worries about tomorrow— not even the powers of hell can separate us from God's love.

—Romans 8:38

An Example to Follow

*There is no other God—there never has been, and there never
will be. I, yes I, am the Lord, and there is no other Savior.
First I predicted your rescue, then I saved you and proclaimed
it to the world. No foreign god has ever done this.*

—Isaiah 43:10-12

The beautiful uniqueness of the God of the Bible is that He does the saving. Every other religion has a cold God who needs to be appeased. Favor must be earned through acts of piety and devotion. You never quite know where you stand, and you certainly have no recourse if you rebel against one of those gods.

But the only true God first promised our rescue, and then carried it out Himself. Jesus became one of us so He could live a sinless life and die in our place. He took our shame, our guilt, our deserved punishment, and suffered on our behalf. It is unthinkable, unimaginable, unfathomable that the Almighty Creator would do all that for wretched rebels like us, but He did.

This beautiful, self-sacrificing God deserves our utmost devotion. There is no one like Him, and therefore His people should be unlike anyone else. Let's proclaim this amazing Savior to the world, to our children, to the people who come across our path today. Let's imitate His sacrificial love, dying to ourselves and living for those who don't deserve our kindness. And let's most of all love our beautiful Savior who gave all for us.

*Since I, your Lord and Teacher, have washed your feet,
you ought to wash each other's feet. I have given you
an example to follow. Do as I have done to you.*

—John 13:14-15

Something New

But forget all that—it is nothing compared to what I am going to do. For I am about to do something new. See, I have already begun! Do you not see it? I will make a pathway through the wilderness. I will create rivers in the dry wasteland.

—Isaiah 43:18-20

By this point in the Bible God had done some pretty amazing things. He had created the world, made a people for Himself, and rescued them from slavery. He had parted the Red Sea and conquered mighty armies. He had made unbelievable promises and kept every one. Yet here Isaiah says, "Forget all that, what's coming next is even better!" God was not done making and keeping promises, and the ones that were coming would show even greater depths of His love.

It's sometimes tempting to live in the past, or to think that God is done with the majority of His work in the world. But that is a mistake. He is constantly carrying out more amazing Exodus-like deliverances in people's hearts so that one day He will be honored throughout the whole world.

Do you believe that God is still at work in the world today? Do you believe that He can make rivers in the dry wasteland of hard hearts? Do you believe that He can refresh you? All of these things are promised, and all of these things are part of what God is doing today. Take Isaiah's advice and look for all the ways God is making a pathway through the wilderness for you.

Those who have been ransomed by the LORD will return. They will enter Jerusalem singing, crowned with everlasting joy. Sorrow and mourning will disappear, and they will be filled with joy and gladness.

—Isaiah 35:10

Like the Morning Mist

I have swept away your sins like a cloud. I have scattered your offenses like the morning mist. Oh, return to me, for I have paid the price to set you free.
—Isaiah 44:22

When we know we've really hurt someone we love, what we want more than anything is to go back in time and undo what we've done. We long for more than forgiveness—we want to erase both the cause and the effect of our sin.

That's what God promises here. Our sins are swept away like they never existed. Our offenses disappear like mist that once it's gone, we forget was even there. How can God promise this? Because He paid the price that freed us from not only the punishment, but from the curse itself. He took our sins and offenses on Himself and did away with them once and for all.

When you think about it, God's plea to return to Him seems like something that shouldn't even need to be said. Why wouldn't we continually go before the One who promises to cast our sins as far as the east is from the west and receive that amazing forgiveness? But of course, we do need the reminder. We take it for granted, forgetting the immensity of our sin. Or we fail to even acknowledge our sin, going about our day thinking we're not all that bad after all. Don't let another minute go by before you ask for God's forgiveness once again.

He has removed our sins as far from us as the east is from the west.
—Psalm 103:12

Every Knee Will Bend

Let all the world look to me for salvation! For I am God; there is no other....
Every knee will bend to me, and every tongue will declare allegiance to me.
—Isaiah 45:22-23

God promised to make a people for Himself, to give them a place, and to rule over them with His protection and provision. At first those covenant promises rested on Abraham and seemed to include only the people of Israel. But there was always a hint that these were promises for other nations, because Abraham was promised to be a blessing to the world, not just the Jews.

Here the promise for the nations is made explicit. God's salvation is for the world, it always was and always will be. One day every knee will bow and every tongue confess the one true God.

Perhaps this is something you have heard so many times your eyes gloss over the words. You may know the verse by memory, but do you really believe it? Do you believe that Jesus is for the group of people you don't like very much, the ones who seem harsh or judgmental? Do you believe that He loves the one who hurt and betrayed you, or the one who has done things so terrible they seem inhuman? More to the point, do you commit to love those people with the love of Jesus that is truly for all?

After this I saw a vast crowd, too great to count, from
every nation and tribe and people and language, standing
in front of the throne and before the Lamb. They were clothed
in white robes and held palm branches in their hands.
—Revelation 7:9

I Will Carry You

I have cared for you since you were born. Yes, I carried you before you were born. I will be your God throughout your lifetime—until your hair is white with age. I made you, and I will care for you. I will carry you along and save you.
—Isaiah 46:3-4

This verse is a promise of God's care throughout life, but it also shows yet another way that God is superior to all the false gods of the nations. Verses 1 and 2 of Isaiah 46 portray people from other nations bending under the weight of the idols they must carry. But contrast, our God carries us.

God's care begins before we are born, for He knows every day of our lives before even one of them comes to pass (Psalm 139:16). And it continues until our hair is white with age and even beyond, to the moment He carries us to His presence where we will live forever.

This is the kind of promise that can help us through the days when life stoops us down beneath its heavy load. When you aren't sure if you can carry on, God promises that He will carry you. He made you, He knows you, He loves you, and He will keep on caring for you every day of your life. Hold fast to that truth when the days are long and the nights are longer. From the first breath you took until your last, God is carrying you along to save you.

He is our God forever and ever, and he will guide us until we die.
—Psalm 48:14

An Assured Outcome

Only I can tell you the future before it even happens.
Everything I plan will come to pass, for I do whatever
I wish. . . . I have said what I would do, and I will do it.
—Isaiah 46:10-11

When you read about all of the amazing things God has promised to do, every now and then you might wonder, *can He really do it?* This is one of the many verses in the Bible that assures us He can.

God's promises are first based on His omniscience. He knows all things and exists outside of time. That's why He can tell the end from the beginning. Just think of all the Bible prophecies that have been fulfilled; they are proof that when God says something will happen, we can trust that it will.

But there is more—God's character ensures that He will keep His promises. A God who could do anything but was not perfect could not be trusted to do what is right. A God who was perfect but not all-powerful would not keep His promises. But our God is both perfect and powerful—He knows what is right, chooses to do what is right, and has the power to do what is right. Everything He plans will come to pass. That is how we know that all the promises of Scripture are certain. The outcome is secure because God is in charge.

But the LORD's plans stand firm forever; his intentions can never be shaken.
—Psalm 33:11

Untarnished Glory

I will rescue you for my sake—yes, for my own
sake! I will not let my reputation be tarnished,
and I will not share my glory with idols!

—Isaiah 48:11

God's overarching purpose is to bring glory to His name, to show off the brilliance of His perfection and the weight of His goodness. That is why He does not punish us as our sins deserve and why He holds back His anger. It would tarnish His reputation of compassion if He gave us what we deserve. It would make Him no better than the false idols worshiped by the pagans.

This promise that God will glorify His own name by rescuing His people comes on the heels of a verse about suffering. There is a furnace of affliction that refines us, but God promises based on His own name and reputation that it will not swallow us up. He will not leave us in the fire too long; He will have compassion and rescue us at just the right time.

What a comfort it is that God's mercy is based not on our deserving—for we will never deserve it—but on God's own name. He is merciful, and thus He cannot but show mercy. He is glorious, and thus He will show His glory in and through our suffering. He is perfect, and thus all His ways toward us are perfect.

I am the LORD; that is my name! I will not give my glory
to anyone else, nor share my praise with carved idols.

—Isaiah 42:8

Peace like a River

Oh, that you had listened to my commands!
Then you would have had peace flowing like a gentle river
and righteousness rolling over you like waves in the sea.

—Isaiah 48:18

So often we think of God's commands as drudgery. We know what the right thing is to do, but we struggle and strain to make ourselves do it. Our spiritual life is characterized by defeat and failure and a sense of guilt.

It doesn't have to be that way. God declares that His commands are the pathway to peace. When we place ourselves in the flow of God's will we will be carried along as if by a gently flowing river into the ways of righteousness and the peace that come from a right relationship with God.

The righteous waves mentioned in this verse are a picture of the way God cleanses us with the blood of Jesus. His sacrifice on our behalf washes away our sins. We inherit His righteousness as our own. This indeed is peace flowing like a gentle river. It is the living water that Jesus promised, wells of righteousness springing up within us, a never-ending source of refreshment and satisfaction. Hear God's plea in this verse and respond. Oh, that we would listen to Him and follow Him in joyful obedience so that we can have His peace and righteousness flowing through us.

Oh, that they would always have hearts like this, that
they might fear me and obey all my commands! If they did,
they and their descendants would prosper forever.

—Deuteronomy 5:29

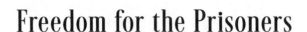

Freedom for the Prisoners

I will say to the prisoners, "Come out in freedom," and to those in darkness,
"Come into the light." They will be my sheep, grazing in green pastures
and on hills that were previously bare. They will neither hunger nor thirst.
The searing sun will not reach them anymore. For the LORD in his
mercy will lead them; he will lead them beside cool waters.

—Isaiah 49:9-10

Jesus began His earthly ministry by quoting Isaiah's prophecies about the promised Messiah (Luke 4:18-19). As He sat in the synagogue and quoted this verse, the Jewish listeners would have immediately known that He was proclaiming Himself to be the Messiah. Only God Himself can set the prisoners free and bring light to the darkness.

These promises are for all who believe in Jesus, who declare in their hearts that He is God. We are freed from the prison of sin, death, and self. We have the light of life. We are His sheep, the ones He feeds in green pastures and satisfies with living water. The tender mercies of God described in this verse are for us.

Which of these promises do you need today? Are you feeling trapped by your sin, doubt, or despair? God says, "Walk in freedom." Are you in the dark, unsure of what you should do or what to believe? God says, "Come into the light." Are you hungry and thirsty? God will lead you to green pastures and quiet waters. Are you feeling seared by the sun? God is your shade. Rest in the mercy of God and let Him quench your thirst with cool water.

The LORD is my shepherd; I have all that I need.

—Psalm 23:1

Never Forgotten

Can a mother forget her nursing child? Can she feel no love for the
child she has borne? But even if that were possible, I would not
forget you! See, I have written your name on the palms of my hands.
Always in my mind is a picture of Jerusalem's walls in ruins.

—Isaiah 49:15-16

Throughout most of Scripture God is presented in male terms—He is our Father and shield and King. Those are images of strength and power and loving care. But in a few places, including this one, He is presented using feminine imagery. His love is tender like a mother's love for her nursing child. There is a sweet gentleness to His care for us.

If you've ever been a nursing mother or been close to one, you know that a mother's body doesn't let her forget about her baby. If she is away too long or hears a baby's cry, her body responds immediately, unconsciously. That is a picture of the way God loves us. Even if it were possible for a nursing mother to forget her child—which we all know it isn't—God could never forget us.

God always remembers us, remembers our needs, remembers our weakness. When we come to Him in prayer He does not need us to remind Him of what we've been doing or asking Him for. Our names are written on the palms of His hands, ever before Him, and our needs are always in His mind. What amazing, intimate love God has for us!

Even if my father and mother abandon me, the LORD will hold me close.

—Psalm 27:10

Favor for a Lifetime

*"For a brief moment I abandoned you, but with great compassion
I will take you back. . . . With everlasting love I will have
compassion on you," says the LORD, your Redeemer.*

—Isaiah 54:7-8

The original blessing pronounced at Creation included multiplication and abundance. Adam and Eve were to "be fruitful and multiply" (Genesis 1:28)—this was God's expression of love to them. Throughout Scripture we see barrenness as a symbol of God withholding blessing, and the miraculous blessing of a child as a symbol of His promise fulfilled.

In Isaiah 54 God describes the covenant of peace that will rest on His people after the Messiah has come, and He does it by comparing the Israel of old to a barren woman. The desolation of an abandoned widow and the bitter disappointment of a woman who longs for a child but can't have one are images for Israel's hopelessness—for our hopelessness apart from Christ.

Contrast that with the new covenant fulfilled in Christ. We no longer live in shame (verse 4). We have the Creator as our husband (verse 5). We have been called back from grief by His great compassion (verse 6). We have so many blessings that we've had to add on to our house to fit them all in (verse 2). These are our realities, the things we can depend on to be true even when our present experience does not match up to our future hope. Rejoice in the glorious blessings of the covenant-keeping God.

*His anger lasts only a moment, but his favor lasts a lifetime!
Weeping may last through the night, but joy comes with the morning.*

—Psalm 30:5

Crowned with Everlasting Joy

The mountains and hills will burst into song, and the trees of the field will clap their hands! Where once there were thorns, cypress trees will grow. Where nettles grew, myrtles will sprout up. These events will bring great honor to the LORD's name; they will be an everlasting sign of his power and love.

—Isaiah 55:12-13

The immediate context of these verses is the triumphant procession that took place when the Jews returned from captivity. God promised to restore the covenant so that His people would once again live under His blessing. God had punished, but He would restore.

In the long term this is a promise for all of us who come to Jesus thirsty to find life (Isaiah 55:1). He leads us out of captivity to sin and death into a place of joy and peace. We are first promised a change in environment: Where once thorns and nettles grew, now there will be cypress trees and myrtles. God redeems what is broken, and the reversal of the curse extends to nature so that even the trees clap their hands. The new heaven and new earth will be places of perfect abundance, peace, and blessing.

More importantly, through Jesus our relationship with God is restored—we are called by His name. We were made to have a relationship with God, and though we severed it through sin, God has restored it in Christ. Let us, then, join the trees and mountains in praising His name!

Those who have been ransomed by the LORD will return. They will enter Jerusalem singing, crowned with everlasting joy. Sorrow and mourning will disappear, and they will be filled with joy and gladness.

—Isaiah 51:11

Hope for the Humble

The high and lofty one who lives in eternity,
the Holy One, says this: "I live in the high and holy place
[and] with those whose spirits are contrite and humble.
I restore the crushed spirit of the humble and revive
the courage of those with repentant hearts."

—Isaiah 57:15

It's not too surprising that the high and lofty One who lives in eternity and is holy would live in a high and holy place. That's where He belongs; it makes sense to us. What does not make sense is the second part of the verse—this high and holy One also lives with those whose spirits are contrite and humble, who are crushed and have no courage.

I don't know about you, but I don't even want to be around myself when I'm feeling low, let alone choose to be with someone else who is down in the dumps. But that's what God chooses, and He does it because that's where we are when we truly realize our need of Him. It is those who have repentant hearts who are ready to receive His help.

If you are feeling crushed and humbled today, know that God is with you. He is even now restoring and reviving you. And if you're not feeling that way, then maybe it's time to reexamine your heart. Do you realize how your sin grieves a holy God? When you grasp the extent of the chasm between you and the holy God, you will be ready to receive the promise of His presence.

The LORD is close to the brokenhearted;
he rescues those whose spirits are crushed.

—Psalm 34:18

The Call That Gets Answered

*Then when you call, the L*ORD *will answer. "Yes, I am here," he will quickly reply.*
—Isaiah 58:9

Even if we are in an important meeting or screening our phone calls, there are a few people who can always get through no matter what—a spouse, a child, or a parent, to name a few. That's the image given in this verse. When we call, the Lord quickly answers. We can always get through. We never get an "out of office" automatic reply or a busy signal.

There is a condition to this verse, given in the verses preceding. At first glance it appears that the condition is that we must be working for justice, but a closer reading reveals that God is asking for more than outward obedience—He is asking for our hearts, for sincere worship and humility.

In one sense, it's not as easy as declaring a fast. We can't fake it with God. Obedience and self-discipline are not enough. But in another sense, it is far easier. All God asks for is what He deserves—the heart He has made from the child He loves. Respond to your heavenly Father's love with love and this promise is for you. When you call, He will quickly respond with, "I am here!"

I will answer them before they even call to me. While they are still talking about their needs, I will go ahead and answer their prayers!
—Isaiah 65:24

A Well-Watered Garden

*The LORD will guide you continually, giving you water when
you are dry and restoring your strength. You will be
like a well-watered garden, like an ever-flowing spring.*

—Isaiah 58:11

Earlier in this chapter Isaiah contrasted true and false worship. True worship is characterized by actions that prove the worshiper's sincerity of heart. Like James said, faith without actions is dead (James 2:17).

So this promise is for everyone who lives out their faith in God. If you are pouring out your life for the sake of the gospel, then God promises to guide you and provide everything you need to fulfill the work. He will give you refreshment when you are spiritually dry and restore your strength so that His energy flows through you like an ever-flowing spring. He will give you everything you need to do His will.

If you're not feeling that fruitful energy from God, then you should ask yourself why. Have you taken on something that He isn't calling you to? Have you forgotten to go to Jesus for living water? Are you resisting His leading? Are you relying on your own wisdom, your own strength? Are you working so hard for God that you have neglected your relationship with Him? God wants for you to experience flourishing in your faith walk, and you can only do that when you are looking for refreshment in the right place.

*Blessed are those who trust in the LORD and have made the LORD
their hope and confidence. They are like trees planted along
a riverbank, with roots that reach deep into the water.*

—Jeremiah 17:7-8

Everlasting Light

No longer will you need the sun to shine by day, nor the moon to give its light by night, for the LORD your God will be your everlasting light, and your God will be your glory. Your sun will never set; your moon will not go down. For the LORD will be your everlasting light. Your days of mourning will come to an end.

—Isaiah 60:19-20

Wherever God's glory appears in Scripture it is accompanied by light. God is light, and in Him there is no darkness—no shadow of confusion or darkness of despair or hiding in shame. He is brilliance and goodness and heavenly glory, all that is right and perfect and pure.

This is part of what makes heaven so beautiful. We will no longer need the light of sun and moon, for though they are beautiful, they are but poor reflections of the bright light of God. We will no longer have night, for there is no end or waning of God's presence. His light is everlasting and unchanging.

It is this brightness of God's glory that ensures the final promise here: an end to all mourning. When we are in the presence of God, there will be no memory of the heartache and sorrow of this world. He will erase it all and wipe the tears from our eyes with His own nail-scarred hands. It is a lot to look forward to, and this same light is ours even now through Christ. We can live in the brightness of His glory today as we seek His presence and walk in His light.

The Word gave life to everything that was created, and his life brought light to everyone. The light shines in the darkness, and the darkness can never extinguish it.

—John 1:4-5

Your True Home

Look! I am creating new heavens and a new earth,
and no one will even think about the old ones anymore.

—*Isaiah 65:17*

There's something about home that settles deep in our souls. Even at the end of a wonderful vacation we get a certain yearning for home. It's where we feel we belong, where we are comfortable and safe—or at least that's what it should be.

When Christ returns and ushers in the next stage of reality, the one where His people live under His perfect rule in the new heavens and the new earth, we will not even think about missing our old homes. Aspects of this earth are wonderful, but they are nothing when compared to what's coming. Our new homes will be more home than anything on this earth ever was, because we are made for the new heavens and new earth and they are made for us.

What difference does this promise make in the here and now? It makes a lot of difference. This world's treasures should remind us that we look forward to an even better treasure. This world's heartaches are lessened as we dwell in the truth that something better is coming. And our love for God and desire to share it with others gains more urgency as we look forward to His return.

I heard a loud shout from the throne, saying, "Look, God's home
is now among his people! He will live with them, and they will be
his people. God himself will be with them. He will wipe every tear
from their eyes, and there will be no more death or sorrow
or crying or pain. All these things are gone forever." And the one
sitting on the throne said, "Look, I am making everything new!"

—*Revelation 21:3-5*

Called for His Glory

*I knew you before I formed you in your mother's
womb. Before you were born I set you apart and
appointed you as my prophet to the nations.*

—*Jeremiah 1:5*

The immediate context of this verse is Jeremiah's calling. God knew him and set him apart before birth for a particular task of prophetic declaration. No doubt this comforted Jeremiah in the many difficult days of his life.

But there is a truth here for us as well. God knew each of us before we were born and has a specific plan and call for us to fulfill. Where you were born, the parents you grew up with, the many circumstances of your life—these are all part of a plan set in place by God Himself. And the thing you are called to do was created with you in mind.

Now, your calling is not as earth-shattering as Jeremiah's. It may look pretty ordinary. Your days may be full of menial tasks that just about anybody could do. Or you may be called to something bigger but always feel inadequate for the task. Whatever God has given you to do in this life, know that it is a calling. Even changing diapers or taking out the garbage can be a noble calling, and it's important to God that you do it for His glory. You were set apart for God's glory; now let His light shine in all you do.

*May the Lord our God show us his approval and make
our efforts successful. Yes, make our efforts successful!*

—*Psalm 90:17*

Something to Boast About

*This is what the LORD says: "Don't let the wise boast in their wisdom,
or the powerful boast in their power, or the rich boast in their riches.
But those who wish to boast should boast in this alone: that they
truly know me and understand that I am the LORD who demonstrates
unfailing love and who brings justice and righteousness to the earth."*

—*Jeremiah 9:23-24*

For the most part, Christians don't boast a lot. That is as it should be, because boasting usually smacks of pride and self-centeredness rather than the humility to which we are called. Often it is about us taking credit for things that are actually gifts from God. But the Bible does encourage one kind of boasting—boasting in God.

A child who is proud of his father will brag to other kids on the playground about how big or important he is. That's the kind of boasting that is encouraged here. It's telling other people that our God is amazing, and does amazing things! Another way of putting it is "glorying in Christ." Hebrews 3:6 talks about "boasting in our hope" (ESV). This kind of boasting brings honor to God and takes the spotlight off of us.

When was the last time you boasted about something God has done in your life? When was the last time your social media feed was full of praise for who God is and the amazing salvation He offers? What could you do today to boast in the God who demonstrates unfailing love and brings justice and righteousness to the earth?

*When people commend themselves, it doesn't count for
much. The important thing is for the Lord to commend them.*

—*2 Corinthians 10:18*

He Will Restore

This is how the LORD responds:
"If you return to me, I will restore you
so you can continue to serve me."

—*Jeremiah 15:19*

Jeremiah was in a dark place. He had declared God's messages of woe to Judah, but no one listened. His ministry appeared to have been worthless, and on top of that he didn't even have any friends. He was in such a dark place he even wished he had never been born.

Perhaps you can relate to his despair. Maybe you, too, see your life's work in shambles around you and wonder if you missed God's call or if He just doesn't care. At least Jeremiah had the sense to go to God with His complaints, and God responded.

The message God gave to Jeremiah, and to all of us who feel worthless and alone, is one of hope. If we return to Him, He will restore us. He will not leave us alone, for He has promised His presence. Beyond that, as long as we have breath, God will give us a means to serve Him. It may be through the testimony of suffering, or the ministry of prayer or service to others, or perhaps we will have a platform for proclamation like Jeremiah did. No matter the exact circumstances, we are promised a relationship with God and a purpose for life. As long as we have those two things, we need never despair.

The LORD is close to all who call on him, yes, to all who call on him in truth.
—*Psalm 145:18*

Flourishing

*Blessed are those who trust in the Lord and have made the Lord
their hope and confidence. They are like trees planted along
a riverbank, with roots that reach deep into the water. Such trees
are not bothered by the heat or worried by long months of drought.
Their leaves stay green, and they never stop producing fruit.*
—*Jeremiah 17:7-8*

Jeremiah 17 contrasts the lives of those who trust in human strength and those who trust in the Lord. It is the difference between fearing God or fearing man, between living for the rewards and accolades of this life or the next, between self-reliance or God-reliance. And the outcomes could not be more different.

Those who rely on human strength are cursed. In choosing to turn away from God they also are rejecting the blessing, joy, and life that He offers. They live in parched places and shrivel like a shrub in the wilderness. There is no life or vitality inside, and so their life purpose—to bear fruit—is stunted.

By contrast, those who trust in the Lord flourish like a tree planted by water. They don't fear scorching sun because their nourishment comes straight from the stream of living water. They are not anxious even in a drought, for they still bear fruit in season. Their life is marked by inner strength and consistent, purposeful living. They provide refreshment and nourishment to those around them, and they are full of vitality and joy.

*The godly will flourish like palm trees and grow strong
like the cedars of Lebanon. . . . Even in old age they will
still produce fruit; they will remain vital and green.*
—*Psalm 92:12, 14*

Near and Far

"Am I a God who is only close at hand?" says the LORD.
"No, I am far away at the same time. Can anyone
hide from me in a secret place? Am I not everywhere
in all the heavens and earth?" says the LORD.

—Jeremiah 23:23-24

This verse promises that God is omnipresent, filling every time and place equally. He is not limited or hemmed in by the constraints of humanity, but rather operates on every scale, large and small, simultaneously. This is the kind of theological idea that makes our heads hurt. What does it mean, and how is this a promise?

It first of all means that there is an unhurried peace to God's ways. His timetable is unlimited, and therefore we do not need to be concerned when things are not working out as quickly as we want. God is still in control, still working His purposes, and His patience is a grace to us and our loved ones. God does not rush us or get impatient with our slow progress in the Christian life— He is at work everywhere, all the time.

It also means that God sees us. Nothing is hidden from His sight. He knows the thoughts and intentions of our hearts. When we are unjustly accused He knows the truth, and when we are fully at fault He knows and still forgives us. Praise God that He knows the truth and loves us still!

I can never escape from your Spirit! I can never get
away from your presence! . . . If I ride the wings of the
morning, if I dwell by the farthest oceans, even there your
hand will guide me, and your strength will support me.

—Psalm 139:7-10

The Higher Way

"For I know the plans I have for you," says the LORD.
"They are plans for good and not for disaster, to give you
a future and a hope. In those days when you pray, I will
listen. If you look for me wholeheartedly, you will find me."
—*Jeremiah 29:11-13*

We're fond of taking this verse on its own and framing it as a promise for our future flourishing. Seek God and good things will happen. In a sense that is true, but not in the way we might hope.

Jeremiah prophesied this verse while the people were in exile. They had been promised by the false prophet Hananiah that their exile would end in two years—which of course wasn't true. So the people of God were dealing with some pretty serious disappointment. Finally God spoke to them. First He told them to settle in where they were, to build houses and families and work hard in the place of exile. Most surprisingly, He told them to pray for their captors and work for the good of the home they shared (Jeremiah 29:5-7). And then He told them this was all part of His good plan.

The place where God has you is not an accident. It is not an obstacle to your flourishing; it is rather the very place where God wants to bless you. He is there in your disappointing circumstances, in the hard things that feel like exile. God knows the plan and is working the plan and promises that it is for your good. But you may need to change your definition of good. In the meantime, settle in and work for the good of the people God has placed next to you. That is God's good plan for you.

"My thoughts are nothing like your thoughts," says the LORD.
"And my ways are far beyond anything you could imagine."
—*Isaiah 55:8*

I Have Drawn You to Myself

Long ago the LORD said to Israel: "I have loved you,
my people, with an everlasting love.
With unfailing love I have drawn you to myself."

—Jeremiah 31:3

John Calvin called it irresistible grace. He didn't mean that God's grace is like a beautiful red velvet cupcake that casts its spell on us. Rather, he was teaching that God's elect are powerless to resist His call to salvation.

You may argue with Calvin's point, and many have, but you cannot read the Bible and deny that God draws us to Himself. While we were dead in sin, Paul tells us, God breathed life into us (Ephesians 2:1). We are powerless to save ourselves and undeserving of God's love, yet He reaches out to us with His everlasting love. The prophet Hosea used the image of a parent leading a child using ropes of kindness and love.

This is a promise for those who feel adrift, unsure of God's care, or concerned for a loved one who seems to be running from God. He draws us to Himself with unfailing love even when we are not seeking Him. He follows after us and calls us back to relationship, back to joy, back to the safety of His love. He did it for the people of Israel, He does it for every one of His children, and He will do it for you. Reach up to Him and you will find that He's already reaching down to you.

For this is what the Sovereign LORD says:
I myself will search and find my sheep.

—Ezekiel 34:11

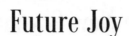

Future Joy

The young women will dance for joy, and the men—old and young—
will join in the celebration. I will turn their mourning into joy.
I will comfort them and exchange their sorrow for rejoicing.

—*Jeremiah 31:13*

This promise straight from God Himself was a promise to His exiled people. He would release them from captivity and bring them back from all the places He had scattered them. They would overflow with shouts and songs of joy as their years of mourning and sorrow were replaced with freedom. Indeed, the description Ezra gives when they laid the foundation stone of the Temple is a fulfillment of this promise (Ezra 3:11).

One day all of us exiles will fully experience this promise in heaven—in this world we experience sorrow, but one day it will be replaced with joy. This isn't just a promise for someday, though. Even now we can experience these promises, the same way those returning exiles did, and the key is to feast on God's good gifts. It's not about the material blessings He may or may not give us, about focusing on the here and now moments that bring us joy, but rather it is about satisfying ourselves in the goodness of God Himself. When we gaze at Him, we realize all that He has done for us and we are filled with grateful praise. He forgives our sins. He reconciled us to Himself at the Cross. He gives us His comforting presence. These are the things that cause us to be radiant with the joy of the Lord even in the moments when we feel like we are in exile.

With praise and thanks, they sang this song to the Lord:
"He is so good! His faithful love for Israel endures forever!"
Then all the people gave a great shout, praising the Lord
because the foundation of the Lord's Temple had been laid.

—*Ezra 3:11*

The New Covenant

"But this is the new covenant I will make with the people of Israel after those days," says the LORD. "I will put my instructions deep within them, and I will write them on their hearts. I will be their God, and they will be my people. . . . And I will forgive their wickedness, and I will never again remember their sins."

—Jeremiah 31:33-34

Up to this point the Old Testament has been about God's covenant promises, first made in the Garden of Eden, then clarified through the family of Abraham. But the people were incapable of keeping their side of the agreement because they were helplessly mired in sin.

So now God unveils the new covenant, which comes through Christ. It was a fresh start for the people of God. Whereas the old covenant was a law written on stone that the people had to try to keep in their own power, the new covenant is written on our hearts and we are empowered by the indwelling Holy Spirit to obey it. Whereas the old covenant was administered by human priests who had to make sacrifices each day for their own sins as well as the sins of the people, the new covenant is mediated by the sinless Christ who made the sacrifice once for all. Whereas the old covenant led to death, the new covenant leads to life.

The crux of the new covenant is that we can be totally, utterly, completely forgiven through the once-for-all, perfect sacrifice of Christ. God forgives our wickedness and forgets our sins, and we live in the full blessing of covenant relationship with Him, with free access to Him through the blood of Christ.

He has enabled us to be ministers of his new covenant. This is a covenant not of written laws, but of the Spirit. The old written covenant ends in death; but under the new covenant, the Spirit gives life.

—2 Corinthians 3:6

Long-Term Hope

I am the LORD, the God of all the peoples of the world. Is anything too hard for me?
—Jeremiah 32:27

These are the same words Jeremiah had said to God a few verses earlier (Jeremiah 32:17). It's an easy question to answer when things are going well—of course God can do anything. But things weren't going well for God's people; they were under siege from the Chaldeans, and they were about to be captured. Was God throwing these words in Jeremiah's face like a taunt?

Far from it, these are words of comfort. Not immediate comfort, but long-term hope. The angel Gabriel declared these same words to Mary just after he told her she would bear God's Son (Luke 1:37). That, too, was a wonderful promise in the long run, as it was part of God's plan for the salvation of the world. But in the short run it would mean for Mary embarrassment, lack of security, and a mother's deepest sorrow as she watched her son die a painful and humiliating death.

Nothing is too hard for God. He can turn any situation into good. But for you, like for God's people in Jeremiah's day and for Mary, it may involve pain, feelings of abandonment, and deep suffering. The promise is that God is in control even of that. He is working good, even now. He loves you and He is working out His plans, even though His ways may involve suffering.

O Sovereign LORD! You made the heavens and earth by your strong hand and powerful arm. Nothing is too hard for you!
—Jeremiah 32:17

Unstoppable Goodness

And I will make an everlasting covenant with them: I will never stop doing good for them. I will put a desire in their hearts to worship me, and they will never leave me. I will find joy doing good for them and will faithfully and wholeheartedly replant them in this land.
—Jeremiah 32:40-41

One aspect of the new covenant established through the work of Christ is that it changes our hearts. Whereas the old covenant was a list of laws the people had to will themselves to obey, the new covenant is all about God changing our hearts so that our dispositions are toward obedience. That doesn't mean that we don't need to work to obey, of course. It is our task to walk in obedience. But it is no longer an uphill climb. God through the Holy Spirit helps us, empowers us, and motivates us to obey. What He commands, He also equips us to do.

There is another wonderful promise to those who are in Christ: God will never stop doing good for us. It is His joy and delight to faithfully care for us and establish us. Think about that for a minute—God delights to do good to you. He is not holding back His blessing or keeping back anything that would be for your good. The perfect good, as defined by the perfectly good God, will be done in your heart and in your life. Even the pain of life is part of God's work to plant you in a faithful relationship with Him.

Now that you belong to Christ, you are the true children of Abraham. You are his heirs, and God's promise to Abraham belongs to you.
—Galatians 3:29

Remarkable Secrets

This is what the LORD says—the LORD who made the earth, who formed and established it, whose name is the LORD: Ask me and I will tell you remarkable secrets you do not know about things to come.
—*Jeremiah 33:2-3*

There is something almost irresistible about a secret. That's why gossip is such a temptation for us. We like to have inside information, to know things that other people don't know. And so there have been, in every generation, those who declare with certainty specific end-times events. Sometimes they go so far as to predict the exact date of Christ's return.

God is the One who holds the future. He made the earth and has determined the time when it will be replaced with a new heaven and a new earth. He is the only one who can predict future events. This verse isn't promising Jeremiah, and certainly not us, that God will reveal the future to us, as if God could be manipulated or controlled.

Here is what it does promise: God knows all things, and He is able to give us understanding beyond our own. Further, we are encouraged to ask Him to do so. Most often this will mean a new insight into Scripture that we hadn't seen before, and sometimes it will also mean an insight into a situation we are asking for God's help in. So go ahead and ask God to reveal Himself and His ways to you, and then wait expectantly for Him to speak to you, as He has promised.

From there you will search again for the LORD your God. And if you search for him with all your heart and soul, you will find him.
—*Deuteronomy 4:29*

Mercy for Each New Day

Yet I still dare to hope when I remember this: The faithful love of the LORD never ends! His mercies never cease. Great is his faithfulness; his mercies begin afresh each morning.
—*Lamentations 3:21-23*

Jeremiah, who was known as the "weeping prophet" because of all the bad things that happened to him and all the bad things he predicted for God's people, had a "hope dare." Doesn't hope often feel like that, as if clinging to it requires an act of courage that not many have? Or perhaps as if it's something so outrageous we don't quite dare to do it?

Here we have the one reason we can dare to have hope, and the one reason it isn't really that daring after all: God's unfailing faithfulness. It is inexhaustible; we can never reach the end of it. Through all time, to all generations, every morning His mercies are fresh. There will never be an end to them. Each new day, each new moment, He is continually offering to us grace upon grace.

Having hope in that kind of God isn't really very daring. In fact, it's the most sensible and wise thing we could ever do. Rest your life on the faithful love of God. He will see you through every joy and trial, every moment of weakness, every sin with His faithful mercy. You can depend on it.

But you, O Lord, are a God of compassion and mercy, slow to get angry and filled with unfailing love and faithfulness.
—*Psalm 86:15*

JUNE

Trust in the **LORD**
with all
YOUR HEART;
do not depend
on your own understanding.
SEEK HIS WILL
in all you do,
AND HE WILL SHOW YOU
which path to take.

PROVERBS 3:5-6

Quietly Waiting

*I say to myself, "The LORD is my inheritance; therefore,
I will hope in him!" The LORD is good to those who
depend on him, to those who search for him. So it is
good to wait quietly for salvation from the LORD.*

—*Lamentations 3:24-26*

Everything in this world, even the things we hold most dear, will, in the end, perish. The one part of our inheritance that lasts forever is our relationship with God. Therefore, that is the thing we should put our hope in, the thing we should place our confidence on, and the thing we should prize above all else. When everything else fades away, He remains. What a precious inheritance He is— something to be thankful for and confident in even when every other support is gone.

When we put our hope in the inheritance we have in Christ, we experience His goodness. If we have other supports to depend on we don't rely on His faithfulness, but in those moments when everything else fails we come to discover He is more than enough.

I think that's the quietness described in verse 26. It is a peaceful, calm, resting hope that God is in control even when our lives seem to be falling apart. When we truly hope in God as our inheritance, we don't panic in the face of difficulty and loss because we know that God's loving care for us is certain. He is faithful, and so whatever happens, our most important support is fully intact.

*LORD, you alone are my inheritance, my cup
of blessing. You guard all that is mine.*

—*Psalm 16:5*

Favor for a Lifetime

Though he brings grief, he also shows compassion because of the greatness of his unfailing love. For he does not enjoy hurting people or causing them sorrow.
—*Lamentations 3:32-33*

It is interesting that the book of laments—of complaints to God—has so many encouraging promises. Here Jeremiah rests His heart in the promise that God longs to bring joy to His people. When He wounds us or allows us to experience suffering, it is done with a loving Father's care and forethought, for our ultimate spiritual good. None of it will be wasted.

That may be of little comfort when you're in the midst of a storm. The grief we experience this side of heaven can be devastating. But we need to keep reminding ourselves of the greatness of God's unfailing love. Yes, even in this, God loves you. Though He brings grief, He also shows compassion, and He does not enjoy causing you sorrow.

God's Word tells us that there will be an end to all the sorrow and suffering you experience; God places limits on it. Over time, even in this life the edges of it will soften. You will begin to see God's sustaining hand in the midst of it and feel His presence. Beyond that, you can rest in the promise that one day every tear will be wiped away, every sorrow erased, every wound healed.

For his anger lasts only a moment, but his favor lasts a lifetime! Weeping may last through the night, but joy comes with the morning.
—*Psalm 30:5*

From Doubt to Faith

But LORD, you remain the same forever! Your throne continues
from generation to generation. . . . Restore us, O LORD, and bring
us back to you again! Give us back the joys we once had!
—*Lamentations 5:19, 21*

Here is the promise upon which all other promises depend: God is eternal. He has no beginning or end, no limits, and He never changes. We can depend on Him because He is immutable. Everyone in our lives may change and let us down, everything we depend on may be torn away, but God remains ever the same, ever faithfully loving us, ever in control.

Even as he expressed this truth, Jeremiah, the writer of Lamentations, didn't feel like it was true. The verse between these two has him asking God why He has forgotten and abandoned His people. Isn't that often the way it is? We know what is true about God, we can even tell others that He is faithful, but when life is hard we question whether it's true for us.

In those moments it is good for us to express the truth—God is on His throne—and then to be honest with Him about the struggle. That's really what lament is, it's expressing the truth about our feelings within the context of faith. It is taking all our doubt to God rather than allowing ourselves to be eaten up by bitterness. Be honest with God and trust Him to restore your joy.

Before the mountains were born, before you gave birth to
the earth and the world, from beginning to end, you are God.
—*Psalm 90:2*

Soft Hearts

*"I will give them singleness of heart and put a new spirit
within them. I will take away their stony, stubborn heart and
give them a tender, responsive heart, so they will obey my
decrees and regulations. Then they will truly be my people,
and I will be their God. . . . I, the Sovereign LORD, have spoken!"*
—Ezekiel 11:19-21

It's a prayer I often pray for myself and my loved ones: "Lord, give us a soft heart toward You!" Those words express my desire that we would hear God's voice and respond, that we would be tenderhearted toward spiritual truth.

Here God promises that He will transform the hearts of those who are His. He will give them unity and will instill in them a responsiveness to Him so that they will hear and respond to His voice. It is a promise that God is at work helping us to obey, that we are not alone in the struggle against temptation and sin.

But there is a condition here. Before God promised new hearts, the people removed "every trace of their vile images and detestable idols." God doesn't force Himself on us; He waits for us to invite Him. And the way we do that is to continually, intentionally root out sin in our lives. We have to remove every trace of the things that lure us away from Him before He can fill our hearts with more of Himself. If you are praying for a soft heart, are you willing to do the work to make your heart ready for God to fill it?

*This means that anyone who belongs to Christ has become
a new person. The old life is gone; a new life has begun!*
—2 Corinthians 5:17

The Reliable Word

For I am the LORD! If I say it, it will happen.

—Ezekiel 12:25

As we slog through our day-to-day existence, it's easy for us to lose sight of what is true. We get drawn into the arguments and doubts of others. We are unknowingly influenced by the cultural assumptions of our day. Or our own trials and tribulations make us doubt what the Bible says.

Today's verse is a simple affirmation of the reliability of God's Word. If He says it, it is so. If He promises it, it will be. Why? Because He is God. If you think about it, all our questions and doubts boil down to one thing: Do we believe that God is who He says He is? If we do, then we will cling to Him in hope even when life seems hopeless. If we don't, then we will doubt everything He says.

Believing in God is the most sensible thing we could ever do. Yes, it requires a leap of faith. But it is a leap into the loving arms of our heavenly Father, into the strong arms of the Almighty Creator. All the promises of the Bible have been answered in Jesus, and we can count on it that the unchanging God will continue to fulfill every one.

It is the same with my word. I send it out, and it always produces fruit.
It will accomplish all I want it to, and it will prosper everywhere I send it.

—Isaiah 55:11

The Savior's Touch

*"I myself will tend my sheep and give them a place to lie down
in peace," says the Sovereign LORD. "I will search for my lost ones
who strayed away, and I will bring them safely home again.
I will bandage the injured and strengthen the weak."*

—*Ezekiel 34:15-16*

This chapter echoes the truths expressed in Psalm 23, Matthew 18, and John 10. God cares for us like a gentle shepherd cares for his sheep. He leaves the 99 to search for us when we are lost. He calls us each by name. He makes us lie down in green pastures and restores our soul. He notices when we are hurt and tenderly binds up our wounds. He even gave His life so that we could be spared. It is a beautiful image, one that we can spend all our days meditating on and never come to the end of its treasures.

Perhaps the most beautiful word in this verse is "myself." God's care for us is personal. He doesn't delegate it to an angel or another human being, though He may bring them alongside to help. God knows us intimately and tailors His care to our individual needs. He is not far off, He is near. God Himself finds just the right place for us to lie down in peace. He touches us with His own hand to bandage our wounds.

Hear the love of your Good Shepherd in these verses of tenderness. He Himself is reaching out to touch and heal you.

*The LORD is my shepherd; I have all that I need. He lets me rest
in green meadows; he leads me beside peaceful streams.*

—*Psalm 23:1-2*

I Will Bring You Back

Therefore, give the people of Israel this message from the Sovereign Lord:
I am bringing you back, but not because you deserve it. I am doing
it to protect my holy name. . . . And I will put my Spirit in you so that
you will follow my decrees and be careful to obey my regulations.
—Ezekiel 36:22, 27

God is bringing you back, but not because you deserve it—He is doing it to protect His reputation. At first glance maybe this doesn't seem like much of a promise, but on a day when you are faced with the ugliness of your sin and the depth of your rebellion against God, this is indeed a beautiful promise.

God will draw us to Himself not based on our worthiness, not based on our likeability, not based on anything changeable, but because of who He is. Our relationship with Him is based on His holiness, which will never change or diminish or fail in any way.

God's holiness is also the basis of our assurance that He forgives us and places His Spirit within us. His actions toward us are designed to bring glory to Himself, and our forgiveness is what brings Him glory. Therefore we can know that we are indeed forgiven. More than that, He puts His own Spirit in us so that we can better obey Him. Isn't it a comfort to know that our relationship with God is dependent on Him rather than on us? Let these words reassure you that God will keep all His promises to you.

The Lord did not set his heart on you and choose you because
you were more numerous than other nations, for you were the
smallest of all nations! Rather, it was simply that the Lord loves
you, and he was keeping the oath he had sworn to your ancestors.
That is why the Lord rescued you with such a strong hand.
—Deuteronomy 7:7-8

A New Life and a New Future

*I will put my Spirit in you, and you will live again and
return home to your own land. Then you will know that I,
the Lord, have spoken, and I have done what I said.*

—*Ezekiel 37:14*

God's people felt like old, dried-up bones. They had deliberately turned their backs on God, and as a result found themselves far away from His presence. It seemed like all hope was gone. But their story wasn't over yet because God hadn't yet fulfilled all His promises to them. And so God gave the prophet Ezekiel a vision of a valley of bones coming back to life. First the bones reattached into skeletons, then they were covered with muscles and flesh, and finally God breathed life into them and they stood straight and tall like a mighty army.

This was God's promise to His exiled people—they would return home and God would breathe His Spirit into them. His face would once again shine on them in blessing, as it had in Moses' day. The end result of all this is that people would know and worship God.

Do you sometimes feel like your bones are old and dried up? The same breath of God that breathed hope and life into His people in Ezekiel's day is available to you. The Spirit of God comes to dwell within you by faith. In Him you will find hope and life and purpose.

*The Spirit of God, who raised Jesus from the dead, lives in you.
And just as God raised Christ Jesus from the dead, he will give
life to your mortal bodies by this same Spirit living within you.*

—*Romans 8:11*

It's All under Control

He controls the course of world events; he removes kings and
sets up other kings. He gives wisdom to the wise and knowledge
to the scholars. He reveals deep and mysterious things and knows
what lies hidden in darkness, though he is surrounded by light.
—*Daniel 2:21-22*

Daniel had interpreted the king's dream, but he knew that the power to do so came from God. Furthermore, the king's dream revealed what Daniel already knew: God is the only true King, the one in charge of all earthly powers and authorities.

In this day and age, so far removed from the time of Daniel, it's easy to forget that God is in control. He seems to be allowing things that ought not to be. There is corruption and abuse of power and so much evil imposed by those in authority.

But God is the source of all wisdom and power, and He controls the course of world events. Every bit of wisdom we have comes from Him, and He reveals it to us according to His will. The promise we can rely on is that there is a good plan, and if things aren't working out according to truth and justice then we just aren't seeing the end of the story yet. Trust in the One who reveals deep and mysterious things and is surrounded by light. He alone controls the course of world events, and He isn't finished writing the story yet. Take courage—the end will be better than you can imagine.

His mighty arm has done tremendous things! He has scattered
the proud and haughty ones. He has brought down princes from
their thrones and exalted the humble. He has filled the hungry
with good things and sent the rich away with empty hands.
—*Luke 1:51-53*

A Forever Kingdom

During the reigns of those kings, the God of heaven will set up
a kingdom that will never be destroyed or conquered. It will crush
all these kingdoms into nothingness, and it will stand forever.
—*Daniel 2:44*

The forever Kingdom is coming. It cannot be destroyed, conquered, or diminished. Its beauty is unparalleled and its justice untarnished. Ultimately, of course, this is the eternal Kingdom of God, the city not made with human hands. It is a place of no more pain, no more sorrow, no more sickness, no more death. The pure Lamb of God will rule there in perfect peace and justice.

But God's Kingdom is already here, for it came when Jesus broke into human history and said, "The Kingdom of God is at hand!" That Kingdom is the one we experience when we put our trust in Jesus and allow Him to rule in our hearts. It is one of righteousness, peace, and joy in the Holy Spirit. It is what happens when we extend God's love to another and spread His redemptive rule on earth. It is what we are asking for when we say, "Your will be done."

Have you fully experienced this Kingdom? If not, choose today to let God rule in your heart and in your life and in your home. Ask for His justice to reign over your church, your city, and your country. There is a "not yet" to God's Kingdom, but there is also an "already" that can be yours through faith in God's promises.

For the Kingdom of God is not a matter of what we eat or drink,
but of living a life of goodness and peace and joy in the Holy Spirit.
—*Romans 14:17*

Promised Hope

I prayed to the LORD my God and confessed: "O Lord, you are a great and awesome God! You always fulfill your covenant and keep your promises of unfailing love to those who love you and obey your commands. . . . The Lord our God is merciful and forgiving, even though we have rebelled against him."

—*Daniel 9:4, 9*

Daniel was one of the exiled Jews, those who experienced the punishment God brought when His people rejected Him. One day Daniel found a copy of Jeremiah's writings and learned that Jerusalem would lie desolate for 70 years—and it had been nearly that long. So Daniel fasted and prayed for an end to their suffering. He asked God to remember His promises and keep them.

When we are suffering, the best thing we can do is remember God's promises. Read them, recite them, memorize them, and trust them. Remind yourself of what is true. Pray God's own promises back to Him. This is how we stay grounded in truth during difficult days. God's character and His promises never change. They are firm through the continual changes in our circumstances.

The key to Daniel's hope—and ours—lies in the fact that God is merciful and forgiving even though we have rebelled against Him. The covenant promises are secure even though we could never uphold our end of the agreement. God has saved us and will bring us safely to eternal life. This is our certain hope for every day of our lives, in good times and bad.

Hope in the LORD; for with the LORD there is unfailing love. His redemption overflows.

—*Psalm 130:7*

Shine like the Stars Forever

Many of those whose bodies lie dead and buried will rise up,
some to everlasting life and some to shame and everlasting disgrace.
Those who are wise will shine as bright as the sky, and those
who lead many to righteousness will shine like the stars forever.
—Daniel 12:2-3

Daniel prophesied about the rise of a series of leaders who would come hundreds of years after him, culminating in Antiochus IV in Daniel 11 and 12. This wicked ruler was nicknamed "the mad one" and systematically persecuted the Jews. In those dark days, God promised a rescuer and a resurrection.

For the Jews there was first a rescue from Babylon—a mini resurrection back to stability and joy. Ultimately there will the final resurrection to eternal life. Both of these are in view here—an "already" fulfillment in this world and a "not yet" fulfillment that will take place when Christ returns.

The truth is, there is an eternity for each of us. The question is whether we will rise up to everlasting life or descend to shame and disgrace. There is no in-between, no third alternative, and no doubt. Those who hear the voice of God's Son, who respond to the call of Jesus to repent of their sins and be saved, will rise to eternal life. This promise is for us the best news ever—regardless of the pain we may experience in this life, we are promised perfect joy in the next as we bask in the presence of God's glory.

Indeed, the time is coming when all the dead in their graves
will hear the voice of God's Son, and they will rise again. Those
who have done good will rise to experience eternal life, and those
who have continued in evil will rise to experience judgment.
—John 5:28-29

A Chosen People

Israel's people will be like the sands at the seashore—too many to count!
Then, at the place where they were told, "You are not my people," it will be said,
"You are children of the living God." . . . God will again plant his people in his land.
—Hosea 1:10-11

The Bible is really one story—God's story of how He is making for Himself a people, creating for them a place, and gracing them with His presence. The promise was first made in the Garden, then expanded to Abraham and his descendants. Here it is echoed once again. God's people will multiply until they are too numerous to count, and they will live together in the land God will give them.

There is more here than just the beauty of the continuity of Scripture. Up to this point Hosea has been predicting judgment to the people who have rebelled against God. They had rejected God's love, and as a result God had called them "not my people" (Hosea 1:9). They were cut off, separated from Him by their sin. But God would restore them. The story was still being written.

Paul quoted this verse to prove God's calling of the Gentiles (Romans 9:26). It is the promise of restoration for each of us who belong to Jesus. Anyone who responds to His invitation of salvation is called a child of the living God. Have you taken hold of this promise for yourself? Are you sharing it with others? The final act of the story is coming soon, and we want to be part of it.

He came to his own people, and even they rejected him.
But to all who believed him and accepted him,
he gave the right to become children of God.
—John 1:11-12

Unfailing Love

*I will make you my wife forever, showing you righteousness
and justice, unfailing love and compassion. I will be faithful to you
and make you mine, and you will finally know me as the Lord.*

—Hosea 2:19-20

There is a beautiful image in Scripture of God betrothing His people to Himself. In the ancient world this would have included all the legal steps of a marriage, including payment of a bride-price by the groom. It is an image of sacrifice and belonging as God woos us to Himself. He loves us with the same kind of unconditional loving affection that a husband has for his beloved bride.

For those who have experienced the failure of earthly romantic love this can be a complicated image, but it can also be a restorative one. Where earthly love fails, God's love never does. It is a forever love, an endless ocean of acceptance and forgiveness.

The end result of God's love is that we will know Him as the Lord. God's longing is for us to know Him even as we are known, to have such an intimate relationship with Him that He is our home, our place of safe landing, our place of assurance from which we can become all we were created to be. God's faithful, unfailing love and compassion make this possible for us. Whatever love story you have—or have not—been a part of here on earth, God's devoted love is even better.

*I saw the holy city, the new Jerusalem, coming down from God
out of heaven like a bride beautifully dressed for her husband.*

—Revelation 21:2

My People

I will show love to those I called "Not loved."
And to those I called "Not my people,"
I will say, "Now you are my people."
And they will reply, "You are our God!"

—*Hosea 2:23*

If you've ever experienced rejection, you can empathize with Israel's situation. They had rejected God, and so He had rejected them. For a time, they were not loved and not His people. They had chosen other gods. But then the true God made a promise that there would be a reversal. In the places they had rejected God, He would call them back. In the areas they had failed, there would be restoration.

This is a beautiful promise. Where you have failed God, He will bring healing. Where you have experienced separation there can be reconciliation. This is what God does—He takes those who are far off and brings them near. He takes those who are enemies and makes them beloved children. He calls those who don't even realize their need and makes them His own.

The only fitting response—for the Israelites in Hosea's day and for us—is to reply, "You are our God!" Respond to God's pursuing, unfailing love with worshipful devotion. Take joy in your new identity: dear children, those who are loved and chosen and ransomed and belong to Him forever. Here in God's family, you are wanted, just as you are.

Once you had no identity as a people; now you are God's people.
Once you received no mercy; now you have received God's mercy.

—*1 Peter 2:10*

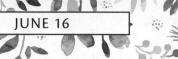

Pressing On

*Oh, that we might know the LORD! Let us press on
to know him. He will respond to us as surely as the arrival
of dawn or the coming of rains in early spring.*

—*Hosea 6:3*

Knowing God is what we all long for, isn't it? In our quest to know Him we have ups and downs, mountaintop highs and dry times where God seems to be silent. We may even have times when we wonder if God even exists. Through it all, if we are honest with ourselves, our deepest desire is to know Him. That's what we were created for.

Here Hosea tells us how we can know God: We must press on to know Him. It's the consistent chasing after God, the day in, day out discipline of placing ourselves under the influence of His Word and His presence that will bring the rains of springtime in our hearts. It may not come when we wish or on our timetable. It may take more pressing on than we thought we were capable of. But at just the right time God will show Himself, and when He does it will be as brilliant and beautiful as the arrival of dawn. The blessing of God's presence always is. Don't give up during the dry times—keep pressing on to know God until He refreshes you. Stick with it until you receive the blessing.

*For I will pour out water to quench your thirst and to irrigate
your parched fields. And I will pour out my Spirit on
your descendants, and my blessing on your children.*

—*Isaiah 44:3*

Plow Your Heart

Plant the good seeds of righteousness, and you will harvest a crop of love. Plow up the hard ground of your hearts, for now is the time to seek the LORD, that he may come and shower righteousness upon you.

—*Hosea 10:12*

Gardening provides rich analogies for the Christian life. Here Hosea compares our hearts to an unused parcel of land. We are to plow up the hard ground of bitterness and dig up the weeds of complacency and worldliness so that we can plant seeds of righteousness. Our hearts must be ready to receive the blessings of God.

Once the ground is plowed it's ready to be planted. The type of seed we plant matters. Are we planting seeds of gentleness, kindness, and love—or are we planting seeds of indignation and harshness? Good seeds of righteousness come from God. They are the fruit of the Holy Spirit's work in our lives, things like joy and peace and patience.

Hosea tells us that the proper tool for plowing up the hard places in our hearts so they will be ready for planting seeds of righteousness is devotion. We must seek God, and now is the time to do so. The promise is that when we seek Him through prayer and Bible reading and Scripture meditation, we will receive showers of righteousness. God doesn't impose Himself on us; He waits for us to ask. Won't you prepare your heart and ask Him to fill it with more of Himself?

You must warn each other every day, while it is still "today," so that none of you will be deceived by sin and hardened against God.

—*Hebrews 3:13*

Ropes of Kindness

I led Israel along with my ropes of kindness and love.
I lifted the yoke from his neck, and I myself stooped to feed him.

—Hosea 11:4

This verse isn't so much a promise that God will do something specific, but a promise of who He is and how He cares for His people. The rebellion of the Israelites can't be overstated. God plucked them from obscurity and promised to make them a great nation and give them land. Over and over again they walked away from Him and suffered the consequences, and each time He rescued them. He promised to be their righteous King and even to live among them.

In response, Israel rejected His rule, disobeyed His commands, and chased after the gods of the nations around them. Their disobedience is shocking. We would like to think that we would have done better, but we do the same thing.

Here is what God did for rebellious Israel, and what He does for us: He leads us with ropes of kindness. He Himself bends down to feed us. There is a gentle firmness to the way God leads us. They are ropes that in some sense we can't escape once we are His. But they are kind. They lead us on paths of righteousness and peace. They keep us from harm and provide just the amount of support we need to be able to walk. Won't you let Him lead you with ropes of kindness?

I have loved you, my people, with an everlasting love.
With unfailing love I have drawn you to myself.

—Jeremiah 31:3

Healed

The LORD says, "Then I will heal you of your faithlessness;
my love will know no bounds, for my anger will be gone forever."

—Hosea 14:4

It's easy for us to go about most days in the mode of self-sufficiency. Most of our material needs we are able to meet. Many of our physical ailments we are able to cure. We can make goals and meet them, plan out a desired future and do what needs to be done to see it realized, and even achieve great things for God—all pretty much in our own power. Of course, in the end, the ability even to take our next breath is dependent on God, and He is the one who enables us to do anything at all. But because He blesses us with so much ability, it is hard for us to truly comprehend how powerless we are.

If we are honest with ourselves, we do have to admit that beyond all our ability is a soul sickness that we can't heal. There is a problem that afflicts each one of us: sin and its consequence, death. We are born in sin and choose sin, and as a result we are destined to be forever separated from God unless He provides the cure. Blessed be His name, He does provide the cure. He has healed us from sin and removed the curse of death. This is boundless love indeed! Today, spend some time remembering and thanking God for all the healing He has brought you, for this life and for the next.

When Jesus heard this, he told them, "Healthy people don't need
a doctor—sick people do. I have come to call not those who think
they are righteous, but those who know they are sinners."

—Mark 2:17

Called to Repent

Don't tear your clothing in your grief, but tear your hearts instead. Return to the LORD your God, for he is merciful and compassionate, slow to get angry and filled with unfailing love. He is eager to relent and not punish.

—Joel 2:13

God's people were experiencing a natural disaster of truly epic proportions. A locust plague was threatening their very existence, compounded by a severe drought. The people were at the end of their resources and the end of themselves, and so they turned to their last resort: God. They threw themselves on the mercy of God, probably with little hope that He would actually respond. After all, their predicament was a just response for their sin.

Joel urged the people to make their repentance sincere. God would not respond to the outward trappings of religion—fasting and offerings—but to sincere repentance of the heart. They needed to tear their hearts, not their clothes.

This is the same thing God wants of us. He doesn't care for rituals if they are not a reflection of the desires of our heart. But when we do sincerely repent and return to God, we find that He is merciful and compassionate, slow to get angry and filled with unfailing love. He longs to forgive, not punish. This may not be the picture of God you grew up with, but it is the true God as He is revealed in the Bible. If you are facing troubling circumstances, throw yourself on this merciful and loving God.

We are made right with God by placing our faith in Jesus Christ. And this is true for everyone who believes, no matter who we are. For everyone has sinned; we all fall short of God's glorious standard. Yet God, in his grace, freely makes us right in his sight. He did this through Christ Jesus when he freed us from the penalty for our sins.

—Romans 3:22-24

Restoring What Was Lost

The LORD says, "I will give you back what you lost. . . . You will praise the LORD your God, who does these miracles for you."
—*Joel 2:25-26*

This verse should not be misconstrued as a promise that you will have everything you want. But God does promise restoration. Jesus told His disciples something similar when He said, "Everyone who has given up houses or brothers or sisters or father or mother or children or property, for my sake, will receive a hundred times as much in return and will inherit eternal life" (Matthew 19:29). God is in the business of restoration, and when He takes something good away from us, He will give it back in abundance.

In the case of the Israelites, they were suffering because of their sin. God sent the forces of nature to judge them and to get their attention. But as soon as they returned to Him, He graciously restored what had been lost.

Here is the promise for us: There is nothing we can lose in this life that will not be more than made up for if we continue to walk with Jesus. It may be restored in this life through the gracious mercies He sends our way. Or it may not be restored until we see Him face-to-face after this life is over. But either way, nothing is ever wasted when we give it up for Him. He will more than repay us for every loss, every sacrifice, every heartache.

For our present troubles are small and won't last very long. Yet they produce for us a glory that vastly outweighs them and will last forever!
—*2 Corinthians 4:17*

Spirit Blessing

Then, after doing all those things, I will pour out my Spirit upon all people.
Your sons and daughters will prophesy. Your old men will dream
dreams, and your young men will see visions. In those days
I will pour out my Spirit even on servants—men and women alike.

—Joel 2:28-29

This promise lasts from verse 28 through 32 and is a prophecy about the final Day of the Lord when Christ returns. The first fulfillment of this promise was at Pentecost in Acts 2, when the disciples were filled with the Holy Spirit after Jesus returned to heaven.

Now, ever since Pentecost, the Holy Spirit lives within each person who has put their faith in Jesus for salvation. The moment we choose to trust in Jesus' sacrifice to save us from sin, we have the presence of God through the Holy Spirit in our lives. We have access to His supernatural power to help us understand the ways of God and obey what He wants us to do.

Too often we overlook the amazing promise of the Holy Spirit. The reality is, the same power that raised Jesus from the grave lives inside you to help you! In your struggle against sin, you are not left without help. In your loneliness, you are not alone. In your confusion, you have a Helper to give you insight into truth. You have an Advocate with the Father who prays for you with groanings too deep for words. Let the Holy Spirit overflow in your heart and your life.

But when the Father sends the Advocate as my representative—
that is, the Holy Spirit—he will teach you everything
and will remind you of everything I have told you.

—John 14:26

Refuge on the Day of Judgment

The LORD's voice will roar from Zion and thunder from Jerusalem,
and the heavens and the earth will shake. But the LORD will be a
refuge for his people, a strong fortress for the people of Israel.

—*Joel 3:16*

The Day of the Lord that Joel prophesied is both terrifying and wonderful. There is no doubt that the roar of God's voice and the thunder of His judgment that will shake the heavens and the earth will be scary to experience. God's limitless power will be on full display.

At the same time, this verse promises that God is a refuge and fortress for His people. For those who love the Lord, the Day of Judgment will be a day when all His promises are fulfilled. We will not be judged, but rather clothed with robes of righteousness. We will receive the full sum of our inheritance in Christ. Everything we have been longing for will be ours.

The two sides of the Day of the Lord have one shared result: God is glorified. Every knee will bow and every tongue confess that He is Lord. There will be no more question about who is in charge, for everyone will see God in His magnificent brilliance and will acknowledge His authority over all things. The choice each person faces is whether they will acknowledge that in this life, while there is time to take refuge in God, or whether they will deny Him in this life and face the full force of the thunder of judgment.

We will all stand before the judgment seat of God. For the Scriptures say,
"As surely as I live," says the Lord, "every knee will bend to me,
and every tongue will declare allegiance to God."

—*Romans 14:10-11*

God's Power Displayed

*For the LORD is the one who shaped the mountains, stirs up
the winds, and reveals his thoughts to mankind. He turns
the light of dawn into darkness and treads on the heights
of the earth. The LORD God of Heaven's Armies is his name!*

—Amos 4:13

This verse may be an ancient hymn, possibly one sung at Bethel. It reminded worshipers that God was not like the false gods of the nations around them. His power is not limited to one location or one people group. Rather, He is God of all things—and therefore He is a righteous judge.

When you spend time in nature you can't help but be reminded of God's power. Those mountains you see—He formed them, just like an artist shapes the contours of clay. The powerful winds that can bring such great devastation—He chooses when to stir them and when to make them fall silent.

The greatest display of God's power is the thoughts and intentions He reveals to us in His Word. That is where we see His power and love that moved Him to save us. That is where we see the vast chasm between light and darkness, between life with God and life apart from Him. And that is where we learn that we can love and adore the Lord of Heaven's Armies as our own dear Father, for His thoughts and intentions toward us are love and peace.

*Who else has held the oceans in his hand? Who has measured
off the heavens with his fingers? Who else knows the weight of
the earth or has weighed the mountains and hills on a scale?*

—Isaiah 40:12

Led out of Exile

Your leader will break out and lead you out of exile,
out through the gates of the enemy cities, back to your own land.
Your king will lead you; the LORD himself will guide you.

—*Micah 2:13*

The prophet Micah had some harsh words for God's people. He told them how they had rebelled against the one true God, and the judgment that was coming because of it. They would be exiled, removed from God's covenant keeping and torn away from the land He had given them.

But even in the midst of despair there was hope. These terrible things would happen, but God would then gather them up again like lost sleep. They would be led home from exile back to the Land of Promise by God Himself. These promises were fulfilled when God brought them back to their land in the days of Ezra and Nehemiah, but they also look toward the true King, Jesus, who would lead them out of their slavery to sin.

If you feel like there is a lot of bad in your life right now, even perhaps the discipline of God, take heart in this promise of hope. Christ has freed you from sin and death, and He Himself guides you each day. He will gather you into His embrace even now as you seek Him, and one day for all eternity. You are headed for an eternal homeland with your forever King who loved you enough to die for you and lives to save you.

Jesus told him, "I am the way, the truth, and the life.
No one can come to the Father except through me."

—*John 14:6*

Nothing to Fear

*Nation will no longer fight against nation, nor train for war
anymore. Everyone will live in peace and prosperity, enjoying their
own grapevines and fig trees, for there will be nothing to fear.
The LORD of Heaven's Armies has made this promise!*

—Micah 4:3-4

We've read this promise before: God will bring peace to the earth. It is a beautiful picture, where weapons are no longer needed and everyone lives in peace and prosperity. Perhaps best of all, there is nothing to fear. We have assurance that this will come to pass because God Himself has promised it.

In the meantime, however, this promise is hard to believe. There are many disputes between nations—and even in our own homes. Around the world many of God's people do not enjoy peace and prosperity. And if we're honest, some of our fears are perfectly legitimate.

So this promise has a lot of relevance in our day-to-day lives. When you look at all that is wrong in the world, take heart: There is a promised end date to all of this. God will have the final word. Today you can live without fear because you know that your God who loves you is working out His perfect plan, for your life and in the world. If it isn't right yet, that's because He isn't done yet. Rest in the assurance that He will finish everything He has promised.

*I have told you all this so that you may have peace in me.
Here on earth you will have many trials and sorrows.
But take heart, because I have overcome the world.*

—John 16:33

The Prince of Peace

But you, O Bethlehem Ephrathah, are only a small village among
all the people of Judah. Yet a ruler of Israel, whose origins are in the
distant past, will come from you on my behalf. . . . And he will stand
to lead his flock with the LORD's strength, in the majesty of the name
of the LORD his God. . . . And he will be the source of peace.

—Micah 5:2-5

This is one of the core prophecies about Jesus. The Messiah would be born in a specific place—Bethlehem in Judah—and would be sent on behalf of God Himself. He would be fully human (a ruler of Israel) and fully divine (in the majesty of God). God in human flesh, come to save His people. This was the historical moment toward which all of human history since the Fall pointed.

The Christmas story is so familiar to most of us that we relegate it to one month a year and allow the sharp edges of it to be softened in cute nativity scenes. We tame it into something we can enjoy as a nostalgic plaything. But this promise upended everything, and it did so in dramatic fashion.

Perhaps today is a good day to reread the Christmas story and appreciate the scandal. God Himself come as a helpless baby, born to impoverished parents who barely had a roof over their heads, worshiped by the lowest of society and mighty kings. God as a toddler, as a teenager, being tempted and tried just as we are. This is your Savior, and He did it for you, so He could be your shepherd. Have you submitted to this radical love?

For a child is born to us, a son is given to us.
The government will rest on his shoulders. And he will be called:
Wonderful Counselor, Mighty God, Everlasting Father, Prince of Peace.

—Isaiah 9:6

Where Is Another God like You?

Where is another God like you? . . . You will not stay angry with
your people forever, because you delight in showing unfailing love.
Once again you will have compassion on us. You will trample
our sins under your feet and throw them into the depths of the ocean!
—Micah 7:18-19

In asking "Where is another God like you?" the prophet Micah is playing off his own name, which means, "Who is like the Lord?" The obvious answer to this rhetorical question—one which has been answered throughout the Old Testament—is there is no one like our God. Then Micah goes on to say what it is that makes the true God unique among the gods of the nations.

Where other gods get angry and must be appeased, God delights in showing love. Where other gods fail because they are merely imaginary creations of the people who serve them, God is unfailing because He is true. Where other gods are selfish, God is compassionate. Where other gods hold grudges, God tramples our sins and throws them into the depths of the ocean.

The next verse in this passage reiterates that God is faithful to fulfill His promises that began with Abraham. From generation to generation, throughout eternity, God delights to show unfailing love to His people. This should cause us to not only fall at His feet in joyful worship, but also show that same kind of forgiving, faithful love to those around us.

O Lord, God of Israel, there is no God like you in all of heaven above
or on the earth below. You keep your covenant and show unfailing
love to all who walk before you in wholehearted devotion.
—1 Kings 8:23

The Jealousy of God

*The LORD is a jealous God. . . . The LORD is slow to get angry, but
his power is great, and he never lets the guilty go unpunished.
He displays his power in the whirlwind and the storm.
The billowing clouds are the dust beneath his feet.*

—Nahum 1:2-3

When taken with the verse we looked at yesterday, this seems to paint a contradictory portrait of God. Is He jealous and angry, or is He compassionate and forgiving? The answer is yes. And the key to why both are true is found in this Scripture verse.

First, God is jealous for our affections. In the same way we would not want a spouse to be indifferent if we were unfaithful to him, we would not want God to be indifferent to our divided heart. And He isn't. He loves us so much that He wants all of us.

Second, God is just. In His perfect holiness He cannot let sin go unpunished. He is powerful enough to deal with sin and holy enough that He is compelled to do so. It is His nature to do everything justly. And really, we wouldn't have it any other way. We don't want a God who is fickle; we want one we can depend on to do what is right. But notice also that God is slow to get angry. There is forbearance and mercy. And that is where we must place ourselves. Let God love you enough to be jealous for your love, and thank Him that though there will one day be justice, there is also plenteous mercy for all who fling themselves on the grace of God.

*The Lord isn't really being slow about his promise, as some
people think. No, he is being patient for your sake. He does not
want anyone to be destroyed, but wants everyone to repent.*

—2 Peter 3:9

The Goodness of God

The LORD is good, a strong refuge when trouble comes.
He is close to those who trust in him.

—*Nahum 1:7*

We often define goodness on our terms. When things are going well we say that we are blessed and thank God for His goodness to us. When trouble comes, we start to doubt and question His ways. That's because we filter our view of God's goodness through our circumstances and emotions.

Here Nahum challenges that perspective by declaring that God is good not because things are going well, but rather because He takes care of us when trouble comes. Goodness is a part of God's unchanging character, and therefore He is every bit as good when we are in trouble as He is when life is going well. In fact, times of trouble can be the times when we see God's goodness most clearly because we fully realize our need for Him.

God is especially near when we trust Him through times of difficulty. When everything else is stripped away and we turn to God as our last hope, we draw close to Him and find that He is our strong refuge. He is indeed good to meet us in our suffering, to draw near when we cry out in pain, to bend low and answer our desperate, wordless cries. In your times of trouble, turn to God and see that He is there and He is good.

Give thanks to the LORD, for he is good! His faithful love endures forever.

—*1 Chronicles 16:34*

THE LORD

is like

A FATHER

to his children, tender &
COMPASSIONATE
to those who fear him.

PSALM 103:13

Waiting for Justice

The LORD replied, "Look around at the nations; look and
be amazed! For I am doing something in your own day, something
you wouldn't believe even if someone told you about it."

—*Habakkuk 1:5*

Habakkuk had cried out to God over and over, and it seemed like God wasn't listening. He seemed to be indifferent to His people's suffering, to the destruction and violence that plagued their nation. God responded to Habakkuk's question, "How long, O Lord?" with these words of hope.

God's response at first seemed encouraging. Be amazed! I am at work! You won't believe what I have in store! But the specifics of the plan were not what Habakkuk was hoping for: God was going to send an even more violent people— the Babylonians—to take His people captive. This did not sound like good news. God's punishment of Israel with the invading Babylonians was perplexing. But it did prove three important things: 1) God is in control of all things, including the ways of rulers and nations; 2) God is just; and 3) He cares about His people.

God is working now, just as He was then, and His good plan is to bring history to a close and usher in a new era when Jesus reigns as King over all. What happens in the in-between time may be confusing and perplexing and distressing, but we can still trust God to love us and bring justice at just the right time. Let these words give you hope as you wait expectantly for that day when He will make all things right again.

The LORD does whatever pleases him throughout all
heaven and earth, and on the seas and in their depths.

—*Psalm 135:6*

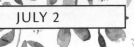

Living by Faith

Look at the proud! They trust in themselves, and their lives are crooked. But the righteous will live by their faithfulness to God.

—Habakkuk 2:4

This verse—"the righteous will live by faith"—is quoted three times in the New Testament (Romans 1:17, Galatians 3:11, and Hebrews 10:38) to draw attention to the fact that salvation is by faith, not by works. Here the contrast is made between the proud, who trust in themselves, and the righteous, who trust in God.

In the end, there are two ways to live. We all live by faith in something; either we trust in ourselves or we trust in God. Those who trust in themselves will always be disappointed. Their lives are characterized by crookedness—since they have no objective standard by which to live—and eventually end in death. Trusting in self is not the pathway to life and peace.

How much better it is to put our trust in God. When we do, He imputes His righteousness to our account and transforms us so that we can live a life of obedience and faith. We have an objective standard to live by and unlimited forgiveness for the times we fail to do so. This indeed is life. Here is God's promise to all who trust in Jesus: You are declared righteous before God and therefore you can live each day, by faith, in joy and peace.

Anyone who believes in God's Son has eternal life.
Anyone who doesn't obey the Son will never experience
eternal life but remains under God's angry judgment.

—John 3:36

Don't Be Afraid of the Hard Things

*For as the waters fill the sea, the earth will be filled
with an awareness of the glory of the LORD.*

—*Habakkuk 2:14*

The verse just before this one promises that the wealth of the nations will turn to ashes. Nothing in this life lasts, not the house we work to furnish or the career we work to build or even the nation we serve. But God's glory lasts forever, and one day the earth's awareness of His glory will be so pervasive that it will span the earth like an ocean. Everyone will know who is in control and who deserves worship and adoration.

The events that Habakkuk prophesied would bring about this far-reaching recognition of God's glory were troubling, to say the least. The Babylonians who had overtaken God's people would receive justice. God would not stand their wickedness forever.

Sometimes God calls attention to Himself through the hard things of life. Kingdoms topple, careers fall apart, families are divided—and through those things God brings Himself glory. He sometimes does it by bringing justice to the oppressors and releasing the captives. But sometimes it is the quiet peace God brings in the midst of pain that shouts His goodness. Even our honest questioning—like Habakkuk's—highlights God's love. So don't be afraid of the hard things. God will reveal His glory, in your life and in the world. He is not silent or absent, He is spreading the awareness of glory.

*The whole earth will acknowledge the LORD and return to him.
All the families of the nations will bow down before him.*

—*Psalm 22:27*

God Is on His Throne

But the LORD is in his holy Temple. Let all the earth be silent before him.
—Habakkuk 2:20

When the prophet Isaiah saw God sitting on His throne, with His robe filling the Temple, he was sure he was going to die (Isaiah 6:1-8). God's glory was so magnificent and so pure that Isaiah for the first time saw the full force of his sin, and he was undone. One day, Habakkuk promises, the entire earth will see God in His holy Temple and fall silent before Him. We will be silent first because of His awesome beauty and holiness, and second because we will see how depraved we are in comparison.

The encouragement here is that God is on His throne, which means He is still in control. Whatever is going on in your life right now, no matter how chaotic and scary and depressing things are, God is in His holy Temple. Everything is okay; the all-powerful, forever faithful and true ruler is still on the throne.

What is the appropriate response to seeing God on His throne? Silence. Let a vision of God on His throne fill your thoughts and cause you to bow in humble adoration before Him. Stop the arguing, the complaining, the struggling and just sit at His feet, grateful that He loves you, He has saved you, and He is in control.

I saw the Lord. He was sitting on a lofty throne, and the train of his robe filled the Temple. Attending him were mighty seraphim, each having six wings. . . . They were calling out to each other, "Holy, holy, holy is the LORD of Heaven's Armies! The whole earth is filled with his glory!" Their voices shook the Temple to its foundations, and the entire building was filled with smoke.
—Isaiah 6:1-4

Joy in Barren Times

Yet I will rejoice in the LORD! I will be joyful in the God of my salvation! The Sovereign LORD is my strength! He makes me as surefooted as a deer, able to tread upon the heights.

—Habakkuk 3:18-19

Habakkuk had been promised that after the days of suffering there would be redemption, but as of yet he had not seen any of God's promises come true. He had to live by faith, not by sight. And so, in the verse just before this one, Habakkuk utters the message of faith: "even though the fig trees have no blossoms, and there are no grapes on the vines . . . yet I." He was saying, "God, I don't see that any of this is about to happen. There is no sign that You are going to keep Your promises. Right now, it all looks hopeless and You seem to not care. Yet—even so—I will rejoice."

Taken in context, this is such a beautiful expression of trust. Habakkuk declares joy and strength even when he doesn't have any objective reason to do so. You might think he's denying reality, but the fact is, he is counting on the true reality of who God is—a reality that is much more solid than anything we can see or touch in this world.

What is your "even though . . . yet I" expression of faith? Even though I have a terminal diagnosis, yet I believe God is good. Even though I can't see how my problem can be solved, yet I will praise the Lord and do what is right. Even though I am perplexed, distraught, and in despair, yet I trust that God is faithful.

Though he slay me, I will hope in him.

—Job 13:15, ESV

You Alone Will Keep Me Safe

The remnant of Israel will do no wrong; they will never
tell lies or deceive one another. They will eat and sleep
in safety, and no one will make them afraid.

—*Zephaniah 3:13*

Zephaniah paints a portrait of redeemed Israel, when Christ returns to rule over His people. At that point in time they will be a purified people, washed clean by the finished work of Christ. And the end result of their purity is that they are safe from every danger and released from every fear.

That's something we wish we had now, isn't it? No more restless, worried nights. No more aches and pains that cause sleep to evade us. No more troubles or sorrows that plague our thoughts. Totally at rest, fully at peace, free from fear.

If we trust in the Lord and His care for us, we can experience that kind of soul rest even now. We can go to bed and sleep peacefully knowing that we have nothing to fear because God loves us and is in control. We can rise in the morning and go about our day with no worry because our heavenly Father feeds the birds and clothes the lilies—and we are of much more value than they are. We can rest in His care because He keeps us safe. The choice is ours: Will we fret about all the what-ifs or will we rest in the assurance of God's sovereign care?

That is why I tell you not to worry about everyday life—
whether you have enough food and drink, or enough clothes
to wear. Isn't life more than food, and your body more than
clothing? Look at the birds. They don't plant or harvest
or store food in barns, for your heavenly Father feeds them.
And aren't you far more valuable to him than they are?

—*Matthew 6:25-26*

The Lord Delights in You with Gladness

For the LORD your God is living among you. He is a mighty savior.
He will take delight in you with gladness. With his love,
he will calm all your fears. He will rejoice over you with joyful songs.
—Zephaniah 3:17

The previous verses outline the reasons why Israel should rejoice: A time of peace is coming and God is going to do great things for His people. But the relationship doesn't end there. God rejoices too—because He actually delights in us with gladness.

There is nothing sweeter than watching a mother sing over her newborn baby. Her whole attention is focused on her beloved child, and she is totally satisfied just being with him. There is no expectation of what the baby will do, just pure love because he exists. That is the picture we have of God's devoted, joyful love here. He lives with us, He delights in us, He calms our fears, and He rejoices over us with singing. It's a beautiful image of God's fatherly love for us.

Is this how you see God? You know He is glorious and holy and just, but do you also know that He just likes to be with you? He's like a loving father who can't wait to get home and play with his kid. When you enjoy Him, He is right beside you, enjoying you right back. You sing songs of worship, but God also sings over you!

I have told you these things so that you will be
filled with my joy. Yes, your joy will overflow!

—John 15:11

A Place of Peace

For this is what the LORD of Heaven's Armies says: In just a little while I will again shake the heavens and the earth, the oceans and the dry land. I will shake all the nations, and the treasures of all the nations will be brought to this Temple. I will fill this place with glory, says the LORD of Heaven's Armies. . . . And in this place I will bring peace.
—Haggai 2:6-9

These verses are quoted in Handel's *Messiah* as prophecies of Christ's coming in judgment. Hebrews 12:26-27 uses the same terminology, "in just a little while," to refer to that event. We are promised that one day not too long from now, after all the shaking is over, there will be peace and the glory of the victorious Christ will be on display for all to see.

The King James Version renders verse 7 as "the desire of all nations." There is some debate about whether this verse refers to earthly treasure being given to restore the Temple or the true treasure of Christ Himself. Either way, what the nations truly desire, whether or not they realize it, is Jesus the Messiah. He is the One who brings eternal peace, and the shaking He does is designed to show us that before it's too late.

The world we live in can be shaken, both on an international scale and in our own corner of the world. Things feel uncertain and out of control. But there is coming a Kingdom that cannot be shaken, one we receive through faith in Christ and look to with hopeful expectation. Live today with that security in the forefront of your mind—God is shaking things up to bring lasting peace.

All of creation will be shaken and removed, so that only unshakable things will remain. Since we are receiving a Kingdom that is unshakable, let us be thankful and please God by worshiping him with holy fear and awe.
—Hebrews 12:27-28

Return to the Lord

Therefore, say to the people, "This is what the LORD of Heaven's Armies says: Return to me, and I will return to you, says the LORD of Heaven's Armies."
—*Zechariah 1:3*

Zechariah prophesied during the time of exile, when God's hand of judgment lay heavy on His people because of their rebellion against Him. Zechariah began by reminding the people of God's anger (Zechariah 1:2), but he didn't linger there. Rather, he immediately began to urge repentance.

Note that God had indeed left His people—that's why He promises to return to them. But it wasn't too late for their situation to be reversed. God would return as soon as the people turned back to Him. They needed a change of loyalty, a reorientation of their lives away from false gods and sin toward the one true God. The repetition of the phrase "the Lord of Heaven's Armies" reminded the people who they would be returning to. Surely you want the almighty God who reigns over heaven as well as earth to be on your side.

God's promise is that if we turn to Him, He turns toward us. As soon as we put our faith in Him, repenting of our sins and committing to obey Him as our Lord, God turns His face toward us. He offers forgiveness, peace, and reconciliation to all who desire to return to Him. Where are you facing right now? Are you turned toward the Lord of Heaven's Armies or against Him?

If at that time you and your children return to the LORD your God, and if you obey with all your heart and all your soul all the commands I have given you today, then the LORD your God will restore your fortunes. He will have mercy on you and gather you back from all the nations where he has scattered you.
—*Deuteronomy 30:2-3*

Springing into Action

*The LORD says, "Shout and rejoice, O beautiful Jerusalem,
for I am coming to live among you. Many nations will
join themselves to the LORD on that day, and they, too,
will be my people. . . . Be silent before the LORD, all humanity,
for he is springing into action from his holy dwelling."*

—*Zechariah 2:10-13*

There is a threefold promise here. First, God promises to live with His people. His presence will bring an era of peace and justice. Second, there will be Gentiles among God's people. The good news is not just for the Jews; the nation of Israel is a blessing to all nations. Third, God is at work. In Zechariah's time they were still in exile. The promises didn't appear to be coming to fruition. But here God said, "I am springing into action!"

Chances are good that there are promises God has made in His Word that don't seem to be true in your life. You can't see the blessing, you can't feel the peace, there is no redemption happening in your life like there is for other people. Here is God's message to you: I am right here with you, you are my dear child, and I am springing into action from My holy dwelling.

You may not see the answers tomorrow, or next year, or in your lifetime. But that doesn't mean they aren't coming. God is at work, He still reigns, and one day you will experience in full all the promises of His Word. Be silent and hope in the God who is springing into action from His holy dwelling.

*Be still, and know that I am God! I will be honored by
every nation. I will be honored throughout the world.*

—*Psalm 46:10*

God's Passionate Love

*This is what the LORD of Heaven's Armies says: My love for
Mount Zion is passionate and strong; I am consumed with
passion for Jerusalem! . . . You can be sure that I will rescue
my people from the east and from the west.*

—Zechariah 8:2, 7

We don't often think about the emotions of God. Somehow it seems like He would be above all that. But while it is true that He is not ruled by His emotions, it is also true that He has them. That's what makes Him a personal God, not a stiff deity who needs to be appeased by our actions.

The word translated *passion* here is also translated "jealous" or "zealous." God loves us so much that He wants us for Himself. His consuming desire is to be our loving Father. And that is what motivates Him to rescue us. The Jews of Zechariah's time looked forward to rescue from their oppressors, a hope that rested in the coming of the Messiah. We can rejoice in our already completed rescue from sin and death through the crucifixion and resurrection of Jesus our Lord and Messiah.

The promise that we are rescued from sin and drawn into the Kingdom of God through faith in Christ is made all the more precious when we come to understand the depth of God's passion for us. He didn't sacrifice Himself out of a sense of duty, but out of love. He doesn't discipline us out of anger, He does it out of a jealous desire for our affections and for our good. This passionate God loves you zealously—what joy there is in that assurance!

*See how very much our Father loves us, for he
calls us his children, and that is what we are!*

—1 John 3:1

Peace to the Nations

Rejoice, O people of Zion! Shout in triumph, O people of Jerusalem! Look, your king is coming to you. He is righteous and victorious, yet he is humble, riding on a donkey—riding on a donkey's colt. . . . Your king will bring peace to the nations. His realm will stretch from sea to sea and from the Euphrates River to the ends of the earth.

—*Zechariah 9:9-10*

This prophecy was fulfilled when Jesus rode into Jerusalem on a donkey shortly before His crucifixion (Matthew 21; Mark 11; Luke 19; John 12). The people shouted and cheered because they thought Jesus was going to set up an earthly kingdom fulfilling all the promises of a time of peace and prosperity. Just a few days later, when it became clear their expectations would not be realized, the same crowd jeered at Jesus and demanded His death.

We may fault the crowds for being fickle and for demanding that Jesus come on their terms, but don't we often do the same thing? The truth is, God has promised peace and justice—but when we experience quite the opposite in this fallen world, we often either lash out in bitterness against Him or doubt the promises and the One who promised them.

Our Savior has come to us, righteous and victorious, humble and self-sacrificing. Let us put our hope in the promises He has made, trusting that they will come true even if we don't see it yet. Let us keep on hoping even when it turns out that the answers don't come in the package we hoped for, entrusting ourselves to the mighty King who promises to return and make everything right in the right time.

A large crowd of Passover visitors took palm branches and went down the road to meet [Jesus]. They shouted, "Praise God! Blessings on the one who comes in the name of the Lord! Hail to the King of Israel!"

—*John 12:12-13*

Prisoners of Hope

*Because of the covenant I made with you, sealed with blood, I will
free your prisoners from death in a waterless dungeon. Come back
to the place of safety, all you prisoners who still have hope! I promise
this very day that I will repay two blessings for each of your troubles.*
—Zechariah 9:11-12

These verses contrast the life of an unbeliever with the life of a believer. Those who through faith in Jesus' death and resurrection have entered into a covenant relationship with God now experience freedom and life. Whereas before they were prisoners of death, trapped in a dungeon of sin, with no source of life or refreshment—now they are in a place of safety, restoration, and blessing. Other versions use the phrase "prisoners of hope" to describe them. They are kept in the stronghold of God's promises.

The covenant promise is an invitation—come back to the hope you have, to the place of safety. Live there, regardless of your emotions or circumstances. When we accept the covenant promises by faith, we are invited into the arms of Jesus Himself, where there is more than double the blessing.

Have you found your way to that place of safety? It's an assurance that even when you experience pain and suffering, you are safe. You are held. You are loved and cared for. You are free to love and be loved by God with no limitations, no stipulations, no fear. You are a prisoner of hope, and that is indeed a double blessing.

*With his own blood—not the blood of goats and calves—he entered
the Most Holy Place once for all time and secured our redemption forever.*
—Hebrews 9:12

Holy to the Lord

And the LORD will be king over all the earth. On that day there
will be one LORD—his name alone will be worshiped. . . . On that
day even the harness bells of the horses will be inscribed with these
words: HOLY TO THE LORD. And the cooking pots in the Temple
of the LORD will be as sacred as the basins used beside the altar.
—Zechariah 14:9, 20

The words HOLY TO THE LORD were inscribed on the turban of the high priest in the Old Testament to denote that he was set apart for God's work. But in the Day of the Lord, when Christ returns, that inscription will be imprinted even on the common things. The harness bells of the horses, which used to announce the coming of a soldier in war, will proclaim the holiness of God. The common tools of household cooking will be transformed into sacred vessels. There will be no distinction between sacred and secular, between holy and profane.

In some sense this is true even now. Believers are identified as a holy priesthood, a people set apart. There is no hierarchy in the Kingdom of God, for we are all equally beloved by the Father.

The things we use each day, even the common utensils of daily life, when used in worship and gospel proclamation, become holy things. In our lives there should be no distinction between sacred and secular because all things can be done for God's glory. This is God's promise to us—that He can make anyone and anything holy, set apart for His service and wholly beloved.

You are a chosen people. You are royal priests,
a holy nation, God's very own possession. As a result,
you can show others the goodness of God, for he called
you out of the darkness into his wonderful light.
—1 Peter 2:9

The Same Yesterday, Today, and Forever

I am the LORD, and I do not change.

—*Malachi 3:6*

God's people had in a sense put God on trial, ending with the accusation, "Where is the God of justice?" (Malachi 2:17). Now God replies, and the crux of His argument is that He is the unchanging Lord of all. Judgment would come, like a refiner's fire, and when it did the people would regret challenging God. Their arguments and complaints would be silenced in the white-hot fire of judgment.

What a comfort it is that God does not change. The God we meet on every page of the Bible is the same God we meet in prayer and the same God we will one day see face-to-face. He is still as life-giving as when He first breathed life into Adam, still as holy as when He appeared to Isaiah, still as loving as when He died on the cross for us, and still as victorious and powerful as when He rose from the dead and ascended into heaven.

In the changes of life, rest in the arms of the unchanging Savior. Come to Him with your questions and doubts, your joys and trials. Come to Him and you will find that He meets you just as He met Moses in his fear, just as He met the woman at the well in her sin, just as He met Peter in his failure. This is a God you can trust with your life.

God is not a man, so he does not lie. He is not human, so he does not change his mind. Has he ever spoken and failed to act? Has he ever promised and not carried it through?

—*Numbers 23:19*

Opening the Windows of Heaven

"Bring all the tithes into the storehouse so there will be enough food in my Temple. If you do," says the LORD of Heaven's Armies, "I will open the windows of heaven for you. I will pour out a blessing so great you won't have enough room to take it in! Try it! Put me to the test!"
—Malachi 3:10

There are two easy ways to misinterpret this promise. The first is to treat it as a proof text for the health-and-wealth gospel. God is not promising that if we bring our 10 percent tithe to the church then we will be repaid with more money than we gave. The other misinterpretation is to think that this is all about money.

What God wants is your heart. He wants you to put Him first because you love Him more than anyone or anything else. And the surest way to know if He is first in your heart is by looking at how you spend your money. It's an issue of trust. Do you trust God enough to give Him the first and best of what you have, or do you give Him the leftovers, the part you don't need? Do you truly believe that everything you have is from Him, and that He will take care of your needs?

This is the only place in Scripture where we are invited to test God, and the word used here has to do with taking a risk to prove our faith. God is inviting us to prove His faithfulness by giving more of our resources away. So go ahead and test Him in this. Give generously, and see if you are not given back far more in blessing and joy.

You must each decide in your heart how much to give. And don't give reluctantly or in response to pressure. "For God loves a person who gives cheerfully." And God will generously provide all you need. Then you will always have everything you need and plenty left over to share with others.
—2 Corinthians 9:7-8

A Special Treasure

"They will be my people," says the LORD of Heaven's Armies.
"On the day when I act in judgment, they will be my own special
treasure. I will spare them as a father spares an obedient child."
—*Malachi 3:17*

The word used here for "special treasure" was first used in Exodus 19:5, at the giving of the covenant at Mount Sinai. God is reminding His people that the promise still holds true, even after all that has happened, after their rebellion, after the exile—after everything, God is still making for Himself a set-apart people. The covenant still stands. God's people will be spared from judgment and spend eternity with Him despite all their wickedness.

Perhaps you don't feel much like a special treasure. You've come face-to-face with your failure and are ashamed of the way you have treated God. You haven't loved Him as you ought, and you have done things you wish you had not done. You don't feel like a treasure, you feel unworthy and unlovable.

God is still calling you. He wants to make you His treasure—something beautiful and valuable and royal. He will remove your shame and treat you as an obedient child, declaring you righteous and beloved. He wants you. All you have to do is turn toward Him in repentance, and He will come running toward you with arms open wide. He is eager to pour out His love and blessing on you. Won't you let Him do it?

The LORD will hold you in his hand for all to see—
a splendid crown in the hand of God.

—*Isaiah 62:3*

No Middle Ground

And she will have a son, and you are to name him Jesus,
for he will save his people from their sins.

—*Matthew 1:21*

This is the moment we've been waiting for since we began in the Garden of Eden. Did you notice it? If you didn't, you are not alone. Jesus stepped onto the pages of human history in near obscurity. It was a promise given in private to a young girl named Mary who wasn't even married yet. Her baby would be born into poverty, with the shame of scandal being whispered about Him wherever His name was mentioned.

And yet, He was the Messiah whose coming was promised on every page of Old Testament Scripture. He was the One upon whom all the Jewish people's hopes were pinned. Indeed, He was their only hope—and their best hope, for He would save His people from their sins.

This is the pivot point of Scripture, for everything up until this moment was looking forward to it, and everything after this moment is looking back to it and forward to the moment when He comes again. It is also the pivot point of your life, for what you do with this Jesus determines everything else about you. Will you rely on Him to save you from your sins? Will you fall in worship at His feet? Or will you reject Him and the life He offers? There is no middle ground.

John saw Jesus coming toward him and said, "Look!
The Lamb of God who takes away the sin of the world!"

—*John 1:29*

Clothed with Joy

God blesses those who mourn, for they will be comforted.
—*Matthew 5:4*

Right at the beginning of His ministry Jesus shocked His disciples by laying out the path of blessing. The concept of blessing would have been very familiar to His listeners. Throughout the Old Testament and on into their present-day culture, fathers blessed their children, speaking forth a vision of the future they hoped God would give.

But now Jesus said that the blessed are those who are poor, sad, and persecuted. How can that be? In what sense can mourning be called a state of blessedness? We certainly don't talk about grief in terms of how blessed we are.

The mourning Jesus had in mind here is the mourning of lament. It is grief laced with faith. It is taking a realistic look at our sinful, fallen state and the fallen world we live in and asserting that this is not how things should be—this is not the way God created the world. That kind of mourning draws us near to God, and when we draw near to Him we experience the supernatural comfort that only He can give. The blessing of mourning comes when we take our sorrows to Jesus and invite Him to heal us. It comes when the veil is pulled back between earth and heaven and we see that God is there. It comes when Jesus reaches down into our pain and uses it for good. This is the blessing Jesus promises will come out of our faith-filled mourning.

You have turned my mourning into joyful dancing. You have taken away my clothes of mourning and clothed me with joy.
—*Psalm 30:11*

The Reward That Lasts

But when you give to someone in need, don't let your left hand know what your right hand is doing. Give your gifts in private, and your Father, who sees everything, will reward you.

—*Matthew 6:3-4*

Jesus hated hypocrisy. The people who gave publicly, blowing trumpets to call attention to their generosity, had received all the reward they would get. By contrast, those who gave secretly, from a sincere love for God and a genuine desire to help others, would be blessed. There is a double promise here: God sees everything, and He will reward acts of humble generosity.

Being misunderstood is painful. When we try to do something kind and our motives are called into question, we want to set the record straight. But we don't have to worry; God sees everything, including our innermost hearts, and He will make things right. The only opinion that matters is God's, and He knows the true desires of our heart.

The reward promised here is pictured in Matthew 25:31-46 as the division between the sheep and the goats at the final judgment. We are saved by faith apart from works, but works naturally follow from true faith. If we are truly saved, we will live a life of increasing obedience. And so Jesus promises that there is a reward for the good things we do, especially the things that flow so naturally from our love for God that we hardly notice we are doing them. Cultivate that kind of generosity, that kind of deep love, because you will never regret giving more to God.

The generous will prosper; those who refresh others will themselves be refreshed.
—*Proverbs 11:25*

Persevering in Prayer

Keep on asking, and you will receive what you ask for. Keep on seeking,
and you will find. Keep on knocking, and the door will be opened to you.
—Matthew 7:7

There is a progression in this verse that describes how we should pray. First we ask, taking our needs and desires to God because we believe that He is the only One who can grant them. Then we seek. This is the desperate prayer we pray when we grow in our relationship with God and realize that what we really need is more of Him, not merely the provision or the healing we are asking for. It is earnest and needy prayer. Finally, we progress to the stage of knocking. This is the consistent wrestling in prayer, the labor of continuing to come to God time after time even when circumstances urge us to give up. It is perseverance born of faith.

Too often we give up on our prayers, assuming that God is saying no to us when we've asked a few times and haven't seen an answer. But what if God wants us to persevere in our relationship with Him, and that is why He asks us to wait? Let us not give up, but keep on asking, seeking, and knocking.

The promises in this verse are that we will receive and find. God won't leave us in the asking and seeking—He will open to us the thing we need most: Himself. Prayer, in the final analysis, is an invitation to a relationship with the God of the universe. So persevere in the work of prayer. Don't give up. You will find Him faithful and true.

You can ask for anything in my name, and I will do it,
so that the Son can bring glory to the Father.
Yes, ask me for anything in my name, and I will do it!
—John 14:13-14

A Father's Love

So if you sinful people know how to give good gifts to your children, how much more will your heavenly Father give good gifts to those who ask him.
—*Matthew 7:11*

The literary construction of comparison is used powerfully throughout the Gospels. Here we are asked to consider, if we as sinful humans give good gifts to our children, then how much more will our heavenly Father do so? And what impact should that have on our prayer life? Jesus pointed out that an earthly parent would never give a stone when their child asked for a loaf of bread, or a snake if they asked for a fish. If human parents lavish good gifts on their children, then how much more does the infinitely more loving God do so?

Yet how often do we treat God as if He were stingy and aloof? We are afraid to ask for something small for fear He won't care, and afraid to ask for something big because we don't think He will give it to us.

Let's stop treating God as a stingy taskmaster and start thinking of Him as He is presented in the Bible—as a loving heavenly Father who longs to give good gifts even more than an earthly parent longs to give good gifts to his child. Ask God for good gifts, and see if He doesn't abundantly bless you with tangible assurances of His love.

Whatever is good and perfect is a gift coming down to us from God our Father, who created all the lights in the heavens. He never changes or casts a shifting shadow.
—*James 1:17*

Much More Valuable

So don't be afraid; you are more valuable to God than a whole flock of sparrows.
—*Matthew 10:31*

Jesus was persecuted and betrayed during His earthly ministry, and He told His followers that they should expect the same treatment. A servant is not greater than his teacher, after all. But then He makes this promise: Don't be afraid, because God will take care of you. Don't be afraid of threats, don't be afraid even of death. God cares for the sparrows, so how much more will He care for you.

For many today this is a hard promise to believe. They have been told they are worthless. They have been abused and misused. They have been beaten down by life, and they think they don't matter to anyone, much less to God. They doubt His love and His care.

Hear this: God considers you valuable. You matter to Him so much that He even has the hairs on your head numbered and keeps track of each one that falls. He cares about everything that happens to you. He is concerned for your needs. He cares about your desires and your dreams, and when He makes His plan for your life, He does it with you in mind. To Him you are a cherished treasure. So don't be afraid; God will care for you as the valued treasure you are.

Look at the birds. They don't plant or harvest or store food in barns, for your heavenly Father feeds them. And aren't you far more valuable to him than they are?
—*Matthew 6:26*

An Easy Yoke to Bear

*Then Jesus said, "Come to me, all of you who are weary
and carry heavy burdens, and I will give you rest. Take my yoke
upon you. Let me teach you, because I am humble and gentle
at heart, and you will find rest for your souls. For my yoke
is easy to bear, and the burden I give you is light."*

—*Matthew 11:28-30*

The requirements of the law were like a yoke resting on the shoulders of believers. Under the old covenant they were heavy weights, and in the end impossible to carry, a burden that crippled God's people with the unyielding demands of the Pharisees' additions to God's law. But Jesus came with a new covenant, and it is a light yoke characterized by rest.

If you ever feel like you can't do everything God is calling you to do, this verse is for you. If you are ever weary from life, unsure if you can continue on, this verse is for you. If you are tired of all the striving and ready to rest, this verse is for you. The things God is asking you to do will not leave you weary and hopeless.

Jesus' demands are light because He carries them for us. He calls us to relationship, not rules. Growth, not regulations. Life, not death. And He does it through the gentle and humble life He lives for and in us. Jesus met the law's demands for us so that we can enter into joyful relationship with Him. He takes our burdens upon Himself, and in exchange gives us peace. Jesus is our rest—have you by faith entered into that relationship of soul rest?

*Loving God means keeping his commandments, and
his commandments are not burdensome.*

—*1 John 5:3*

Faith as Small as a Mustard Seed

*"You don't have enough faith," Jesus told them. "I tell you
the truth, if you had faith even as small as a mustard seed,
you could say to this mountain, 'Move from here to
there,' and it would move. Nothing would be impossible."*

—Matthew 17:20

The disciples had just seen the Transfiguration. They were on a serious spiritual high, full of wonder and awe. And then they encountered unparalleled spiritual defeat—they were unable to cast a demon out of a boy. Perhaps the worst blow of all was that Jesus reprimanded them by saying that they needed more faith. They were confused and discouraged.

Here is the encouragement, for them and for us: All they needed was the tiniest grain of faith. It wouldn't take much, just the smallest beginning of trust, the merest hint of the growth that would come, a germ of faith. If they had just that tiny spark of belief, they would be able to not only cast out demons, but move mountains.

Do you sometimes share the disciples' feeling of discouragement and failure? Do you wonder why your faith isn't moving the mountains in your path? The key is that the seed of faith engages the power of God. It wasn't up to the disciples, and it isn't up to us, to move the mountain; it is up to God. And He moves the mountains He chooses, when He chooses. So take heart. Water the fledgling seed of faith within you and trust the results to the God who spoke the mountains into being.

*For the LORD is a great God, a great King above all gods. He holds
in his hands the depths of the earth and the mightiest mountains.*

—Psalm 95:3-4

The Power of Community

I also tell you this: If two of you agree here on earth concerning anything you ask, my Father in heaven will do it for you. For where two or three gather together as my followers, I am there among them.
—Matthew 18:19-20

The emphasis in this chapter is on community. Jesus first described the attitudes that lead to community (Matthew 18:1-14), then gave instructions for church discipline (Matthew 18:15-17), all with the goal of maintaining unity, purity, and peace in the body of Christ. Then He made this promise, which gets to the purpose of Christian community: to be God's presence on earth. The key to effective and unified Christian community is prayer, yet how often we neglect to do it.

There is power in community. God lives within each believer, and when several gather together to agree in prayer, His presence is especially near. There is a sweetness to the prayers and a particular effectiveness to them. God has promised His presence and His power when we gather together to pray.

This promise should spur us to gather with other believers for the purpose of prayer. Don't let the urgent pressures of daily life prevent you from making it a priority; give it the same importance Jesus did. The time you spend praying with other believers will do more to advance the gospel than any amount of planning and strategizing and work. God gave us the blueprint for effective ministry—let's follow it!

Confess your sins to each other and pray for each other so that you may be healed. The earnest prayer of a righteous person has great power and produces wonderful results.
—James 5:16

Prayers That Get Answered

You can pray for anything, and if you have faith, you will receive it.
—Matthew 21:22

This is a verse that can be easily misused. We want to stay in control, and so we fixate on the part we think we can dictate: our faith. We think that if we can just force our faith to grow, we can have whatever we want. And we have some firm ideas on what is best for us, so we can easily come up with a laundry list of things to ask for.

Fortunately, God doesn't work that way. He loves us too much to give us something that would be bad for us, and He loves us enough to send us hard things we wouldn't ever choose for ourselves in order to grow us into the people we were created to be.

While we might sometimes wish that we could get an affirmative answer to every prayer we utter, in reality what we really want is for God to do what only He can do—what is best for us, what will turn out best in light of eternity, and what will bring Him the most glory. Those prayers He always answers. So pray expecting God to do big things, and pray trusting that He will only do the big things that are for our ultimate good and His eternal glory.

You can ask for anything in my name, and I will
do it, so that the Son can bring glory to the Father.
Yes, ask me for anything in my name, and I will do it!
—John 14:13-14

Humility before Exaltation

The greatest among you must be a servant. But those who exalt themselves will be humbled, and those who humble themselves will be exalted.
—Matthew 23:11-12

We often see the truth of this verse played out in real life. The arrogant people get caught in an embarrassing scandal while the humble hard worker is eventually promoted to a position of honor.

But it doesn't always work that way—sometimes the wicked prosper and injustice seems to be rewarded. At times like that, it is comforting to know that God will one day humble those who exalt themselves. Some people get the message and humble themselves before God in repentance. Others will be humbled at the final judgment. Either way, justice will be done according to God's will and in His timing.

The challenge for us is to put our humility into action by seeking greatness through service. The highest and most sought-after job in the church should be the lowliest job of service, not one of leadership. Our primary goal each day should be to figure out how we can serve others, not analyze how we have been mistreated. True greatness is found in humble sacrifice. If we live this way, seeking humility rather than looking for ways to build ourselves up, God will exalt us.

But among you it will be different. Whoever wants to be a leader among you must be your servant, and whoever wants to be first among you must be the slave of everyone else. For even the Son of Man came not to be served but to serve others and to give his life as a ransom for many.
—Mark 10:43-45

Run with Endurance

The one who endures to the end will be saved. And the Good News about the Kingdom will be preached throughout the whole world, so that all nations will hear it; and then the end will come.
—Matthew 24:13-14

Hanging on to faith can be really hard. We have doubts. Our once-warm relationship with God grows cold. Our prayers go unanswered, and we feel like they are unheard. Our feeble trust in God's plan is choked out by the cares of this world. Life can be hard—really hard—and it can make us angry with God. Only a few will endure to the end and be saved, but the reward for doing so is well worth the cost.

There is another promise here, and it is one that makes enduring to the end a little easier. You see, often the thing that causes our faith to falter is mistrust in God's ways. We have questions about why God allows suffering, or what happens to those who never have the chance to hear the gospel. But God promises that the Good News will be preached throughout the world, giving every people group a chance to believe. Which is really another way of saying that 1) God is merciful and wants everyone to be saved, and 2) our faith in Him will see us through to the end. When we believe this about God, our faith is strengthened. If your faith is feeling a bit ragged, cling to the Savior of the world who has made a way for everyone to be saved and who will see you through to the end.

Let us strip off every weight that slows us down, especially the sin that so easily trips us up. And let us run with endurance the race God has set before us. We do this by keeping our eyes on Jesus, the champion who initiates and perfects our faith. Because of the joy awaiting him, he endured the cross, disregarding its shame. Now he is seated in the place of honor beside God's throne.
—Hebrews 12:1-2

Listening to Understand

To those who listen to my teaching, more understanding will be given. But for those who are not listening, even what little understanding they have will be taken away from them.

—Mark 4:25

It's a promise and a warning. If we listen, we will understand more and more of God's Word and His ways. We know this from experience—what we focus on fills more and more of our mind. But if we close up our ears to God's voice, we will understand less and less. Eventually we won't even hear Him speaking. I don't know about you, but I want to grow in understanding rather than losing what little clarity I have and becoming more confused.

So how can we listen to God better? This is where spiritual disciplines come in: Bible reading, prayer, and meditating on Scripture are all methods for hearing God's voice. The key is consistency, listening each day for God's direction so that our mind is more and more saturated with the timeless truths of Scripture. The more we attend to God's Word, the more His glory will fill our vision. The more His glory fills our vision, the less we will be concerned with the things of this world that don't last. And the less we will suffer from anxiety and worry and stress because we will care more for the things of God than the things of earth.

My sheep listen to my voice; I know them, and they follow me.

—John 10:27

Overcoming Unbelief

"What do you mean, 'If I can'?" Jesus asked. "Anything is possible if a person believes."
—Mark 9:23

You can almost hear a hint of indignation in Jesus' words. What do you mean, "If I can"? The very question is ludicrous—God can do anything. Or as the children's catechism puts it, "God can do all His holy will." Anything that is consistent with God's character, with His purity and holiness and love, is within His power to do.

But there is one way we can hinder God's power. Anything is possible on the condition that we believe. A few chapters earlier, we read that "because of their unbelief, he couldn't do any miracles among them" (Mark 6:5). God does His work in response to our faith. It's not that He can't do what He wants apart from our meager faith, but if we believe in Him then He will get the glory for the good things He does, and that is His main goal.

So what is your "if God can"? What is that thing that you aren't sure God can do, the thing that seems too big and amazing for God to do? He can do it. Do you dare to believe? Will you stake everything on God's power? If you are struggling to do so, pray the prayer of the father in Mark 9: "I do believe, but help me overcome my unbelief!"

It is impossible to please God without faith. Anyone who
wants to come to him must believe that God exists
and that he rewards those who sincerely seek him.
—Hebrews 11:6

My

GRACE

IS ALL YOU NEED.

My *power*

WORKS BEST

in weakness.

2 CORINTHIANS 12:9

Everything Is Possible with God

*Jesus looked at them intently and said, "Humanly speaking,
it is impossible. But not with God. Everything is possible with God."*

—Mark 10:27

Jesus had just debunked the disciples' belief that material wealth was a sign of God's blessing, and that therefore those who are rich in this world have a fast track to entering heaven. Jesus said that the opposite is in fact true: Those who are rich in this world may find it harder to find eternal life because they don't realize their need of God and therefore do not turn to Him in faith.

Here is the promise: God is able to save anyone. What is humanly impossible—paying the price for our sin—is possible with God. He brings rich people to the end of themselves so that they turn to Him. He calls sinners—the self-righteous who at first think they can earn their way to heaven and the utterly depraved who everyone can see don't deserve it. Any of us can be saved, we just have to realize that humanly speaking it is impossible and believe that we can only find life through Jesus.

Do you realize how impossible your salvation is? Do you appreciate how little you deserve it, and how desperately you need Jesus? Remind yourself today that humanly speaking it is impossible, but with God everything is possible. And then thank Him for this impossible, indescribable gift.

I know that you can do anything, and no one can stop you.

—Job 42:2

Investing in What Lasts

Heaven and earth will disappear, but my words will never disappear.
—Mark 13:31

We are surrounded by reminders of our mortality. Possessions rust and decay and are consumed by moths. Time ravages our bodies and steals our health. Seasons come and go. Even the mountains shake and quake and fall into the sea.

How comforting to know that the best things last forever. At the end of time, the only things remaining will be God, His Word, and His people. This is the promise we cling to when everything is falling apart. God's promises are secure. The things He has revealed about Himself are dependable for all time. And He will keep us safe to the end.

If you're wondering where to spend your time and energy today, this verse will point you in the right direction. Invest in the eternal things. Material possessions won't last and our bank account is only good for our lifetime—but the people we can bless and minister to are eternal beings made in the image of God, and anything we can do to point them toward redemption and wholeness is well worth the effort. Entertainment and pleasure are quickly forgotten, but time spent in God's Word marks us for eternity. Your relationship with Him will far outlast anything else, so dive in deep to that.

My life passes as swiftly as the evening shadows. I am
withering away like grass. But you, O LORD, will sit on your
throne forever. Your fame will endure to every generation.
—Psalm 102:11-12

Son of the Most High

He will be very great and will be called the Son of the Most High.
The Lord God will give him the throne of his ancestor David.
And he will reign over Israel forever; his Kingdom will never end!

—Luke 1:32-33

This same title—Son of the Most High—is later used by the demon-possessed man in Mark 5:7. It is the truth of who Jesus is, uttered by angels and demons alike. The question is, will we worship Him as the Son of the Most High who is our Savior and Lord and Friend, or will we utter His name in derision and fear like the demons? One leads to life, the other to death.

Jesus can offer us life because He is on the throne. He reigns in victory, having overcome death once and for all through His sacrifice on the Cross. This is the promise that makes possible every other promise. Jesus is the Most High God who reigns forever; therefore every promise is yes in Him. He has the authority and the power to do everything He has said He will do, culminating in the promise to rule in perfect justice over His redeemed people in the new heavens and the new earth.

Have you bowed in worship before the Son of the Most High who reigns forever? He is worthy of all praise and honor and glory, in this life and the next.

Therefore, God elevated him to the place of highest honor
and gave him the name above all other names, that at the
name of Jesus every knee should bow, in heaven and on earth
and under the earth, and every tongue declare that
Jesus Christ is Lord, to the glory of God the Father.

—Philippians 2:9-11

Release for the Captives

The Spirit of the LORD is upon me, for he has anointed me to bring Good News to the poor. He has sent me to proclaim that captives will be released, that the blind will see, that the oppressed will be set free, and that the time of the LORD's favor has come.

—*Luke 4:18-19*

It was a bold proclamation. Jesus was saying that He was the promised Messiah, the one who had been first prophesied to Adam and Eve in the Garden, who would crush the head of Satan and bring an end to evil. The promises were being fulfilled right there in the synagogue in the tiny village of Nazareth.

Notice who this Good News is for. It isn't for the rich and powerful, the political elite, or even the religious. Jesus came for the poor, for the captives, for the blind and oppressed. Jesus comes to those from every walk of life who know how desperately they need Him.

We don't like to think of ourselves in these terms, but this is who we are apart from Christ. We are impoverished of soul. We are held captive by sin and death. We are spiritually blind. We are oppressed by our own sin and the sins of others. Jesus comes to us in our need and brings us Good News. Release. Sight. Freedom.

Have you acknowledged who you are apart from Jesus? If you have, then all Jesus promises here is true for you. Rejoice in the good news that you are saved. Live in the freedom Christ has bought for you. Bask in God's favor. This is who you are now because Jesus came for you.

To all who mourn in Israel, he will give a crown of beauty for ashes, a joyous blessing instead of mourning, festive praise instead of despair. In their righteousness, they will be like great oaks that the LORD has planted for his own glory.

—*Isaiah 61:3*

Returned Gifts

*Give, and you will receive. Your gift will return to you in full—pressed down,
shaken together to make room for more, running over, and poured into
your lap. The amount you give will determine the amount you get back.*

—*Luke 6:38*

We are encouraged to give generously, and promised that God will be generous with us in return. But in context this verse isn't talking about money at all, it is talking about forgiveness. Jesus had just said, "Do not judge others, and you will not be judged. Do not condemn others, or it will all come back against you. Forgive others, and you will be forgiven" (Luke 6:37). Jesus is saying that we can't out-forgive God. Whatever mercy we might extend to another is nothing when compared to the mercy God has shown to us.

Are you extending this kind of generous forgiveness toward others? That's the condition of this promise. If you have a judgmental, unforgiving heart, you will find that you are treated in kind. Moving God's heart of forgiveness involves humble repentance, and that necessarily includes acknowledging that you are every bit as much of a sinner as those who have hurt you.

When you acknowledge that truth about yourself, God will pour out His mercy on you so abundantly that it is pressed down, shaken to make room for more, running over, and poured into your lap. No matter what you have done, no matter how judgmental you have been toward others, God gives you so much mercy that you can't hold it all. That's how generous God is—will you let His generosity flow through you onto others?

*But you, O LORD, are a God of compassion and mercy,
slow to get angry and filled with unfailing love and faithfulness.*

—*Psalm 86:15*

Victory

Look, I have given you authority over all the power of the enemy,
and you can walk among snakes and scorpions and crush them.
Nothing will injure you. But don't rejoice because evil spirits
obey you; rejoice because your names are registered in heaven.
—Luke 10:19-20

The disciples had just returned from a mission trip, and they were feeling pretty good about themselves because they had been able to cast out demons. Jesus responded that they shouldn't be surprised at this power, and in fact, they should expect even more power over the forces of evil.

The authority over evil promised here is based on the victory of Christ, not on the disciples' abilities. They had power over demons when they used Jesus' name, and it was because of the promise made all the way back in the Garden of Eden that Jesus would crush the head of the serpent. It had nothing to do with their talents or their strategies. Jesus is the One who overcomes the evil one, and victory comes from relying on His power rather than our own.

When we live out of our identity as children of God, we can have this kind of miraculous victory over the enemy as well, but we must remember that Jesus is the One who conquers evil. It is His victory at the Cross that defeats Satan and his minions. We have the great privilege of sharing in His victory, but we must not treasure the gift more than the giver. Today, live out the victory that is yours in Christ, but rejoice even more in the fact that your name is registered in heaven.

We are not fighting against flesh-and-blood enemies, but against
evil rulers and authorities of the unseen world, against mighty powers
in this dark world, and against evil spirits in the heavenly places.
—Ephesians 6:12

Seeking the Right Things

For everyone who asks, receives. Everyone who seeks, finds.
And to everyone who knocks, the door will be opened.

—*Luke 11:10*

Much of life is about acquiring things. If you think about what you spent your time on yesterday, my guess is that a lot of it was about meeting your needs and the needs of your family, whether those needs were physical or emotional or spiritual. The problem is, so much of what we seek isn't the right thing. So often we don't know what we really need—or we do know what we need but it's not what we want.

Here God promises that we will get everything we need if we persist in prayer. We will receive, we will find, and doors will open to us, all through the promise that comes a few verses later in Luke 11:13—the Holy Spirit. Whatever it is we think we need, what we truly need most of all is the power of God, the peace that passes understanding, and guidance for daily life. In other words, what we really need in every situation is more of the Holy Spirit.

What are you seeking today? What do you keep asking for when you pray? What door do you need opened? Jesus says, persist in prayer. Keep at it, even when you don't seem to be getting an answer. He will give you all the best gifts, and along with that He will give you what you need most of all—Himself.

I will ask the Father, and he will give you another Advocate, who
will never leave you. He is the Holy Spirit, who leads into all truth.

—*John 14:16-17*

Look at the Birds

And the very hairs on your head are all numbered. So don't be afraid;
you are more valuable to God than a whole flock of sparrows.

—*Luke 12:7*

The Mighty God, the Creator of all things, has the hairs on your head numbered. He knows about everything that is going on in your body, all the processes at work and the moment one of them starts to malfunction. He also knows everything that is happening in your life, even the things you don't understand and even the things you don't know about yet.

As if that weren't enough, He actually cares about all those things more than you can imagine. That is why you don't need to fear the past, the present, or the future. The God who bothers to keep track of the hairs on your head will also surely care for all your needs.

This is what it means to be a child of God. You are known, you are loved, you are treasured. If you allow this truth to penetrate your soul, it will give purpose to your life. It will make you eager to serve God and give you the confidence to do so with joy. It will transform the way you treat yourself and those around you. Sit with this truth today and let it really sink in.

Look at the birds. They don't plant or harvest or store
food in barns, for your heavenly Father feeds them.
And aren't you far more valuable to him than they are?

—*Matthew 6:26*

Generous God, Glorious Future

So don't be afraid, little flock. For it gives your
Father great happiness to give you the Kingdom.

—*Luke 12:32*

Even among Christians there is a common misconception that God is a far-off King, unconcerned with the daily affairs of believers. Or perhaps we think He is involved in our lives, but more as a judgmental taskmaster than a loving Father. This verse tenderly banishes all such lies.

God is our Good Shepherd, and He thinks of us as a flock of little sheep. He patiently bears with our weaknesses, binds up our wounds even if they are caused by our own foolishness or stubbornness, and anticipates our every need. He leads us in safe paths, toward a glorious future. He is also a loving Father who does all things for our good—even discipline.

Here's the best part: God takes great joy in giving us the Kingdom. He is not holding out on us. He is not keeping back part of the blessing. All of the Kingdom, all of the joy and all of the peace and all of the victory, is ours in Christ. He eagerly lavishes it on us. As you go about your day today, do it with this picture in mind. Fear not, for it is the Father's great pleasure to give you the Kingdom!

Just as my Father has granted me a Kingdom, I now grant you
the right to eat and drink at my table in my Kingdom.

—*Luke 22:29-30*

Found

For the Son of Man came to seek and save those who are lost.
—Luke 19:10

Have you ever been truly lost? In this day and age, with cell phones almost always within reach, most of the time we know where we are and can find our way back to where we want to be. But that doesn't mean we don't experience lostness—it just means it may take us longer to realize how lost we really are.

When we realize that we have done something wrong that can't be made right, that is being lost. When we realize we are out of sync with those around us and perhaps even unable to process our own thoughts and feelings, that is being lost. When we don't know what to do or where to go next, that is being lost.

Lost is who you are apart from Christ, but He came to find you. He took on human flesh to seek you and to save you, and when you accept the free gift He offers you don't have to live in the land of the lost anymore. In Him you can find freedom from sin, release from guilt and shame, forgiveness as vast as the ocean, and a path forward to new life. What was lost is found in Jesus.

Jesus answered them, "Healthy people don't need a doctor—sick people do. I have come to call not those who think they are righteous, but those who know they are sinners and need to repent."
—Luke 5:31-32

Making the Most of the Time

So when all these things begin to happen, stand and look up, for your salvation is near! . . . Heaven and earth will disappear, but my words will never disappear.
—Luke 21:28, 33

We read verses like these and we seesaw between two extremes. Either we live so much for the day when Christ returns that we ignore the important work before us, or we get so wrapped up in our day-to-day existence that we neglect to "stand and look up." Both approaches are wrong. Somehow we have to remain alert to the signs of the times while also fulfilling our call and making the most of the time.

We can find some of the balance between living in the "already" of God's Kingdom and the "not yet" of the new heavens and new earth by focusing on God's enduring Word. The promises, warnings, and commands found in Scripture will outlast this earth. There we are reminded of the inherent value in each human being and the truth that we have an eternal destiny toward life or death. There we are taught to appreciate the beauty of creation and its Creator. There we are encouraged to behold the holiness of God and live in submission to His will. And there we are commanded to participate in God's redemptive plan for the world while eagerly awaiting His return. Embrace the tension between "already" and "not yet" by immersing yourself in God's eternal Word.

We . . . wait with eager hope for the day when God will give us our full rights as his adopted children, including the new bodies he has promised us.
—Romans 8:23

Offered in Obedience

And now I will send the Holy Spirit, just as my Father promised. But stay here in the city until the Holy Spirit comes and fills you with power from heaven.
—Luke 24:49

These were Jesus' last words in Luke, a promise that the down payment of their salvation was coming. Jesus was reiterating the promise that He was sending an Advocate, a Helper, God's presence to dwell in His people. This promise is fulfilled in Acts 2, which is volume two of Luke's account.

This promise is also fulfilled in each individual believer at the moment they place their faith in Jesus for salvation. When we choose to follow Him, the Holy Spirit comes to dwell within us. He reminds us of truth (John 14:26), prays for us (Romans 8:26), grows our character (Galatians 5:22-23), and gives us hope (Romans 15:13). He comforts us and give us peace (John 14:18, 27). Perhaps best of all, the Holy Spirit is proof that we belong to God (Ephesians 1:4; 2 Corinthians 1:22).

The question is, will we respond to the Holy Spirit's work? It is up to us to listen to the promptings of the Spirit. We can quench them by resisting, or we can follow, obey, and grow. If you want to receive all the gifts the Spirit offers, you must offer yourself up in obedience—then the promises are yours.

The Holy Spirit produces this kind of fruit in our lives: love, joy, peace, patience, kindness, goodness, faithfulness, gentleness, and self-control.
—Galatians 5:22-23

Belonging

But to all who believed him and accepted him,
he gave the right to become children of God.

—*John 1:12*

Adoption is a beautiful thing. Children who are unable, for one reason or another, to be raised by their birth parents are given a new home, a new name, a new identity. They are no longer left alone, but now belong to loving parents. They suddenly have an extended family, many people to shower them with affection. They are chosen and given a secure future.

That's what happens to us when we choose to follow Jesus. We were once isolated, enemies of God, friendless and alone, but now in Christ we become beloved children with all the rights and privileges that attend to that status. We simply believe, and suddenly we belong.

Is this the identity you're living out of today? You are loved. You belong. You have been chosen to be part of a family. You have brothers and sisters, aunts and uncles, and a great Father who loves you like crazy. One day you will inherit the Kingdom of your Father, and even now you get to participate in the life of the Kingdom. You might sometimes feel alone or unloved, but this is the truth about who you are and where you're headed. Believe it and live it.

For his Spirit joins with our spirit to affirm that we are God's
children. And since we are his children, we are his heirs.
In fact, together with Christ we are heirs of God's glory.

—*Romans 8:16-17*

A Gift to Accept

For this is how God loved the world: He gave his one and only Son, so that everyone who believes in him will not perish but have eternal life.

—John 3:16

This is love: God gave His one and only Son so that we can have eternal life with Him. It's a truth so familiar that we almost gloss over it, as if this weren't a love so extreme that we can't imagine it. What parent would ever sacrifice their child—their one and only child—for the sake of an enemy? Especially for an enemy that they know will betray and reject them? This is the unthinkable, unimaginable love God has for us.

The promise is that because of the gift God gave in Christ, we have eternal life. All we have to do is say, "Yes, I accept that gift You gave. And in return, I will give back to You the life You gave to me, the life You saved by dying in my place." It's not a fair trade at all, but it sure works out well for us. Why would anyone reject this love? And yet so many do, and those who make that choice remain under God's justified wrath. They are destined for death because they have rejected the offer of eternal life.

If you haven't yet accepted God's love, offered in the person of Jesus Christ, and the payment He made on your behalf to save you from sin and give you eternal life, won't you do it today? The moment you declare that you believe in Him, you have the gift of eternal life.

This is real love—not that we loved God, but that he loved us and sent his Son as a sacrifice to take away our sins.

—1 John 4:10

Fountain of Living Water

But those who drink the water I give will never be thirsty again.
It becomes a fresh, bubbling spring within them, giving them eternal life.
—John 4:14

Jesus is speaking to a Samaritan woman with a sordid past. She is the last person anyone would expect Him to even associate with, and here He is saying that she can have living water overflowing from her heart to eternal life. If even she, with her low social standing and theological arguments and life of immorality was offered this promise, then surely it is for us as well.

The bubbling spring Jesus offers is an eternal supply of refreshment and life. It continues forever by its own internal mechanism, ensuring that as soon as a need arises, it is met. Christianity is not about external rules or spiritual refreshment doled out in bite-size pieces. It is meant to be a continuous flow of life that springs up from within and fills us with God's power, presence, and peace.

If you're feeling dry and parched, cling to this promise. The moment you placed your trust in Jesus for salvation, He gave you this fountain of living water. It's there, you just need to tap into it. Let Jesus fill you with His peace and joy. Read your Bible and discover His words of life. Let Him refresh you with cleansing waters of forgiveness and release.

On the last day, the climax of the festival, Jesus stood and shouted
to the crowds, "Anyone who is thirsty may come to me! Anyone
who believes in me may come and drink! For the Scriptures
declare, 'Rivers of living water will flow from his heart.'" When
he said "living water," he was speaking of the Spirit, who would
be given to everyone believing in him. But the Spirit had not yet
been given, because Jesus had not yet entered into his glory.
—John 7:37-39

Free from Condemnation

I tell you the truth, those who listen to my message and believe in God who sent me have eternal life. They will never be condemned for their sins, but they have already passed from death into life.

—John 5:24

There is so much theology to unpack in this little verse. Jesus had just been accused of blasphemy by the religious elite for healing on the Sabbath, and then gave a discourse on His connection with God the Father to show that as creator of the Sabbath, He has every right to do the work He chooses to do on that day. Furthermore, Jesus said that He also has authority to give life and to judge. In short, He was claiming equality with God.

Here is the part that applies to you, and to me. If we have listened to Jesus and believe in God, we have eternal life. Right now, we are experiencing the start of the life we will have forever, a life of being in relationship with God through the work of Christ. And the most notable thing about this life is that we are free from condemnation. The sin we were born into and the sins we commit do not carry the death sentence they used to have.

We often think of eternal life and freedom from condemnation as part of our future, but this verse tells us that they are our present reality as well. You don't have to live in guilt and you don't have to fear death. You have eternal life, you are free from condemnation, and you have passed from death to life—this is who you are right now and who you will be forever.

Jesus told her, "I am the resurrection and the life. Anyone who believes in me will live, even after dying. Everyone who lives in me and believes in me will never ever die. Do you believe this, Martha?"

—John 11:25-26

Satisfied

Jesus replied, "I am the bread of life. Whoever comes to me will never be hungry again. Whoever believes in me will never be thirsty."

—*John 6:35*

Every human being on the planet knows the sensations of hunger and thirst. We know what it feels like to be desperate for sustenance, to feel like we might faint from hunger, or to be so parched on a hot day that we will give anything for a drink of water. And we know what it is to be satisfied with ice-cold water and a delicious meal with close friends.

When Jesus told the crowds that He is the Bread of Life, it was an image they could all identify with. But it seems like an impossible promise. We are fickle and weak creatures; how is it that we can be permanently satiated? The answer lies in the Who behind the promise. Jesus doesn't offer us a pat answer or a temporary fix, He offers us Himself. Our deepest need and true longing is actually a need for Jesus. The joy and rest we find in Him has no limits, no bottom, no end. And apart from Him we can't find true joy and rest.

What are you hungry for? What is making you feel empty and parched? Bring it to Jesus. Feed on Him. Turn to Him for your satisfaction and your source of life. The sustenance He offers is forever. If you feast on Him you will never be soul-hungry again. If you believe in Him you will never thirst. He alone can truly satisfy your longing.

The Spirit and the bride say, "Come." Let anyone who hears this say, "Come." Let anyone who is thirsty come. Let anyone who desires drink freely from the water of life.

—*Revelation 22:17*

A Free Invitation

Anyone who believes in me may come and drink! For the Scriptures declare, "Rivers of living water will flow from his heart."
—*John 7:38*

It was the last day of an important religious festival, a day of solemnity, and Jesus stood up and cried in a loud voice, "Anyone who is thirsty may come to Me!" He was declaring Himself to be God, the fulfiller of every longing and every promise.

The invitation Jesus offers is for anyone who realizes their need, anyone who longs for something more, anyone with unsatisfied desire for fulfillment and peace. Social status, race, religious background—none of it matters. Anyone who thirsts is invited to come to Jesus.

The invitation is combined with a promise: satisfaction. Jesus will fill us up with an endless supply of life-giving refreshment through the Holy Spirit. Turn to Him and be filled, not with dead, standing water from a well, but with living water, bubbling up from within. This is newness of life and eternal refreshment.

The day Jesus offered this invitation and promise was the day of the festival that commemorated the Israelites' entrance into a "land of springs of water." It was also the only day when water was not poured. The connection is clear. Where earthly comforts fail, where religion falls short, Jesus gives true life forever. If you're tired of being thirsty and of trying to find your own source of water, come to Him and receive this promise to have rivers of living water flowing through you.

Is anyone thirsty? Come and drink—even if you have no money! Come, take your choice of wine or milk—it's all free!
—*Isaiah 55:1*

The Light of the World

Jesus spoke to the people once more and said, "I am the light of the world. If you follow me, you won't have to walk in darkness, because you will have the light that leads to life."

—*John 8:12*

Darkness represents confusion, hiding, fear, evil, and shame. It is a metaphor for our times of depression, despair, and doubt. All the fears and unknowns and problems we face in this journey called life are dark nights of the soul. Jesus bursts into our darkness to bring light—spiritual sight and bright hope, everything that is pure and good and leads to abundant life.

Jesus proclaimed these words during the Festival of Shelters, when Jews commemorated their years of wandering in the desert—year after year when they didn't know where they were going or what was coming next, only that God was leading them. Jesus stood beneath the flickering lights of the Temple and declared Himself to be the source of light, the One who guides us into the light of God's presence.

That leaves us with a choice. Will we walk in the light that leads to life or continue to stumble in the dark, wondering where we are and where we're going? Jesus promises freedom from fear and bondage through the pure light of His presence. We don't need to grope around in the darkness, unsure of who we are or what we should do, because Jesus shows us the truth. We don't need to hide in shame, for Jesus has forgiven us. Come to the light of the world, follow Him, and you will have the light that leads to life.

The Word gave life to everything that was created, and his life brought light to everyone. The light shines in the darkness, and the darkness can never extinguish it.

—*John 1:4-5*

The Truth Will Set You Free

Jesus said to the people who believed in him, "You are truly my disciples if you remain faithful to my teachings. And you will know the truth, and the truth will set you free."

—*John 8:31*

The promise "you will know the truth, and the truth will set you free" is often separated from the condition: if you are disciples of my teaching. In other words, it is our study of the Bible with the intention to obey that helps us discern truth from error and frees us from futility. The more you know the Bible, the more you will understand truth and be free from the grip of sin and falsehood.

The people Jesus was speaking to thought they were free. They had never been imprisoned and were in fact part of the religious elite. But in reality, they were still slaves to sin. What they needed was to become a part of God's family so that they could be truly free.

Your place in God's family is secure. You are His child forever, and because of that status you can live a life of freedom. Jesus has freed you from the compulsion to sin. He has given you His Word so you can know His heart. He has given you a new heart and a new mind that can discern truth and walk in it. He has freed you from the fear of death and given you a secure hope. He has released you from the need to please others or to earn His favor. Now, walk faithfully in your freedom!

Jesus told him, "I am the way, the truth, and the life. No one can come to the Father except through me."

—*John 14:6*

A Rich and Satisfying Life

Yes, I am the gate. Those who come in through me will be saved. They will come and go freely and will find good pastures. The thief's purpose is to steal and kill and destroy. My purpose is to give them a rich and satisfying life.
—*John 10:9-10*

We talk a lot about life goals, both the overarching purpose to our lives and the sometimes trite things we want to do before we die. If you are a Christian, your main goal is to glorify God and live for Him. God has a goal, too, and it is to give you a rich and satisfying life. The irony is, you can only find the rich and satisfying life you want by living for God. When you seek your life, you lose it, but when you lose your life for Him you find it.

Many times we think of God as a taskmaster, placing demands on us and not caring about our comfort. It is true that God has a different perspective on what makes for a rich and satisfying life, and our comfort in this life is not His number one priority. But in the end His perspective is the right one and it is our view that is skewed. True satisfaction comes from doing what we were made to do—worshiping our Creator. The good life is found in submitting to the plans God has for us, plans that are for our welfare.

Let God define your best life. Rest in the promise that His purposes for you are good. He is working even now to help you find a rich and satisfying life, one where you are your best self and you are doing what you were made for.

And this same God who takes care of me will supply all your needs from his glorious riches, which have been given to us in Christ Jesus.
—*Philippians 4:19*

Guided on Right Paths

I am the good shepherd; I know my own sheep, and they know me.
—John 10:14

This is the kind of promise we can spend a lifetime resting in and meditating on. Jesus is our Good Shepherd. He does for us all the things that a good shepherd does for his sheep. When we wake up in the morning, He takes us to safe places where we can have our needs met. When we lose our way, He seeks us out until He finds us, then brings us back home. When we get hurt, He bandages our wounds and carries us until we can walk again. When we are in danger, He protects us. Whatever we need, He gives us.

Even better than being cared for by this Good Shepherd is the fact that we are known by Him. We sometimes struggle to know ourselves, and we only rarely find someone who really "gets us." Yet God knows us even better than we can ever know ourselves or be known by others. His knowledge of us is intimate, loving, and eternal.

Best of all, we can know God. This isn't an impersonal knowledge about Him, but a personal connection, a two-way relationship. We can share our thoughts and feelings with Him and He actually wants to listen to our ramblings. In response, He is delighted to reveal Himself to us. He draws near to us when we draw near to Him. The Shepherd who cares for us so well knows us, loves us, and enables us to know Him.

The LORD is my shepherd. . . . He renews my strength. He guides
me along right paths, bringing honor to his name.
—Psalm 23:1, 3

Safe in God's Hands

I give them eternal life, and they will never perish. No one can snatch them away from me, for my Father has given them to me, and he is more powerful than anyone else. No one can snatch them from the Father's hand.

—John 10:28-29

Even those who came to faith in Christ early in life sometimes struggle with doubt. Am I really saved? If I were truly saved, wouldn't I be better at living the Christian life? Why do I keep messing up if I belong to God? This verse dispels all such insecurities.

Your salvation doesn't rest on anything you did in the past or anything you are doing right now. You could never earn it, and you will never ever deserve it. You are saved because of what Jesus did. Period, end of story. And you can never lose what Jesus has done for you because He is the eternal, unfailing Lord of all. Praise God that it's not up to us!

Separate your feelings from the facts. If you have placed your faith in Jesus, you are held safe in God's hands forever. Nothing can pry His fingers apart and steal you away. Rest in the secure grasp of God's love for you and let it give you confidence to live a life of peace and joy. Your status is secure and your eternal destiny is sure. Whatever circumstances may be making you feel insecure are just that—temporary circumstances that are guiding your feelings. The truth is, you belong to God. You always have and you always will.

He will keep you strong to the end so that you will be free from all blame on the day when our Lord Jesus Christ returns. God will do this, for he is faithful to do what he says, and he has invited you into partnership with his Son, Jesus Christ our Lord.

—1 Corinthians 1:8-9

Salvation in Christ Alone

Jesus told him, "I am the way, the truth, and the life.
No one can come to the Father except through me."

—*John 14:6*

It is human nature to want to chart our own course and set our own rules. We've twisted the God-given authority mandate of Genesis into a lust for power. That's why this verse is so hard for many people to accept. We want there to be multiple ways to God. We want to be able to come to Him on our terms. We think that a sincere heart ought to be enough. And we certainly don't want to humble ourselves enough to admit that we can't bridge the gulf between us and God that we've caused by our sin.

But that's not how it works. If God is God, we have to come to Him on His terms—and that is through Jesus. His death on the cross in our place and resurrection to glory is the only way we can be reconciled to God. He is the only way, the only truth, the only life, and we can't come to God if we refuse to come through Him.

If you turn this verse around, you see the beauty of what Jesus offers us. There is a way! There is an absolute truth! There is eternal life, and you can have it! The only requirement is that you humble yourself before God and receive the gift Jesus offers—Himself. He gives us so much, and He requires so little. Will you come to Him and let Him set the agenda?

I am the gate. Those who come in through me will be saved.
They will come and go freely and will find good pastures.

—*John 10:9*

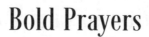
Bold Prayers

You can ask for anything in my name, and I will do it,
so that the Son can bring glory to the Father.
Yes, ask me for anything in my name, and I will do it!

—John 14:13-14

This is a challenging verse. Those new to the faith want to claim the promise that God will do anything we ask without really paying attention to the rest of the verse. They ask for big things and expect their big God to answer. But they often fail to filter their requests through the grid of what will bring God glory. They want Him to fulfill their own selfish desires without surrendering their desires to Him.

On the other hand, those who have been Christians for a long time sometimes stop asking God for things. We become so afraid of asking for the wrong thing that we don't ask anything at all. Or we offer a blanket "Your will be done" without actually praying for anything specific. And then we wonder why our relationship with Him grows cold.

God wants us to come to Him like a child comes before their loving father, and that means asking Him for things and expecting Him to respond. Spend some time in prayer today, asking for big things. Ask God to do great things in you and through you. Ask Him for healing, for reconciliation, for peace and joy. Ask Him to help you find significance and meaning in life and to guide you in paths of wisdom. Most of all, ask Him to bring glory to Himself. God loves to hear your prayers, and He loves to answer them.

Keep on asking, and you will receive what you ask for. Keep on seeking,
and you will find. Keep on knocking, and the door will be opened to you.

—Matthew 7:7

Our Advocate

*And I will ask the Father, and he will give you another Advocate, who
will never leave you. He is the Holy Spirit, who leads into all truth.*
—*John 14:16-17*

The word for *advocate* means "called alongside." It refers to a legal advocate, someone who offers a person's defense on their behalf. The first person to fill this role is Jesus, and when He returned to glory the Holy Spirit came to be this for us in a permanent capacity. The Holy Spirit makes our case before God, declaring that we are His children. He is God's presence in and among us, with us to encourage and instruct and help—just as Jesus did for His followers.

The Holy Spirit isn't promised to everyone, only to those who recognize Him. These words are addressed to those who love Jesus (John 14:15). If you love Jesus, the Holy Spirit dwells within you as your comforter and teacher. Whether you feel close to God or not, He is with you every moment.

Do you live with a sense of God's presence? Do you think of your body as a temple of the Holy Spirit (1 Corinthians 6:19-20)? It is both a comfort and a challenge—God is with you every moment, present in everything you are doing. That means He is there to comfort you in trials but is also being dragged along when you offer yourself as an instrument of sin. The good news is the Holy Spirit is there to help you in your weakness and empower you to do what is right, you just have to allow Him to lead you into the truth.

*Don't you realize that your body is the temple of the
Holy Spirit, who lives in you and was given to you by God?
You do not belong to yourself, for God bought you with
a high price. So you must honor God with your body.*
—*1 Corinthians 6:19-20*

The Gift of Peace

I am leaving you with a gift—peace of
mind and heart. And the peace I give is a gift the world
cannot give. So don't be troubled or afraid.

—John 14:27

What is the best gift anyone has ever given you? Perhaps it was something you had been wishing for or something you didn't even know you wanted. God promises the best gift of all, something that gets us through good times and bad: peace of mind and heart. The biblical word for peace is *shalom*, and it refers to the work Jesus does to restore humankind into relationship with God. It is a sense of everything being right and whole. Really, it's a word that captures the satisfaction of all our longings, that moment when you let out a contented sigh because all is right with the world.

The kind of peace that Jesus gives is something you can't find anywhere else. When you've exhausted all the earthly answers and found them insufficient, turn to Jesus and find *shalom*. He's the only One who can offer it; there are no substitutes. When we experience the *shalom* of Christ we are freed from troubling thoughts and fears. We realize that nothing else matters compared to the joy of being at peace with God and with ourselves. *Shalom* is knowing we are loved, we are forgiven, we are cared for—and therefore we have nothing to fear. It is being untroubled and unafraid even in troubling circumstances. This is the gift of peace Jesus offers us.

Don't worry about anything; instead, pray about
everything. Tell God what you need, and thank him for
all he has done. Then you will experience God's peace,
which exceeds anything we can understand. His peace
will guard your hearts and minds as you live in Christ Jesus.

—Philippians 4:6-7

Abiding in Christ

Yes, I am the vine; you are the branches. Those who remain in me, and I in them, will produce much fruit. For apart from me you can do nothing.
—John 15:5

When Jesus commanded us to remain in Him, He used a word that describes an intimate and enduring relationship. The word "abide" is used in many translations, and it gets at the sense of the word. Our ongoing relationship with Christ ensures that we will grow and bear fruit. We are secure and productive because of God's work in and through us, because His presence and power are running through our veins like sap through the branches of a tree and producing life.

There is a warning here as well. Like many promises in Scripture, this one is conditional. We will produce much fruit if we satisfy the condition: abiding in Christ and letting Him abide in us. The fruitfulness happens naturally as long as the branch remains in its environment. The sun, the water, the nutrients, and the care of the gardener all work together to ensure that there is a harvest. The branch's only job is to stay attached to the vine. But if the branch is severed from the vine, it dies. It is utterly helpless to do what it was made to do if it loses its connection with the vine.

If you're hoping for greater fruitfulness, abide in Christ. Put your energy into sustaining an intimate relationship with Him. Submit to His work in you even when it involves painful pruning. That is where you will find life, nourishment, and the ability to produce the fruit of righteousness.

The Holy Spirit produces this kind of fruit in our lives: love, joy, peace, patience, kindness, goodness, faithfulness, gentleness, and self-control. There is no law against these things!
—Galatians 5:22-23

The Promise of Joy

So you have sorrow now, but I will see you again;
then you will rejoice, and no one can rob you of that joy.

—*John 16:22*

This life is full of sorrow, and none greater than that of the disciples as they witnessed the Crucifixion. All their hopes were dashed. They had trusted Jesus and now He was letting them down, or so they thought. Jesus acknowledged this and gave them permission to mourn. It is right and legitimate to grieve the things in this world that are not as they should be. Even Jesus, who knew the end of the story, experienced sorrow. He wept at Lazarus's tomb even though He knew He would raise him from the dead (John 11:35).

But Jesus didn't leave the disciples in their sorrow, and He doesn't leave us there either. There is sorrow now, but we are assured of rejoicing later if we trust in His promises. The things we experience now are like birthing pangs on the way to future restoration when Jesus returns. The anguish we feel now will be forgotten when we see Him face-to-face.

The best part is that no one can rob us of this kind of joy. Not even the tragedies that afflict us. Nothing can separate us from God's love now, and nothing can take away the promise that we will one day be rescued from the curse. Don't let anyone rob you of the joy you have in Christ today. Rest in it, rely on it, and cling to it. Jesus will return, and from that day you will experience full joy forever.

As he spoke, he showed them the wounds in his hands and
his side. They were filled with joy when they saw the Lord!

—*John 20:20*

He Has Overcome the World

Here on earth you will have many trials and sorrows.
But take heart, because I have overcome the world.

—John 16:33

Jesus first promises that in this life we will have trials and sorrows. That's part of the curse of sin—things are not as they should be, not as God created them. I suppose there is some comfort in knowing that what we are facing is not unusual, others go through it as well, and it doesn't take God by surprise.

The real comfort, however, is in the last part of the verse: Jesus has overcome. Have peace and take heart even when you face those trials and sorrows, because God wins. The curse is lifted, and even though Jesus hasn't yet returned to claim and restore every part of creation, the final outcome is secure. He already won at the Cross, and the empty tomb proves it.

What is your trial or sorrow today? Even in the face of crushing grief, even in the face of unimaginable tragedy, even if you are persecuted and destitute, take heart. Find peace in Jesus and let Him draw near to you in your suffering. He has won the victory and overcome, and you are assured of a good future if you trust in Him.

Can anything ever separate us from Christ's love? Does it
mean he no longer loves us if we have trouble or calamity,
or are persecuted, or hungry, or destitute, or in danger, or threatened
with death? . . . No, despite all these things, overwhelming victory
is ours through Christ, who loved us. And I am convinced that nothing
can ever separate us from God's love. No power in the sky above or in the
earth below—indeed, nothing in all creation will ever be able to separate
us from the love of God that is revealed in Christ Jesus our Lord.

—Romans 8:35-39

Holy Spirit Power

But you will receive power when the Holy Spirit comes upon you. And you will be my witnesses, telling people about me everywhere—in Jerusalem, throughout Judea, in Samaria, and to the ends of the earth.

—Acts 1:8

You have been promised Holy Spirit power, a supernatural ability to know what is right and do it. The same power that raised Jesus back to life lives inside you. But this promise isn't for your own benefit, it is for the spread of the gospel. You have the power of the Holy Spirit so that you can be witnesses of God's glory to the ends of the earth.

Is your vision as big as God's promise? He doesn't give you this surpassing power so you can build your own empire or fulfill your dreams—He does it so you can complete the work He came to do, to reconcile people to Himself.

That doesn't mean the only thing we should be about is evangelism. God gives us a wide array of gifts and has a unique purpose for each of us. But the overarching goal in everything we do is to spread His glory throughout the earth. Whether that means cooking meals for the homeless or for your family, whether it means preaching to a congregation or being kind to your server at McDonald's, whether it is turning a profit in business so you can support missionaries or being a missionary yourself, use the Holy Spirit power God has given you to be a witness. Tell someone about all He has done for you!

On the day of Pentecost all the believers were meeting together in one place. Suddenly, there was a sound from heaven like the roaring of a mighty windstorm, and it filled the house where they were sitting. Then, what looked like flames or tongues of fire appeared and settled on each of them. And everyone present was filled with the Holy Spirit and began speaking in other languages, as the Holy Spirit gave them this ability.

—Acts 2:1-4

I am leaving you
WITH A GIFT –
PEACE OF MIND

and heart.
And the peace I give
IS A GIFT
the world cannot give.
SO DON'T BE TROUBLED
OR AFRAID.

JOHN 14:27

Times of Refreshment

Now repent of your sins and turn to God, so that your sins may
be wiped away. Then times of refreshment will come from the presence
of the Lord, and he will again send you Jesus, your appointed Messiah.
—Acts 3:19-20

Peter has just reminded the listening crowd that they rejected and killed the holy and righteous One, Jesus Christ, the author of life—but God raised Him from the dead (Acts 3:14-15). Now he offers them a chance to wipe the slate clean. If they repent and turn back to the God they have turned their backs on, their sins will be wiped away. Though they have denied and killed the Son of God, He offers them forgiveness and eternal life.

There is great irony here—they had tried to kill the author of life who is not only the source of life but also their only hope for eternal life. But there is also such great promise. A wiping away of every wrong thing we have done. Times of refreshment—isn't that what we all long for and seek after? The very presence of the Lord, and the guarantee of His return. These are great and precious promises.

If you long for these things, if you know that you need a fresh start and the refreshment that only comes from a new beginning with God, then do what this verse says. Repent of your sins and turn back toward God. Seek Him rather than all the world's solutions to de-stress and find satisfaction, and you will find that you receive true forgiveness, deep refreshment, hope for the future, and great joy in God's presence.

He canceled the record of the charges against us
and took it away by nailing it to the cross.
—Colossians 2:14

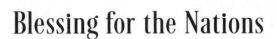

Blessing for the Nations

You are the children of those prophets, and you are included in the covenant God promised to your ancestors. For God said to Abraham, "Through your descendants all the families on earth will be blessed."

—Acts 3:25

I t's been a while since we've been reminded of the covenant promises, but here they are again. Way back in Genesis, thousands of years before the events of the book of Acts, God had promised a rescuer and a blessing. The theme recurred through every book of the Bible, and here Peter connects the dots for his listeners and for us: Jesus was the promised rescuer, the One descended from Abraham who would bless all families on earth.

The blessing of God, forgiveness through Jesus Christ and eternal life with Him, is for all. It isn't just for your little enclave of like-minded friends. It isn't just for the people you think might respond, or those you think deserve it. The gospel is good news for all families on earth.

That leaves us with a mission. We are to share the great hope we have, the amazing promises we've been reading about all year. Whom can you tell? Pick some people you think might want to hear about it, and then add some people to your list whom you wouldn't normally discuss spiritual things with. Who knows—one of them might join the great roar described in Revelation 7 that will take place at the end of time, when all God's people stand around the throne and praise Him.

This promise is to you, to your children, and to those far away—all who have been called by the Lord our God.

—Acts 2:39

The Message of Good News

This is the message of Good News for the people of Israel—that
there is peace with God through Jesus Christ, who is Lord of all.

—*Acts 10:36*

In our everyday vocabulary "good news" might be as minor as a positive report at work or as major as a medical test that turns out to be benign. Big or small, all good news pales in comparison to the Good News of the gospel, stated so succinctly here by Peter: There is peace with God through Jesus Christ.

In order to appreciate how truly great this news is—the best news ever—we need to fully comprehend how desperate our situation is apart from Christ. We are enemies of God. We have rebelled against His perfect law and rejected His love. We are dead in our sins, helpless to please God and destined for eternal death. Our situation is utterly hopeless apart from Christ's death in our place.

So here is the Good News: If we accept Christ's sacrifice on our behalf, believing that He is the Son of God and that He now reigns in glory, we are at peace with God. Our sins are removed as far as the east is from the west. We inherit the righteousness of Christ as if it were our own. We have become children of God. We are no longer slaves to sin but are destined for eternal life with God. You've heard this so many times you probably take it for granted, but you shouldn't. Meditate today on who you are apart from Christ and who you are in Christ so that you can truly rejoice in the best news ever.

But now you have been united with Christ Jesus. Once you were
far away from God, but now you have been brought near to him
through the blood of Christ. For Christ himself has brought peace to us.

—*Ephesians 2:13-14*

Soul Freedom

Brothers, listen! We are here to proclaim that through this man Jesus there is forgiveness for your sins. Everyone who believes in him is made right in God's sight—something the law of Moses could never do.
—Acts 13:38-39

Reading through the law of Moses in Leviticus, you get an overwhelming sense of heaviness. There are so many laws. It would be hard enough to keep them all straight, let alone obey them all. It was a burden too heavy for the people to bear, and even if they could obey every word it could never make anyone righteous.

Imagine the freedom in hearing these words if that was your frame of reference, if your entire life had been spent trying so hard to measure up and you knew that you never would. Perhaps you can relate to the Jews' feelings of inadequacy and hopelessness. Here is the promise of hope: Everyone who believes in Jesus is forgiven and made right. Where the law failed, Jesus succeeded. He fulfilled the law's demands that we never could, and because of Him we can live in freedom. We are enough.

If you're burdened under a stack of religious obligations and feeling hopeless, let these words speak freedom to your soul. You are forgiven, now go and forgive others. You are right in God's sight, now live like the beloved child you are. Release yourself from the voices that say you are not good enough and hear God telling you that you are more than enough for all He is asking you to do.

The law was our guardian until Christ came; it protected us until we could be made right with God through faith. And now that the way of faith has come, we no longer need the law as our guardian.
—Galatians 3:24-25

Believing in Jesus

*They replied, "Believe in the Lord Jesus and you will
be saved, along with everyone in your household."*

—*Acts 16:31*

The testimony of Paul and Silas, their constant prayers and songs even while they languished in prison, had touched the jailer. When a crisis came, an earthquake followed by the assurance that all the prisoners were accounted for and none had escaped, the jailer was ready to commit his life to their God.

This verse is beloved for its simplicity—believe in Jesus and you will be saved. It's a promise that we don't have to earn our salvation (after all, we never could deserve it), nor do we have to participate in a religious ritual to ensure it (although there certainly is a place for church practices and sacraments, as evidenced by the fact that the jailer is baptized right after this). All we need to do is put our faith in Christ.

But it isn't really as simple as it seems at first, is it? Believing in Jesus means trusting that His way is best, even if we don't understand it and even if it causes us great suffering. Believing in Jesus means standing up for Him even if it harms our career, damages our relationships, or puts our life in danger. Believing in Jesus means living for Him day in and day out, even when it's difficult or boring or costly. Believing in Jesus means resting in Him and living for Him—which brings joy and fulfillment and total satisfaction if we will stand firm to the end.

*For this is how God loved the world: He gave his one and only Son,
so that everyone who believes in him will not perish but have eternal life.*

—*John 3:16*

A Strong Anchor

And this hope will not lead to disappointment. For we know how dearly God loves us, because he has given us the Holy Spirit to fill our hearts with his love.

—Romans 5:5

We are no strangers to disappointment, are we? We learn early in life that the toy we so desperately desire does not live up to the advertisers' promises. Later we learn that people also disappoint us; they can never fulfill all of our hopes for them.

How wonderful it is that the hope we have in Christ does not disappoint. In fact, it's better than we can imagine. He is always faithful, His promises always come true, and the deeper we go in our understanding of who He is, the more beautiful He becomes. His glory shines ever brighter. We may be temporarily disappointed by the circumstances God allows, but we can never be ultimately disappointed by God Himself. No matter how high our hopes are, He is better. All of this is guaranteed by the Holy Spirit. His presence in our hearts reminds us of how very much God loves us.

If you're feeling disappointed these days, if things haven't turned out as you had dreamed, rest in this promise: God will never disappoint you. Your hope in Him is never in vain. He loves you dearly, and He has given the Holy Spirit to remind you of that—especially in the moments when you are disappointed by life.

I pray that God, the source of hope, will fill you completely with joy and peace because you trust in him. Then you will overflow with confident hope through the power of the Holy Spirit.

—Romans 15:13

Raised to Life

Since we have been united with him in his death,
we will also be raised to life as he was.

—Romans 6:5

Christians are resurrection people. This is our ultimate hope, our ultimate destiny, our ultimate reality. One day we will be raised to new life, in the same way Jesus was raised to new life after the Crucifixion. We will receive new and improved bodies that will never decay or die. And we will live with God forever. This is what we live for and what the martyrs died for.

It is right that we live in this hope, but we must not neglect the reality of the first part of this verse: We are united with Christ in His death. In a metaphorical sense this means that we associate ourselves with His sacrifice on the cross. But it means more than that. It also means that we willfully put to death our sins, that we die to ourselves, that we live the reality of the Resurrection rather than participating in the deeds of the flesh that enslaved us in our former life.

This is the tension of our everyday existence as believers. Our bodies carry death but also the promise of life. Creation groans under the curse of decay but will one day be restored. And we can choose, moment by moment, to live in resurrection power.

For when we died with Christ we were set free from the power
of sin. And since we died with Christ, we know we will also
live with him. We are sure of this because Christ was raised
from the dead, and he will never die again.

—Romans 6:7-9

Living Free

We know that our old sinful selves were crucified with Christ so that sin might lose its power in our lives. We are no longer slaves to sin. For when we died with Christ we were set free from the power of sin.
—Romans 6:6-7

It's amazing how many Christians walk around with a sense of defeat. While it is true that we all have our besetting sins, those habits of thought or action that we seem to fall into again and again no matter what we do, we don't have to live defeated. Christ has won the victory, and His victory is ours.

The key to living in victory rather than defeat is embracing our true identity: We are no longer slaves to sin, but rather slaves to righteousness. We will still sin, and the struggle against our sin nature is a battle we must fight each day. But that is not who we are anymore. Our sinful selves died with Christ, and so the longer we walk with Him, the less those sins have a hold on us. The pattern of our lives is characterized more and more by obedience to His ways as He changes us from the inside out.

Don't live like a slave to sin, live like a free person. Embrace your identity as one who is dead to sin and alive to righteousness. Sin is powerless over you because Christ has defeated it. Your job is to live out the reality that is already yours, through the power God provides.

My old self has been crucified with Christ. It is no longer I who live, but Christ lives in me. So I live in this earthly body by trusting in the Son of God, who loved me and gave himself for me.
—Galatians 2:20

No Condemnation

So now there is no condemnation for those who belong to Christ Jesus.
And because you belong to him, the power of the life-giving Spirit
has freed you from the power of sin that leads to death.

—Romans 8:1-2

Which voices condemn you? Is there a voice inside that throws all your past failures in your face each time you have a moment of self-reflection? The voices of critical parents who never approved of you, no matter how hard you tried? The experts in your professional life who compare you to an impossible standard? So-called friends on social media who live in a constant state of criticism and moralistic outrage? The truth is, we don't have to look far to find condemnation.

Here is God's promise: None of those voices can touch you now that you belong to Christ. Plug your ears to all of it. You are free. No more condemnation, no more shame, no more hiding, no more death. God has declared you forgiven and righteous, so those old labels of failure, defeated, not enough, and never-going-to-amount-to-anything don't fit you anymore.

I think there is no verse in the Bible that is as freeing as this one. There is no condemnation. You belong to Christ, and He has freed you from the power of sin that leads to death. Meditate on this glorious truth until His voice is the only one you hear. Let Him speak over you these words of life: You are no longer condemned, because you are Mine and I have set you free.

I will give repeated thanks to the LORD, praising him to everyone. For he
stands beside the needy, ready to save them from those who condemn them.

—Psalm 109:30-31

Raised with Christ

The Spirit of God, who raised Jesus from the dead, lives in you.
And just as God raised Christ Jesus from the dead, he will give life
to your mortal bodies by this same Spirit living within you.

—Romans 8:11

There is nothing more heart-wrenching than standing at the deathbed of someone we love. Everything in us screams out that this isn't the way it was supposed to be. We know, deep in the core of our being, that death is not a natural part of the creation God declared to be good.

That is why this verse is such a comfort. Death has been swallowed up by life. Jesus is the resurrection and the life, and our assurance that we will one day be raised to new life is secured by Him. Our hope in the Resurrection does not rest in any earthly power; we know that we will be raised with Christ because the same Spirit who raised Jesus from the dead lives in us.

This is the promise that can give us strength to press on even in the face of tragic death. The Spirit of God is alive and well, even when our bodies return to the dust from which we came. There is life after death, and when the believer dies they are, to paraphrase Billy Graham, more alive than ever because the Spirit that raised Jesus from the grave will also raise them.

The trumpet will sound, the dead will be raised imperishable, and we
will be changed. For the perishable must clothe itself with the
imperishable, and the mortal with immortality. When the perishable
has been clothed with the imperishable, and the mortal with immortality,
then the saying that is written will come true: "Death has been swallowed
up in victory." Where, O death, is your victory? Where, O death, is your sting?

—1 Corinthians 15:52-55, NIV

An Opportunity for Great Joy

*Since we are his children, we are his heirs. In fact, together with
Christ we are heirs of God's glory. But if we are to share his glory,
we must also share his suffering. Yet what we suffer now is
nothing compared to the glory he will reveal to us later.*

—*Romans 8:17-18*

Our position as a child of God carries with it rights, privileges, and responsibilities. We are adopted siblings of the Lord Jesus Christ, and as such we will inherit the Kingdom He promised. The glory that Jesus received after His death and resurrection will one day be ours. That is incredible to think about—the glory of a magnificent winter sunset or a majestic mountain pales in comparison to our reward when Christ returns to take us home.

The responsibility is that we must participate in the sufferings of Christ. Peter makes clear the connection between our suffering now and the glory later: "Trials make you partners with Christ in his suffering, so that you will have the wonderful joy of seeing his glory when it is revealed to all the world" (1 Peter 4:13). We can't have the glory later without suffering now. We have to persevere in the battle against sin and overcome. We must surrender to the refining process God puts us through to make us mature in the faith.

But we are assured in the same breath that it is all worth it. Our suffering now is nothing in comparison to the glory later. So press on in your trials. Count it joy to participate in the sufferings of Christ. And look forward with eager longing to the day when God will wipe every tear and you will inherit all the Kingdom promises.

*Dear brothers and sisters, when troubles of any kind come your way,
consider it an opportunity for great joy. For you know that when
your faith is tested, your endurance has a chance to grow.*

—*James 1:2-3*

Groanings Too Deep for Words

And the Holy Spirit helps us in our weakness. For example, we don't know what God wants us to pray for. But the Holy Spirit prays for us with groanings that cannot be expressed in words.
—*Romans 8:26*

Have you ever been in such despair and confusion that you can't even pray? Perhaps God has seemed to be silent for a long season, and prayer is a chore you find no joy in anymore. The rare times when you talk to God at all, it is a duty, just one more thing to check off the to-do list.

Here is the word for you: The Holy Spirit is praying for you, right now. When you are at your weakest, when you don't know what to pray for, He speaks on your behalf. The Holy Spirit is right now standing before the throne of God and speaking up for your needs with groans that are deeper and more effective than any prayer you could ever compose on your own. God feels for you and speaks for you.

Isn't that a great comfort? With prayer support like that, how could you not take advantage of the great privilege of speaking with God as a friend, as a dear Father, as your beloved? Whether you don't know what to say to Him or you have lots to say, enter boldly into His throne room knowing that your prayers are given words and wings by the very Spirit of God.

Let us come boldly to the throne of our gracious God. There we will receive his mercy, and we will find grace to help us when we need it most.
—*Hebrews 4:16*

God Intended It for Good

And we know that God causes everything to work together for the good of those who love God and are called according to his purpose for them.
—*Romans 8:28*

If you don't already have a life verse, this might be a good one to choose. It starts out with a note of confidence: This is what we know. We can stand on this truth when circumstances tempt us to believe otherwise or when our entire life lies in shambles around our feet. This is true regardless of what we feel.

God is using every circumstance in your life, the painful and the pleasant, for your good. It is all part of a plan, and the plan is a good one because it was created in the mind of our perfectly good Savior. There is no tear wasted, no brokenness that will be left unmended, no pain that doesn't have a purpose. God is working everything into a tapestry of His design, and it will be beautiful. There is a why behind your suffering—thanks to the Who behind everything.

One good way to make this verse your own is to look back at your life and remember God's faithfulness in the past. Think of those things that seemed so painful at the time, but that you can now look back on with appreciation, if not outright thanksgiving. Think of those missed opportunities that put you in just the right place for something even better, or those devastating tragedies that God has used for His glory. Let those remembrances give you courage for whatever comes as you cling to God's promise that His plan is for your good.

You intended to harm me, but God intended it all for good. He brought me to this position so I could save the lives of many people.
—*Genesis 50:20*

God Is for Us

What shall we say about such wonderful things as
these? If God is for us, who can ever be against us?

—*Romans 8:31*

At the end of an entire chapter about God's amazing grace and all the blessings He has given us both now and for eternity, Paul urges us to consider the secret weapon of the Christian. This is the reality that stills all our anxiety and silences our accusers: God is for us. And with Him on our side we can't lose. Really, that's all that needs to be said. No evil power in the supernatural realm or on earth can overcome us because we are on God's side, and His side has won the victory.

As further proof that we have all we need in Christ, Paul follows up with these words: "Since he did not spare even his own Son but gave him up for us all, won't he also give us everything else?" (Romans 8:32). God has already given us the highest and best gift of all—His Son. Of course He will also give us everything else that is good for us.

Do you live in this reality? God, the Creator and sustainer of all things, is on your side. There is no accusation, no threat, no danger that can stand against you. Everything happens according to the will of God, and He is for you. What do you have to fear?

But you will not even need to fight. Take your positions;
then stand still and watch the LORD's victory. He is with you,
O people of Judah and Jerusalem. Do not be afraid or discouraged.
Go out against them tomorrow, for the LORD is with you!

—*2 Chronicles 20:17*

Inescapable Love

No power in the sky above or in the earth below—indeed,
nothing in all creation will ever be able to separate us from
the love of God that is revealed in Christ Jesus our Lord.

—*Romans 8:39*

In the verses just before this, Paul lists off all the things he personally has experienced that a witness might offer as proof that God did not love him. As if hearing their accusations, he asks, "Does it mean God no longer loves us if . . . ?" You can fill in the blank—if we suffer with disease, heartbreak, betrayal, indescribable loss, total failure, does that mean God doesn't love us?

It can feel like it. But the truth is, nothing can separate us from God's love. Our circumstances and heartaches do not mean God doesn't love us. In fact, He proves His love by comforting us in the midst of those things and bringing us out on the other side. He proves His faithfulness by using all that pain for our good.

If you're feeling separated from God's love, cling to this verse. Say to yourself, "I am convinced that nothing can ever separate me from God's love. Neither death nor life, neither angels nor demons, neither my fears for today nor my worries about tomorrow—not even the powers of hell can separate me from God's love" (Romans 8:38). There is nothing you can do and nothing that can happen to you that could make Him stop loving you. Let these words be your anthem as you fight against all the forces that try to pull you away from the God who loves you and make you doubt His goodness.

May you have the power to understand, as all God's people should,
how wide, how long, how high, and how deep his love is. May you
experience the love of Christ, though it is too great to understand fully.

—*Ephesians 3:18-19*

Overflowing with Confident Hope

I pray that God, the source of hope, will fill you completely with joy and peace because you trust in him. Then you will overflow with confident hope through the power of the Holy Spirit.
—Romans 15:13

How would you like someone to describe you? I think "overflowing with confident hope" would be a good goal. Imagine if your friends, coworkers, and family members thought that you were so full of the Holy Spirit and so assured of God's love that your default setting was optimism and peace.

This verse offers the prescription to make that habit of attitude a reality: Trust God. That is the action step here, the only one in this verse. The promises that follow that decision are that you will be completely filled with joy and peace and overflow with confident hope. It sounds like a high return on a simple decision, doesn't it?

Except trusting God isn't always easy. It is a day-by-day, moment-by-moment act of the will, and often it's a battle. Trust is choosing to believe God's promises even when all the available evidence tells you they aren't coming true. It is surrendering your future, your dreams, your plans to God because you choose to believe that His plans for you are better than your own. It is believing what He says about you—that you are forgiven, beloved, and capable of good works through the power of the Holy Spirit. It is choosing to submit to the ways God breaks you because you believe that He will remake you. Do you want to overflow with confident hope? Trust God, and you will.

Don't let your hearts be troubled. Trust in God, and trust also in me.
—John 14:1

Rejoice in our confident hope. Be patient in trouble, and keep on praying.
—Romans 12:12

Warrior of Peace

The God of peace will soon crush Satan under your feet.
—*Romans 16:20*

It seems like an oxymoron. The God of peace is going to crush someone? Isn't that the opposite of peace? Well, not if the one being crushed is actively seeking to prevent us from having peace. This is God righteously defending His people against evil. God brings us peace by crushing Satan.

What this verse is really promising is an end to everything that is wrong in the world. A righting of the universe back to the perfection it had at the moment God spoke it into existence. An end to injustice, persecution, and oppression. A renewal of peace between God and humankind as well as between humans. No more sadness, no more sin, no more Satan.

If you're feeling defeated today, remember that God wins. If you're feeling depressed at the state of world events, remember that Satan's days are numbered. Jesus won at the Cross, and that means we can have peace in our hearts and be assured that one day He will return to rule over the new heavens and new earth in perfect peace and justice. Fight the injustices in your world today with the confidence of someone who knows they are on the winning side.

And I will cause hostility between you and the woman, and between your offspring and her offspring. He will strike your head, and you will strike his heel.
—*Genesis 3:15*

Eyes on Jesus

*He will keep you strong to the end so that you will be free from
all blame on the day when our Lord Jesus Christ returns.*

—*1 Corinthians 1:8*

Marathoners know that the key to a race isn't the beginning, it's the end. If you collapse a few yards from the finish line then you might as well not have run at all. This verse promises that God takes on the responsibility for getting us across the finish line of life. When we choose to follow Him, He commits to keeping us and sanctifying us so that we will grow in faith throughout our lives.

Right now you're probably thinking about people who seemed to be walking the life of faith and then fell away. What about them? Well, marathoners will also tell you that the beginning of the race determines a lot about the end of it. To carry the metaphor into our Christian walk, our spiritual habits—or lack thereof—will set us on a path to success or a path to failure. If we neglect to spend time with God and stop paying attention to our spiritual growth then we are putting our souls at risk. If we fail to live in authentic community and let other believers speak into our lives, we might not finish well. After all, Judas spent a lot of time with Jesus and he didn't finish well.

If your goal is to stand before Christ at the end of time free from all blame, then you are positioned to finish well. Trust God to help you stay strong and submit to His work in your life and you will be running to win.

*Therefore, since we are surrounded by such a huge crowd of witnesses
to the life of faith, let us strip off every weight that slows us down,
especially the sin that so easily trips us up. And let us run with endurance
the race God has set before us. We do this by keeping our eyes
on Jesus, the champion who initiates and perfects our faith.*

—*Hebrews 12:1-2*

Unimaginable

That is what the Scriptures mean when they say,
"No eye has seen, no ear has heard, and no mind has imagined
what God has prepared for those who love him."

—*1 Corinthians 2:9*

Many of us memorized this verse as a promise of the glories of heaven, but in its context Paul is contrasting the world's wisdom to God's wisdom. Apart from the ministry of the Spirit we are unable to understand the mystery of the blessings we have in Christ. The experience of this world and the power of our senses to comprehend it are not sufficient to help us understand the ways of God; only God's Spirit can prepare us for that.

There is something about the Christian life that can't be explained, it can only be experienced. When we have peace and calm in the midst of suffering or hope in the face of deep sorrow, it doesn't make sense to the watching world. Only those who have the Holy Spirit can comprehend it.

Likewise, the plans of God are only understood through the power of the Holy Spirit. Paul goes on to say, "No one can know God's thoughts except God's own Spirit. And we have received God's spirit (not the world's spirit), so we can know the wonderful things God has freely given us" (1 Corinthians 2:11-12). There is a beautiful mystery in our relationship with God, one that we can, in some sense, grasp through the ministry of the Holy Spirit but will never plumb the depths of. So dive in! Live the mysterious beauty of a life lived with God; it is far more glorious than you can imagine.

But it was to us that God revealed these things by his Spirit. For
his Spirit searches out everything and shows us God's deep secrets.

—*1 Corinthians 2:10*

A Holy Temple

Don't you realize that all of you together are the
temple of God and that the Spirit of God lives in you?
—*1 Corinthians 3:16*

In other places Paul mentions that each individual believer is a temple of the Holy Spirit (1 Corinthians 6:19). Here we learn that there is a corporate component as well. The collective body of Christ, the church both local and worldwide, is a temple of God.

Think about that for a minute. When you gather on Sunday morning for worship, it is as holy a moment as it was when God filled the Temple in the Old Testament. Even if the instruments are out of tune and the pastor fumbles his words, God is there. When you are in a long meeting with other church members to make decisions about the church's finances, you together are a temple of God.

It puts things into perspective, doesn't it? That was Paul's intent as he wrote to the unruly Corinthian church. Take care with what is taught and how you relate to one another, for you are God's presence on earth. Stay away from petty arguments and jealousy and divisive attitudes. Act like the holy place that you are. And give your fellowship with other believers the same importance God does—if it is a holy moment, treat it with the reverence and priority it deserves.

Together, we are his house, built on the foundation of the apostles
and the prophets. And the cornerstone is Christ Jesus himself. We are
carefully joined together in him, becoming a holy temple for the Lord.
—*Ephesians 2:20-21*

A Way Out

The temptations in your life are no different from what others experience. And God is faithful. He will not allow the temptation to be more than you can stand. When you are tempted, he will show you a way out so that you can endure.

—*1 Corinthians 10:13*

Temptation can make us feel very alone. Sin by its nature isolates us, and the further down the path of wrongdoing we go, the more our shame makes us want to hide. We end up feeling like we are the only one who has fought this particular struggle, and when we fight alone we often lose the battle.

This verse promises that we are not alone in our temptation. Even Jesus faced the same temptations (Hebrews 4:15). As soon as we internalize that truth, the temptation begins to lose its power. It's no longer an insurmountable challenge; others have faced it and overcome, so we can too.

But there is more. The real power of this verse is in the next phrase. God is faithful. Because He is faithful, He will not give you more temptation than you can stand up to. He will give you a way out. Do you hear that, Christian? That temptation you keep falling prey to is not in charge of you. You don't have to give in. In fact, you have supernatural weapons to wage war against it. God has promised to help you find a way to withstand it, you just have to ask Him.

God blesses those who patiently endure testing and temptation. Afterward they will receive the crown of life that God has promised to those who love him.

—*James 1:12*

Made like Him

Now we see things imperfectly, like puzzling reflections in a mirror, but then we will see everything with perfect clarity. All that I know now is partial and incomplete, but then I will know everything completely, just as God now knows me completely.

—1 Corinthians 13:12

There are a lot of things that are unclear to us in life. We catch glimpses of God's glory in creation and in His Word, but we don't grasp all of it. We see, as Amy Carmichael put it, the edges of His ways, but not the full picture. Paul used the metaphors of childhood and a dim mirror to illustrate the understanding of God we have this side of eternity. Our limited vision is often frustrating, but it grows in us a greater longing to see more of God.

There are two promises here. First, we do have beautiful glimpses of God and His ways. The Holy Spirit gives us insight and understanding into things we could not grasp without supernatural help. God is not hiding from us; we can and should seek greater understanding, and He gives it freely.

Second, we have the promise that one day we will know everything completely. God will reveal all of His glory, majesty, and love to us. There will be perfect clarity to everything we have experienced when we see Him face-to-face. Someday it will all make sense. What a day that will be! Even better, God knows it all now. He knows us completely and He sees everything that happens to us. There is no dimness or imperfection or ambiguity in God's vision. Therefore, we can trust Him and His ways—forever.

So all of us who have had that veil removed can see and reflect the glory of the Lord. And the Lord—who is the Spirit—makes us more and more like him as we are changed into his glorious image.

—2 Corinthians 3:18

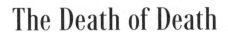
The Death of Death

*Then, when our dying bodies have been transformed
into bodies that will never die, this Scripture will
be fulfilled: "Death is swallowed up in victory."*

—1 Corinthians 15:54

While it may be true that more people fear public speaking than death, I think it's safe to say that all of us consider death an enemy. We work to make our bodies healthy so we can stay active as long as possible. We use the expertise provided by the medical field to help us stay alive and feeling good.

What a wonderful promise it is, then, that death will be swallowed up by victory in our bodies. When God transforms our earthly bodies into heavenly ones, we will no longer be prisoners of a dying body. We will be clothed in immortality and equipped to live on in perfection. Death does not have the final word in the life of a Christian. It is swallowed up, like a whirlpool that absorbs everything that comes near it and sends it to the depths of the ocean, never to be seen again. The ravages of disease and death will be no more.

If you are in a season of loss or illness, take heart. Jesus lives and so shall we, death will be no more. Even if the worst happens, this is the hope that secures us like an anchor to our real life, our eternal existence with God where there will be no more death or dying or sorrow or tears. Embrace this never-ending life God has given you.

And the last enemy to be destroyed is death.

—1 Corinthians 15:26

Strong and Immovable

So, my dear brothers and sisters, be strong and immovable.
Always work enthusiastically for the Lord, for you know
that nothing you do for the Lord is ever useless.

—*1 Corinthians 15:58*

There are a lot of days where we wonder if all our work is accomplishing anything. The chores are never done. The inbox is always full. The garden is once again full of weeds. What is the use of all our toil "under the sun," as the writer of Ecclesiastes put it?

In the end, we are really searching for meaning, for a greater purpose than ourselves. We long to know that what we're doing has a point. And here Paul says that we have a guarantee that our labors can have eternal worth. The key is that our work should be done both enthusiastically and for the Lord. We can take joy and pride in what we do, even if it is a menial task that never gets done and no one will ever see, if we do it for the Lord. He isn't honored by the things we do grudgingly or with a complaining spirit, but if we do those same tasks with a heart of gratitude they become acts of worship.

What work has God given you today? Rejoice in it. Sing while you do the dishes, thank God for the interruption of a friend in need, offer an encouraging word when you return those emails. Nothing you do for the Lord is ever useless.

Work willingly at whatever you do, as though you were working for the
Lord rather than for people. Remember that the Lord will give you an
inheritance as your reward, and that the Master you are serving is Christ.

—*Colossians 3:23-24*

Purpose in Suffering

All praise to God, the Father of our Lord Jesus Christ. God is our merciful Father and the source of all comfort. He comforts us in all our troubles so that we can comfort others. When they are troubled, we will be able to give them the same comfort God has given us.

—*2 Corinthians 1:3-4*

The word used here for *comfort* refers to coming alongside in response to a call for help. Too often we confuse comfort with being comfortable. But in fact we have no need of God's comfort if we are comfortable. The goal of the Christian's life is to be comforted by God—to have His peace and love—not to live a comfortable life this side of eternity.

The comfort God gives us is not for us only, it is meant to be shared. When He gives us a particular trial, He often later places us in positions where we can reach out to those who are suffering in the same way. The cancer mom is the only one who can really understand the pain and uncertainty another cancer mom is facing. The husband who has lost a wife is the only one who can say with any authority to another grieving widower that the crushing sorrow really does get better.

God's promise here is that you will be comforted in your troubles, and that He will then use the pain you have endured to comfort others. In other words, your suffering has at least two purposes: to draw you nearer to the heart of God and to draw others nearer to His heart as well. In your pain, cry out to your merciful Father—He has promised to draw near to you and bring you through it.

Even when I walk through the darkest valley, I will not be afraid, for you are close beside me. Your rod and your staff protect and comfort me.

—*Psalm 23:4*

The Promise to End All Promises

For all of God's promises have been fulfilled in Christ with a resounding "Yes!" And through Christ, our "Amen" (which means "Yes") ascends to God for his glory.

—2 Corinthians 1:20

In a very real sense this verse is the promise to end all promises. Paul is saying that Jesus is proven to be the Son of God, the promised Messiah, because every promise God made in the entire Old Testament came true in Him. Resoundingly so. There can be no doubt about whether Jesus is the Christ because He fulfilled every prophecy, every promise. Our response, through Christ, is "Amen"—which means "confirmed and agreed, it is so." And when we respond to God's promises in this way, God is glorified.

There is great encouragement here. Our hope is not in vain, for we have placed our trust in the One who fulfills every promise with a resounding "Yes!" That includes every promise we've looked at in this book and all the ones we didn't have space to consider here. God promised to be with you always—check. He promised to give you eternal life—check. He promised that in Christ He has overcome death and reconciled you to Himself—check, check. And Jesus stands at God's right hand interceding for you—check.

Today, let your life resound with an Amen! Believe all these promises to the core of your being and live as if they were all fulfilled, because they have been in Christ.

[Jesus Christ] is the one who mediates a new covenant between God and people, so that all who are called can receive the eternal inheritance God has promised them. For Christ died to set them free from the penalty of the sins they had committed under that first covenant.

—Hebrews 9:15

Transformed by Glory

So all of us who have had that veil removed can see and reflect the glory of the Lord. And the Lord—who is the Spirit—makes us more and more like him as we are changed into his glorious image.
—*2 Corinthians 3:18*

When God gave His law through Moses, it was accompanied by so much glory that Moses had to cover his face with a veil so the people would not be overcome with the brilliance of God that lingered on him. But that old covenant was comprised of external laws that could not give life. Now we have the new covenant, the ministry of the Spirit that is written on our hearts and transforms us from the inside out. It is far more brilliant and glorious because it is able to give life.

The moment we put our trust in Jesus, the veil is removed from our hearts. Through the miraculous work of the Holy Spirit we are able to see the glory of God. We can suddenly understand God's Word in a way we couldn't before. We can comprehend God's love for us for the first time. And that process of beholding God's glory, of gazing at Him, changes us. We can't leave a true encounter with God unchanged. Seeing His glory transforms us so that we reflect His nature and imprint to the world around us.

Are you gazing at God so that you can see how glorious He is? Are you spending time just being with Him and beholding His beauty? If so, then the experience will change you to be more and more like Him.

This means that anyone who belongs to Christ has become a new person. The old life is gone; a new life has begun!
—*2 Corinthians 5:17*

Light in the Thin Places

*We now have this light shining in our hearts, but we ourselves
are like fragile clay jars containing this great treasure. This makes
it clear that our great power is from God, not from ourselves.*
—*2 Corinthians 4:7*

The fragile clay jar mentioned here was a common household object that was often used as a metaphor for human weakness. It was used for daily tasks such as gathering and storing water, but was easily broken. Maybe that's a metaphor for your life right now—common, useful, but oh so fragile. Perhaps even a little cracked.

Those thin places in your life, the little cracks and fissures caused by daily use, are the very places where God's light shines through. They are the things God uses to display His glory. The reason He uses our weaknesses is because that is how people will know that the power comes from Him. He gets the glory when we let other people see our limitations and failures and how God has helped us overcome.

Are you constantly working to cover up your weaknesses, to shore up your cracks so no one will notice them? Is self-sufficiency your greatest aim? Are you trying to live the Christian life without God's help? Stop the struggle. The fragile places in your heart are what God wants to use to show off His power. Let His light shine out through the thin places. Give Him room to show off. Stop hiding your weaknesses and let the glory of Jesus shine through you.

*[God] said, "My grace is all you need. My power works best
in weakness." So now I am glad to boast about my
weaknesses, so that the power of Christ can work through me.*
—*2 Corinthians 12:9*

Indestructible

We are pressed on every side by troubles, but we are not crushed.
We are perplexed, but not driven to despair. We are hunted down,
but never abandoned by God. We get knocked down, but we are not
destroyed. Through suffering, our bodies continue to share in the death
of Jesus so that the life of Jesus may also be seen in our bodies.
—2 Corinthians 4:8-10

My guess is that you haven't experienced all the struggles Paul described here, the things he and his companions suffered through. But I bet you've felt like this before. Pressed on every side. Perplexed. Hunted down. Knocked down. Suffering even to the point of death. Maybe you've felt all that in the same week.

Here is God's promise: You will not be crushed. You will not be driven to despair. You will never be abandoned by God. You will not be destroyed. Your body, though marred by death, displays the life of Jesus.

It is good to acknowledge the struggles you are going through. After all, those things are part of life, and sometimes naming them helps them lose some of their power over your emotions. But in doing so you must also acknowledge the hope of God's promises. A helpful exercise is to personalize this verse: "I am pressed by ___, but I am not crushed. I am perplexed by ___, but I am not driven to despair. I feel like I am being hunted down, but God will never abandon me. I have been knocked down by ___, but I am not destroyed. My suffering allows me to share in the death of Jesus so that my body will display His life!"

That is why we never give up. Though our bodies are dying,
our spirits are being renewed every day. For our present
troubles are small and won't last very long. Yet they produce
for us a glory that vastly outweighs them and will last forever!
—2 Corinthians 4:16-17

Future Vision

So we don't look at the troubles we can see now; rather, we fix our gaze on things that cannot be seen. For the things we see now will soon be gone, but the things we cannot see will last forever.

—*2 Corinthians 4:18*

In this hurried life it's easy to get tunnel vision. We have so many urgent demands on our time, so many people who need things from us, so many struggles of our own, that often the only thing we are able to think about is the next task before us. We have little time to plan for the future, let alone to devote to spiritual things. Paul urges us to look up and fix our gaze on the unseen spiritual realities, on the things that last forever.

Maybe the fact that the things we see now will soon be gone doesn't seem like a very good thing. After all, there are wonderful parts of life, things that give us a glimpse of the glory awaiting us in eternity. And we don't want our work here to be meaningless (of course, God promises that anything we do for Him has eternal value—1 Corinthians 15:58). But isn't it a relief to know that all the sin, all the futility, all the mistakes, all the pain will soon be gone?

Here is what does last forever: the love we have for God and for others; the relationships we have with other believers; the faith and hope we have in Christ; God's love; and His Word. In short, all the beautiful things we experience now that pull back the veil on eternity. Fix your gaze there, and let the struggles and heartaches of this life fade into a blur.

*Faith shows the reality of what we hope for;
it is the evidence of things we cannot see.*

—*Hebrews 11:1*

OCTOBER

THE LORD IS
GOOD,
A STRONG REFUGE

when trouble comes.
He is close to those who
trust in him.

NAHUM 1:7

Strength Renewed

For we know that when this earthly tent we live in is taken down (that is, when we die and leave this earthly body), we will have a house in heaven, an eternal body made for us by God himself and not by human hands.

—*2 Corinthians 5:1*

We try to look up and fix our gaze on eternal things, but we are continually brought back down to earth by the frailty of our bodies. As Isaiah reminded us, even youths get tired and weary (Isaiah 40:30). We get sick and our flesh reminds us that we are made of dust, and to dust we shall return.

That's why we need the hope of this promise. Our bodies, miraculous though they are, are merely tents. They were not designed to last forever. Those physical signs that our lives here are temporary are actually blessings, because they remind us that what is waiting for us is better—eternal bodies made by God himself. We will be clothed in immortality, perfected and whole, with no curse of decay and death hanging over us.

Remind yourself of this promise tonight when you are bone-weary and longing for sleep. Or when you stand at the bedside of someone ravaged by disease. Or when you are waiting for the results of a medical test, waiting to find out whether your life is about to change dramatically. You have a house in heaven, an eternal body made for you by God Himself. Better things are in store.

Even youths grow tired and weary, and young men stumble and fall; but those who hope in the LORD will renew their strength. They will soar on wings like eagles; they will run and not grow weary, they will walk and not be faint.

—*Isaiah 40:30-31, NIV*

New Life

This means that anyone who belongs to Christ has become
a new person. The old life is gone; a new life has begun!
—2 Corinthians 5:17

Paul is building an argument in the verses just preceding this one. He is defending his ministry against false accusations, ending with the assertion that "Christ's love controls us" (2 Corinthians 5:14). The logic goes like this: Because Christ died for us, we have died to our old life and now live for Christ. Now everything looks different—our whole frame of reference changed when we were saved. In summary, "the old life is gone; a new life has begun."

I wonder how many of us think about this transformation we have undergone. So often our lives don't look very different from our good-hearted non-Christian neighbors. We enjoy the same TV shows, we spend our Saturdays doing the same things, perhaps we have the same rules for our children.

That's not how it should be. If we are in Christ, if we truly belong to Him, there should be something fundamentally different about us. We have a different lens through which to view our world and our experiences and the people around us—the lens of God's eternal love. We have a different standard of morality—the standard of Scripture. We have a new heart, one that is a temple of the Holy Spirit. We view people as eternal souls made in the image of God and possessing inherent worth. We are controlled by the love of Christ, and that should make all the difference in our attitudes and actions.

Do not let any part of your body become an instrument of evil
to serve sin. Instead, give yourselves completely to God, for you
were dead, but now you have new life. So use your whole body
as an instrument to do what is right for the glory of God.
—Romans 6:13

Don't Hold Back

God will generously provide all you need. Then you will always
have everything you need and plenty left over to share with others.
—*2 Corinthians 9:8*

The promise comes at the end of this verse—God will give us everything we need, enough that we have something to share with others. The condition comes in the verses just before—we must first give generously. It's counterintuitive. How can we give if we don't have enough for ourselves?

If we wait to give until we have "enough," we will never give. Our needs will expand as our resources grow. That's why God asks us to give generously first, and when we do He will give us what we need and some more left over to give even more. God is asking us to step out in faith. Do we trust Him to provide for our needs, or are we really placing our trust in our savings account and full pantry?

Sometimes I think we make excuses for not giving more. We say we don't want to put God to the test, so we take care of our families and then discover that we don't have much left over to give. But it's not testing God to take Him at His word. He said that if we give generously and cheerfully, He will provide enough for our needs and more to give even more. If you want to harvest a rich crop of joy, give everything God calls you to give, not holding anything back. After all, He hasn't held back even His own Son.

The generous will prosper; those who refresh
others will themselves be refreshed.

—*Proverbs 11:25*

A Thorn in the Flesh

Each time he said, "My grace is all you need. My power works best
in weakness." So now I am glad to boast about my weaknesses,
so that the power of Christ can work through me.

—*2 Corinthians 12:9*

I think all of us can relate to Paul as he prayed for his "thorn in the flesh" to be removed. We all have something we are sure we would be better off without. A constant temptation or addiction. A weakness, whether physical or mental. A life circumstance that holds us back from what we think would be a life of more effective Kingdom service.

Ultimately, accepting our "thorn in the flesh" is an act of trust in God's sovereignty. Do you believe that He can do all things, and that everything He does is for your ultimate good and His glory? If so, then the thing you beg God to remove that He does not is the thing He will use to show His power. Trust that He is dealing with you graciously, as He always has before and has promised to always do in the future, and surrender to what He has allowed.

Instead of praying for your thorn to be removed, start praying that God will use it. Ask Him to show His power when you are powerless. Ask Him to be gracious in your weakness. Ask Him to use the difficult things in your life to reveal His glory. And then stop fighting against it, stop trying to hide it, and let God show up and show off in your weakness.

I take pleasure in my weaknesses, and in the insults, hardships, persecutions,
and troubles that I suffer for Christ. For when I am weak, then I am strong.

—*2 Corinthians 12:10*

Out with the Old Self

*My old self has been crucified with Christ. It is no longer I who live,
but Christ lives in me. So I live in this earthly body by trusting
in the Son of God, who loved me and gave himself for me.*

—*Galatians 2:20*

The "old self" Paul is talking about here is the old life he mentioned in 2 Corinthians 5:17. At the moment of salvation, we take on Christ's death and with Him rise to new life. There is a fundamental shift in our identity, from enemy of Christ to child of God. It is not just about the eternal life we will spend with Him but also the life we have now.

The new life we have in Christ means that instead of living for ourselves, we live for God. Everything about us changes. We are transformed into people who want to do what's right and who have the power to do what's right because the Holy Spirit lives inside us. The longer we walk with Jesus, the more we look like Him and the less we look like the world.

Of course, we still sin. We must continually put off the old self and put on the new (Ephesians 4:22-24). We choose each moment whether we will live in the new nature or the old. That's why this promise is so important. It says that whether or not we live it every moment, the truth is that our old self is dead. God lives inside us and helps us put to death the deeds of darkness that are part of our old, sinful nature. Our task—and our joy—is to stop living like the dead person we were and start living like the fully alive person we are now.

*We know that our old sinful selves were crucified with Christ so that
sin might lose its power in our lives. We are no longer slaves to sin.
For when we died with Christ we were set free from the power of sin.*

—*Romans 6:6-7*

Rescued

*But Christ has rescued us from the curse pronounced
by the law. When he was hung on the cross, he took
upon himself the curse for our wrongdoing. For it is written
in the Scriptures, "Cursed is everyone who is hung on a tree."*
—Galatians 3:13

The verse quoted here comes from Deuteronomy 21:23, which stated that criminals executed in public were under God's curse. When Jesus died on the cross, He was taking upon Himself the curse God uttered in the Garden of Eden when Adam and Eve sinned. In other words, the method of Christ's death was what made it an adequate ransom to free us from the curse of sin and death.

Most of us go about our day thinking we are pretty good people. Our sins are small—little attitudes or thoughts and the occasional cross word. But when we think about ourselves in that way we are misunderstanding the concept of holiness. Any blot ruins the bright white of sinless perfection. Whether the sin is big or small, it deserves the full wrath of God. Apart from Christ's ransom, we were under the same curse as the worst murderer in history.

Understanding God's holiness and the curse we lived under helps us better appreciate the sacrifice Jesus made for us. He took upon Himself the curse we deserved for our "little" sins and our big ones. He was crushed for our sins and wounded so we can be made whole. He took upon Himself all the wrath of God that we deserved. What a rescue we have received!

*All of us, like sheep, have strayed away. We have left God's paths
to follow our own. Yet the Lord laid on him the sins of us all.*
—Isaiah 53:56

One in Christ

And all who have been united with Christ in baptism have put on Christ, like putting on new clothes. There is no longer Jew or Gentile, slave or free, male and female. For you are all one in Christ Jesus. And now that you belong to Christ, you are the true children of Abraham. You are his heirs, and God's promise to Abraham belongs to you.
—Galatians 3:27-29

In the Kingdom of God, we're all wearing the same clothes. Every Christian has put off their old self and put on Christ. Each of us was wearing filthy rags until we were clothed with the righteousness of God. When you think of it that way, the distinctions we make based on social status, race, or worship preferences are pretty insignificant. We are all one in Christ. This is the reality, whether we experience it in our world or not.

Don't miss the end of this verse—God's promise to Abraham that is now ours was that He would make him a blessing to all nations. Guess how that happens? If we live like the new creations we are, breaking down the barriers society sets up between people. We are all one in Christ Jesus, heirs of the same promise, no matter our race, gender, or social standing. Let's bless the nations by living that out. What does that look like in your life? Perhaps it means fighting social injustice. Perhaps it means making a new friend who looks and acts a lot different than you do. Perhaps it means adopting a posture of listening rather than one of judgment. Perhaps it means consciously putting off old attitudes and prejudices and putting on the new clothes of loving your brothers and sisters in Christ.

Christ is all that matters, and he lives in all of us. Since God chose you to be the holy people he loves, you must clothe yourselves with tenderhearted mercy, kindness, humility, gentleness, and patience. . . . Above all, clothe yourselves with love.
—Colossians 3:11-12, 14

Adopted

Now you are no longer a slave but God's own child.
And since you are his child, God has made you his heir.

—*Galatians 4:7*

One of the most common images used in Scripture for our condition before salvation is slavery. It still sometimes feels like we are enslaved to our evil desires, incapable of denying ourselves. We want to do what is right but feel powerless to do so.

There is an equally powerful image for who we became when we put our faith in Jesus. We lost our old title of slave and gained the title "child of God." We no longer have to do what our flesh tempts us to do, for we have become a beloved son or daughter. We no longer have to offer sacrifices to appease an angry God, for He is now our heavenly Father. We are free to love, free to serve, free to do what is right—and unlike sin, those things bring true joy.

The challenge for us is to live out of this new, true identity. Until Jesus returns to claim us once and for all, we still have the choice to live like a slave of sin. That's why we need to claim this promise daily, even hourly: I am no longer a slave to sin, at the mercy of my passions. I am a child of God and an heir to all His promises.

God sent [his Son] to buy freedom for us who were slaves
to the law, so that he could adopt us as his very own children.
And because we are his children, God has sent the Spirit of
his Son into our hearts, prompting us to call out, "Abba, Father."

—*Galatians 4:5-6*

The Fruit of the Spirit

*So I say, let the Holy Spirit guide your lives. Then you won't be doing
what your sinful nature craves. . . . But the Holy Spirit produces this kind of fruit
in our lives: love, joy, peace, patience, kindness, goodness, faithfulness,
gentleness, and self-control. There is no law against these things!*
—**Galatians 5:16, 22-23**

There is a battle in the Christian life. Even after we've converted to the winning side—God's side—and have the Holy Spirit living inside us to help us wage war, we are still in a battle. And we sometimes lose, giving in to what our sinful nature craves. Those moments can be very discouraging, and that's when we need this promise.

The Holy Spirit bears fruit in us. It's not "if we do these things then the Holy Spirit might help us." There is no condition. The Holy Spirit produces this kind of fruit. It is a natural process, one that takes place in varying degrees depending on the conditions, but it is the natural progression of the Christian life. If we are in Christ, we will exhibit more and more of the fruit of the Spirit.

Now, that is not to say that we can't hamper the process. That's where the command to "let the Holy Spirit guide your lives" comes in. We have the power to create conditions for growth or to quench the growth. The more we listen to the Holy Spirit, the more we put ourselves under God's Word, the more fruit we will have. If we refuse to listen, the Holy Spirit will back away and advise us less and less. The choice is ours: Will we plant ourselves near the source of life and let the growth happen, or will we cut off the buds before they can bloom?

*I am the vine; you are the branches. Those who remain in me, and I in
them, will produce much fruit. For apart from me you can do nothing.*
—**John 15:5**

Don't Give Up

*Let's not get tired of doing what is good. At just the right time
we will reap a harvest of blessing if we don't give up.*

—*Galatians 6:9*

Do you ever just get tired of doing the right thing? You try to win someone over by being kind even when they are rude, but they just seem to get even more angry. You are honest and honorable, but you get passed over for a promotion while the people who lie and cheat succeed. You are faithful and loyal, but you still get betrayed. Sometimes you just want to quit.

The promise for those moments of weariness in doing what is good is that at some point there will be a harvest of blessing. One day God will make things right. You will never regret doing the right thing, but you will very likely regret doing the wrong thing even in this life, and most certainly you will regret it when you stand before the throne of God.

Don't give up! Keep doing what's right. Get encouragement from those who are running the race beside you. Let God refresh you with His Word. Pick yourself up, dust yourself off, and keep fighting the good fight of the faith. One day, perhaps even today, it will all be worth it. God is on His throne, and He is pleased with your obedience. Don't let yourself quit when you are so close to the finish line.

*Therefore, since we are surrounded by such a huge crowd of witnesses
to the life of faith, let us strip off every weight that slows us down,
especially the sin that so easily trips us up. And let us run with endurance
the race God has set before us. We do this by keeping our eyes on Jesus,
the champion who initiates and perfects our faith. Think of all the hostility
he endured from sinful people; then you won't become weary and give up.*

—*Hebrews 12:1-3*

#Blessed

All praise to God, the Father of our Lord Jesus Christ, who has blessed us with every spiritual blessing in the heavenly realms because we are united with Christ.
—Ephesians 1:3

It's a common hashtag: #blessed. Usually people post it when their circumstances are matching up to their expectations or hopes. New job, #blessed. Wonderful kids, #blessed. Something good is happening, and they give glory to God who is the giver of all good gifts.

The truth is, in Christ we are always blessed. With our limited vision we think that blessing is about the good things in life. But really, it's about the good things we have in Christ, and those things are ours whether or not our circumstances are living up to our expectations. He has given us every spiritual blessing in the heavenly realms—what more could we want? We might be suffering greatly, but we still have every spiritual blessing in the heavenly realms because we are still united with Christ.

Every day is a good day to count your blessings. But be sure to count the ones that really matter: You are loved. You are saved. You are forgiven. You are healed in all the ways that matter most—on the inside. It's great to be thankful for your dear family and friends, but it's even better to know how blessed you are in Christ even if all those things are taken away. Which blessings are you most thankful for today?

Let all that I am praise the LORD; may I never forget the good things he does for me. He forgives all my sins and heals all my diseases. He redeems me from death and crowns me with love and tender mercies. He fills my life with good things. My youth is renewed like the eagle's!
—Psalm 103:2-5

Chosen and Beautiful

*Even before he made the world, God loved us and
chose us in Christ to be holy and without fault in his eyes.*
—*Ephesians 1:4*

Do you ever imagine what it would have been like to witness creation? There was nothing, an empty void, and then God spoke the universe into existence. Suddenly there was light and dark, ocean and land, bluebirds and kittens, and it was beautiful and very good.

But here's the thing—even before He made that great big beautiful world, God loved us, chose us, and promised to make us holy. Before there was a place where God would one day breathe life into humanity, He knew that one day there would be you and me and all the saints who have gone before us, and He loved us already. Like a parent eagerly awaiting the coming of a child, He was already in love. It kind of blows your mind, doesn't it?

What do you think of yourself today? Chances are good that you are frustrated by some of your faults, perhaps down on yourself about a thing or two. Hear this word from the Lord: You were loved and chosen before time began. That's how much God cares for you. And He has made you holy and without fault through Christ. Be encouraged today by God's great, expansive, unimaginable love for you that started before the foundation of the world and makes it possible for you to spend forever with Him.

*For you are a holy people, who belong to the LORD your God. Of all
the people on earth, the LORD your God has chosen you to be his own
special treasure. The LORD did not set his heart on you and choose you
because you were more numerous than other nations, for you were the
smallest of all nations! Rather, it was simply that the LORD loves you.*
—*Deuteronomy 7:6-8*

The Seed of God's Promises

The Spirit is God's guarantee that he will give us the inheritance he promised and that he has purchased us to be his own people. He did this so we would praise and glorify him.

—*Ephesians 1:14*

When you make a big purchase, such as a house or a car, you usually put down a portion of the cost and take out a loan for the rest of it. The down payment guarantees that you are serious about the purchase and will make the rest of the promised payments until the loan is paid off.

The Holy Spirit is like a down payment from God to us. The Spirit's presence in our lives is absolute confirmation that God will fulfill every promise He has made. It is the proof that we belong to Him and that He will one day return to take full possession of the people He has bought with His blood. The Spirit within us is the seed of God's promises, which will come into full bloom when Christ returns to take us home. There is a little supernatural flame within us that will burst into full glory when we see Him face-to-face.

Some days it feels like a small flame indeed, in danger of flickering out. But God has guaranteed all His promises. If you have felt the warmth of the Spirit confirming Scripture in your heart, if you have been moved to lovingkindness in a difficult relationship, if you have grown in peace and joy as you walk with God, then you have experienced the down payment and can know without a shadow of doubt that God will keep you till the end.

So you have not received a spirit that makes you fearful slaves. Instead, you received God's Spirit when he adopted you as his own children. Now we call him, "Abba, Father."

—*Romans 8:15*

Boasting

*God saved you by his grace when you believed. And you can't take
credit for this; it is a gift from God. Salvation is not a reward for
the good things we have done, so none of us can boast about it.*
—*Ephesians 2:8-9*

It is human nature to want to take credit for our accomplishments. Feeling good about something we've worked for is what helps us press on and take on the next challenge. But there is one thing we must never take credit for: our salvation. In ourselves, we are spiritually dead. There is nothing we can do to breathe life into our dry bones. We are cut off, separated from God, and no amount of effort can bridge the gap. Our situation is hopeless and we are helpless to do anything about it.

But God rescued us. He gave us a gift. We did not earn it, and we certainly do not deserve it. God did for us what we could not do for ourselves: He lived a perfect human life and then took the penalty for our sins. If we realize how desperately we need this gift, we will also realize that we dare not try to take credit for it—or boast about our goodness as if it is anything other than the work of God in us.

There is something we can boast about, though, and that is in what God has done. Tell everyone you know what He has done for you. Talk about all the times you were at your weakest and God showed up in strength. Tell them how you were lost, and now you have been found; or how you were blind to spiritual truth, and now you can see because God is your light.

*This is what the Lord says: "Don't let the wise boast in their wisdom,
or the powerful boast in their power, or the rich boast in their riches.
But those who wish to boast should boast in this alone: that they
truly know me and understand that I am the Lord."*
—*Jeremiah 9:23-24*

God's Masterpiece

*For we are God's masterpiece. He has created us anew in Christ Jesus,
so we can do the good things he planned for us long ago.*
—*Ephesians 2:10*

An artist spends days, months, even sometimes a lifetime on their masterpiece. Just the right color here, a bit more shading there, all done with love for the process as well as the finished product. There is intentionality and delight in equal measure in each brushstroke.

That is what God is doing in you, right now, this very day. You are a masterpiece that communicates His message and blessing to the world. Each trial you face, each triumph you celebrate, each circumstance in your life, is working toward this end: You are a new creature who lives out all the good things God has planned for you.

It is a great joy to know how intentional God's work is in you. Nothing is arbitrary, nothing is wasted. At the same time, it is inspiring and challenging to know that God has planned good works for you to walk in. You have a responsibility to live up to the investment God is making in you. So enjoy the process, knowing that God is doing everything in your life with purpose and planning. Submit to the master Artist's work in you. And then walk, with boldness and love and commitment, in the paths He is making for you so that you can proclaim the glory of the Master to everyone you meet.

*And I am certain that God, who began the good work within you, will continue
his work until it is finally finished on the day when Christ Jesus returns.*
—*Philippians 1:6*

Opening Your Heart

Then Christ will make his home in your hearts as you trust in him.
Your roots will grow down into God's love and keep you strong.
And may you have the power to understand, as all God's people
should, how wide, how long, how high, and how deep his love is.
May you experience the love of Christ, though it is too great to
understand fully. Then you will be made complete with all the
fullness of life and power that comes from God.

—Ephesians 3:17-19

Even though Paul himself was enduring great suffering, his pleadings for the Ephesians in these verses are more prayer than promise. It is a great model for how we can pray real, solid, meaningful prayers for those we love rather than just always relying on the "God bless so-and-sos" or the list of physical needs they are facing. These are prayers that reach into the soul and spirit of our loved ones.

There is promise here as well. These things are attainable. With God's help, we can create habits and heart postures that make a home for Christ in our hearts. When we do that, we will have roots that grow deep into God's love and keep us fruitful during the dry seasons. We will have power to understand the bigness of God's love for us and to experience Christ's love, though it is too great for us to fully comprehend. And we can be complete with all the fullness of life and power that comes from God.

Is this what you long for, in your own life as well as for those you love? Then make Christ at home in your heart. Read your Bible. Pray deeply. Submit joyfully. Live devotedly. Trust Him fully, and these spiritual realities can be yours in full measure.

Jesus replied, "All who love me will do what I say. My Father will
love them, and we will come and make our home with each of them."

—John 14:23

Exceedingly Abundantly More

Now all glory to God, who is able, through his mighty power at work within us, to accomplish infinitely more than we might ask or think.
—*Ephesians 3:20*

What are you longing for today? What are the things you really need God to do for you? Most days, if we let ourselves go there, we are carrying around in our heart a desire or need that we almost don't dare express because we aren't really sure that God can do it—or that He will do it for us.

God is able—because He has all power—to accomplish not just what we ask or think or dream, but infinitely more. The Greek translation is "exceedingly abundantly." It's as though Paul can't even express the greatness of God's power to work good in and for us. Our longings are not too big for Him, they are too small. We want healing for our bodies, but God offers healing for our souls that lasts into eternity. We ask for help to make it through another day with our depression or anxiety, but God wants to walk us through it to the other side. We don't dare to ask Him to repair a relationship, but what He wants is to bring reconciliation and unity.

Give yourself some time and space today to look at those deep longings of your heart and ask God to show you what He wants to do in them. He may have far bigger plans than you can imagine! Trust the God who does exceedingly abundantly above anything you can imagine with your inmost longings and desires, and see what He will do.

No eye has seen, no ear has heard, and no mind has imagined what God has prepared for those who love him.
—*1 Corinthians 2:9*

People of Light

*For once you were full of darkness, but now you have
light from the Lord. So live as people of light!*

—*Ephesians 5:8*

Paul contrasts our former way of life with our way of life after trusting in Christ by using the image of darkness and light. Before Christ we were full of impurity, filthiness, and immorality. The things we desired and did were shameful and secretive. Our lives were futile, and we were under the wrath of God.

But now that the light of Christ lives within us, we are characterized by all that is good and right and true. We can discern what is right and have the power to do it. We are full of gratitude rather than bitterness, and we walk in love following the example of Christ. The light of Christ affects every relationship in our lives—those in the home and those outside it—and illuminates the world around us with the glory of God.

Are you living out the light of Christ? Are your actions and attitudes informed and shaped by Christ's example of sacrificial love? Are you discerning about how to live? Submissive to those God has placed in authority over you? The light of Christ changes everything about the way we view ourselves and the way we interact with the world if we allow Him to help us live as people of light.

*Because of God's tender mercy, the morning light from heaven is about
to break upon us, to give light to those who sit in darkness and
in the shadow of death, and to guide us to the path of peace.*

—*Luke 1:78-79*

Strong in the Lord

*Put on every piece of God's armor so you will be able
to resist the enemy in the time of evil. Then after
the battle you will still be standing firm.*

—*Ephesians 6:13*

The Christian life is a battle. We wage war against the spiritual forces of darkness, against flesh-and-blood enemies who are seeking our downfall because we love Jesus, and even against our own weakness. Behind every one of those battles is Satan, who prowls around like a roaring lion looking for someone to devour.

There are two promises in this verse. First, we are promised help in the battle against sin and evil. God has given us a whole array of weapons: the belt of truth, the armor of righteousness, the shoes of the gospel of peace, the shield of faith, the helmet of salvation, and the sword of the Spirit—God's Word. And, of course, we have God's presence and supernatural help to withstand temptation.

But there is more, and perhaps this is the most encouraging promise of all: There is an end to the battle, and when the end comes we will be standing firm. We win because Jesus won at the Cross. As long as we have put ourselves on His side by trusting in Him for salvation, we are promised that His armor is enough to keep us safe until the end. Now, that doesn't mean that we will win every battle. Sometimes we will put our armor down and choose to stop fighting. But as long as we belong to Jesus, at the final day we will have the victory. So suit up and keep fighting!

Be strong in the Lord and in his mighty power.

—*Ephesians 6:10*

Not Done Yet

And I am certain that God, who began the good work within you, will continue his work until it is finally finished on the day when Christ Jesus returns.

—Philippians 1:6

We are unfinished products, like a half-painted canvas or a manuscript that hasn't found its last chapter and needs some editing. That's kind of comforting, isn't it? God knows we're not done yet. The rough edges are not hidden from His sight. And He won't quit working on us until the day Christ returns.

There is in this promise deep encouragement that God is intimately involved in our spiritual growth. He sees with a loving Creator's eyes how we need to grow, He desires to see the masterpiece of our lives completed perfectly, and He is in every moment actively involved in our lives to accomplish it. But there is also a challenge. Will we work with the process, or will we hamper it? Will we surrender to God's ways even when they cut us in painful ways? Do we trust that He is in control and is working for our good? Or will we become lazy in our spiritual walk and bitter when things are difficult?

God is at work in you, and all His ways are good. You can trust Him to use every circumstance in your life to help you become the person He created you to be. And you have the great honor of helping the process along by joyfully submitting to His expert shaping and disciplining yourself to walk in His ways.

May the God of peace . . . equip you with all you need for doing his will. May he produce in you, through the power of Jesus Christ, every good thing that is pleasing to him.

—Hebrews 13:20-21

Transformed Thoughts

*For God is working in you, giving you the
desire and the power to do what pleases him.*

—*Philippians 2:13*

We talked yesterday about God's promise to finish the work He began in you. Today's verse describes what that work looks like. How can we know God is doing something when our spiritual lives so often feel dry and unproductive?

God works in us by transforming our desires. As the months and years go by you should notice that you live a little less for yourself and a little more for others. You should find yourself wanting to spend time reading the Bible and praying. You should discover a passionate desire to spend time with God's people and use your gifts to serve the church. Those are all signs of a healthy spiritual life, and taking periodic inventory of where you are is a good habit to make sure you're on track.

Even more than transforming our desires, God also empowers us to do what is right. The Holy Spirit helps us do what God asks us to do. That is especially comforting when God is prompting you to reach out to an unbelieving friend and you're not sure how they will react, or when you know you need to make a radical life change for the sake of the gospel that others don't understand. Whatever step of obedience you know you need to take, God will help you. He's right beside you to help you, behind you to protect you, and in front of you to lead the way.

*Don't copy the behavior and customs of this world,
but let God transform you into a new person by changing
the way you think. Then you will learn to know God's
will for you, which is good and pleasing and perfect.*

—*Romans 12:2*

Eternal Longing

*But we are citizens of heaven, where the Lord Jesus Christ lives.
And we are eagerly waiting for him to return as our Savior.
He will take our weak mortal bodies and change them into
glorious bodies like his own, using the same power with which
he will bring everything under his control.*

—*Philippians 3:20-21*

Do you remember how eagerly you waited for things when you were a child? Whether it was your birthday or reaching a vacation destination after a long journey, you probably repeatedly asked your parents how many more days or hours until the anticipated event. That's the kind of eager longing Paul says we should have for Christ's return. It should be the thing that fills our imagination, that we plan and prepare for, that we joyfully anticipate.

Our longing for eternity is not something we have to manufacture—although our eagerness will grow as we meditate on the promises of God and spend time basking in His presence through worship and study. Rather, we have a natural longing for God's presence because as Christians we are citizens of heaven. We no longer quite fit in here on earth, and in our heart of hearts we sense that. Here we are surrounded by death and dying, but we are made for immortality. Here we are frustrated by the triumph of evil over good, and it makes us long for the coming of God's perfect Kingdom.

Let your longing for eternity grow this week. When you are weighed down by physical weakness, let it cause you to long for the glorious body God is preparing for you. As you glimpse God's glory in a majestic sunset or a beloved child, let it make you eager for more, knowing that heaven will be all that and so much more.

*We look forward with hope to that wonderful day when the
glory of our great God and Savior, Jesus Christ, will be revealed.*

—*Titus 2:13*

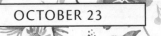

The Antidote to Worry

Don't worry about anything; instead, pray about everything. Tell God what you need, and thank him for all he has done. Then you will experience God's peace, which exceeds anything we can understand. His peace will guard your hearts and minds as you live in Christ Jesus.

—*Philippians 4:6-7*

There aren't many situations in life that couldn't benefit from a little more peace. We worry about everything, from getting out the door on time to that nagging health problem we hope doesn't turn out to be something big. We could use peace in our relationships and peace after a long day. These verses not only promise that we will experience God's peace—and that it is bigger and deeper than we can imagine—they also tell us the secret of attaining this peace.

Prayer. It's the antidote to worry and the gateway to peace. We can do it anytime, anywhere, and ask for anything we want. So then, why don't we do more of it? I think it's because the very nature of prayer goes against our desire for independence. In prayer we have to admit that we are, in the end, helpless. We have to acknowledge that we don't know what's best and that we aren't as in control as we like to think we are. We want to do something to fix our problems, not sit and pray about them.

But if we want peace, if we want real answers, then prayer is the only way. It releases our anxiety. It reminds us to trust God. It reorients our hearts to submit to God. Don't use prayer as a last resort, go there first. Start your day by laying your burdens at the throne of God and you will experience His peace.

Give all your worries and cares to God, for he cares about you.

—*1 Peter 5:7*

The Secret of Contentment

I can do everything through Christ, who gives me strength.
—Philippians 4:13

Emblazoned on a workout T-shirt this verse seems to be encouraging us to lift heavy and run fast. Whatever my goal, I can do it through Christ. But in the context of Scripture it is far more than that. The previous verses read, "I have learned how to be content with whatever I have. I know how to live on almost nothing or with everything. I have learned the secret of living in every situation." This, then, is a promise that with Christ's help we can be content.

Imagine the freedom of being able to honestly say that you can be content regardless of your circumstances. No feelings of entitlement or jealousy, no greedy grasping for more. I can do everything—even be content with my lot in life—with the strength God provides. This attitude of surrendered thanksgiving is possible through the power of Christ.

Have you learned the secret of contentment? It starts with submitting to God's plan, trusting that He is in control and gratefully receiving from His loving hand whatever He gives you. But you can't do this alone, you need God's help. Maybe this week rather than praying for God to give you what you think you need, you can ask Him to help you be content. And then look around at all the things you have to be thankful for.

Don't be afraid, for I am with you. Don't be discouraged,
for I am your God. I will strengthen you and help you.
I will hold you up with my victorious right hand.
—Isaiah 41:10

Generous Provision

And this same God who takes care of me
will supply all your needs from his glorious riches,
which have been given to us in Christ Jesus.

—Philippians 4:19

Paul had already shared with the Philippian believers the secret of being content (Philippians 4:11-12). Now he promises that as they foster an attitude of contentment and generously give of their resources, God will repay them. It's all connected: If we realize that we can be just as happy with little or with much, then we are willing to give what we have to help those in need. When we do that, God gives us back far more in spiritual blessings than the meager financial gift we gave. The generous giver always ends up benefiting in God's equation.

Trusting God's supply is acting out our belief that He has an unlimited supply. There is no end to what God can give us. The God we trust is the creator of all things, the One who owns everything that exists. His riches are indeed glorious. Therefore, He can give us everything we need and more.

Unfortunately, we often forget these truths. We wonder if God will take care of us like He takes care of others, or as He has in the past. We quickly lose perspective and lose faith. Don't let that happen. Look at how God provided for Paul, look at how He provided for others you know, and be encouraged to trust that He will also take care of you. This same God will supply all your needs from His glorious riches.

Seek the Kingdom of God above all else,
and he will give you everything you need.

—Luke 12:31

Rescued from Darkness

[God] has rescued us from the kingdom of darkness and transferred us into the Kingdom of his dear Son, who purchased our freedom and forgave our sins.

—Colossians 1:13-14

There is so much to be grateful for in these verses. We have been rescued from the kingdom of darkness. We have a new home and a new family in the Kingdom of God. Our freedom has been purchased and our record wiped clean.

Yet we so often take all this for granted. In the buzz of daily life we fail to see the amazing things God has done for us. We gripe and grumble about inconsequential earthly matters and do not have thankful hearts for all the amazing gifts we have in Christ.

Today, spend some time meditating on these truths as if for the first time. Think about all the things you have been rescued from, all the "there-but-for-the-grace-of-God-go-I" things you see in the world. Gaze on the brilliant glory of God and marvel at the fact that He has a place prepared for you in heaven. He has a special name for you, and it is written in the book of life. Think on the wrath of God that you deserved and be grateful for the freedom Christ purchased for you. And let all these truths give you abundant joy. No matter what is going on in your life, no matter how dire your circumstances or how great your fears, know this truth: In Christ you are rescued, you belong, and you are free.

You are a chosen people. You are royal priests, a holy nation, God's very own possession. As a result, you can show others the goodness of God, for he called you out of the darkness into his wonderful light.

—1 Peter 2:9

Flawless

Yet now he has reconciled you to himself through the death of Christ in his physical body. As a result, he has brought you into his own presence, and you are holy and blameless as you stand before him without a single fault.
—*Colossians 1:22*

Imagine yourself standing before the throne of God. There He is, so brilliant and glorious you can't even look at Him. What does He say about you? If you are reconciled to Him through faith in Christ's death—in other words, if you believe that Christ died for your sins—then He declares that you are holy. Blameless. Faultless. You were a condemned criminal, deserving of death, His enemy, full of evil thoughts and actions. But in Christ you have received His perfect record. You can stand before God and receive His words of affirmation and love.

Perhaps you have been on the receiving end of negative comments about yourself. Maybe you think of yourself as less than. Maybe every time you look in the mirror you are confronted with your shortcomings. Satan whispers in your ear that you are unworthy, that these promises don't apply to you, that God can't possibly love you.

Don't you believe those lies. Hear these promises of God and declare the truth about who you are. If you have received Christ's death as the payment for your sins, you are holy and blameless and stand before God without a single fault. When God looks at you, He declares you to be perfect. Beautiful. Enough. His dear child. Beloved. Without fault or flaw. Wanted. Precious.

And so, dear brothers and sisters, we can boldly enter heaven's Most Holy Place because of the blood of Jesus.
—*Hebrews 10:19*

Christ in You, the Hope of Glory

The riches and glory of Christ are for you Gentiles, too.
And this is the secret: Christ lives in you.
This gives you assurance of sharing his glory.
—*Colossians 1:27*

Other Bible versions translate the last part of this verse as "Christ in you, the hope of glory." That more poetic rendering gets at the heart of the Christian life in seven brief words. Through the Holy Spirit, Christ lives in us, and that assures us that our hope is not in vain; one day we will reign with Him in glory.

It is, as Paul says, a mystery how God's glory can dwell in such fallen creatures as us. The dailiness of our lives—cleaning the dishes, going to work, fixing the things that break, making dinner—these things can easily overshadow the wonder of the Christian life. But if we focus on this great mystery, how much more meaning our lives will have. Even in the most mundane activities of life we carry with us Christ and the hope of glory.

The shekinah glory—the same holy presence that dwelt in the Holy of Holies—lives in you. Let that truth lift your gaze this day. Let it inform your choices about what you will do, where you will go, how you will work, and what you will think about. Most of all, let it assure you that one day you will have the inexpressible joy of seeing Jesus face-to-face and hearing Him say, "Well done."

The Spirit of God, who raised Jesus from
the dead, lives in you. And just as God raised
Christ Jesus from the dead, he will give life to your
mortal bodies by this same Spirit living within you.
—*Romans 8:11*

Heavenly Vision

Your real life is hidden with Christ in God.
And when Christ, who is your life, is revealed to
the whole world, you will share in all his glory.

—*Colossians 3:3-4*

What do you think of when you hear the phrase "real life"? Usually it's a reference to the challenges we face. *That's life*, we think when things don't go our way. Grown-ups deal with real life, the bills and the responsibilities of making a living. The Bible encourages us to think of real life differently. This life is a shadow, the Bible tells us, while the reality is heaven, where Christ sits at the right hand of the Father. Our real life isn't here on earth, it's hidden above in the heavenly places. And our responsibility is to live life on earth in such a way that our gaze is fixed on the real life that awaits us.

This already-but-not-yet concept is woven throughout Scripture, and it's a challenge to live it out. We want the glory now; we don't like to wait a whole lifetime for it. But part of being people of the promise means taking on this challenge to accept with patience this in-betweenness. We need to daily remind ourselves of what is real and what is shadow. Real is Christ reigning as King. Shadow is the political battles we fight right now. Real is creating a nurturing environment for our kids to learn about Jesus. Shadow is their accomplishments and accolades. Real is our devotion to Christ. Shadow is the paycheck we work for each day. The shadows aren't worthless, but the reality is worth far more.

Since you have been raised to new life with Christ,
set your sights on the realities of heaven, where
Christ sits in the place of honor at God's right hand.
Think about the things of heaven, not the things of earth.

—*Colossians 3:1-2*

Loving Judgment

[Jesus] has rescued us from the terrors of the coming judgment.
—1 Thessalonians 1:10

If you read through end-times prophecies in Daniel and Revelation, the future can be a little scary. As the King James version translates Hebrews 10:31, "It is a fearful thing to fall into the hands of the living God." Some people even reject Christianity because they can't reconcile God's judgment with His love.

The truth is, a God who didn't care enough to right every wrong wouldn't be very loving. Just think of the public outcry when a murderer goes free on a technicality. By the same token, a God who was just but didn't provide a way for us to be forgiven wouldn't be very loving. Fortunately, God is both loving and just, and we know that because of the promise in this verse.

Judgment Day will be terrifying for those who fall under God's wrath. But every believer has already been rescued from that. We won't have to pay the penalty for our sins because Jesus paid it for us. For us, then, Christ's return will be a day of joyful reunion. We will meet our Savior, the One we already know and love from studying His Word. We will be welcomed with open arms by our heavenly Father, and He will declare to us His love in a way that is personal and tender. Rejoice today that you have been rescued from the terrors of the coming judgment, and look forward with joy to the day you will meet the One your soul adores.

For God chose to save us through our Lord Jesus
Christ, not to pour out his anger on us.
—1 Thessalonians 5:9

Triumphant Return

*For the Lord himself will come down from heaven with a commanding
shout, with the voice of the archangel, and with the trumpet
call of God. . . . Then we will be with the Lord forever.*
—*1 Thessalonians 4:16-17*

It's hard to read about the coming of Christ without getting a little emotional. This life is so full of death and sorrow that declaring the bedrock truths of our future hope is a moving experience. These aren't just idle hopes—these are the realities of what is to come. The death we experience now won't last. Eternal life will have the final word, and it will be better than we can imagine or dream.

I don't know what struggle or crisis you are facing today, but I do know the hope that will help you get through it: Christ will return. One day there will be a trumpet blast and a shout and the thundering voice of God that sounds like rushing water, and you will be with Him forever if you have trusted in Jesus for salvation.

None of us can know what tomorrow holds. There may be triumph or there may be heartbreak. We may be surprised by good news or blindsided by sudden tragedy. But we do know what comes on the day after all the tomorrows. There will be an end to all this, and for us who are in Christ it will be the consolation of every hope and dream we've ever had.

*It will happen in a moment, in the blink of an eye,
when the last trumpet is blown. For when the trumpet
sounds, those who have died will be raised to live forever.
And we who are living will also be transformed. For our
dying bodies must be transformed into bodies that will never die;
our mortal bodies must be transformed into immortal bodies.*
—*1 Corinthians 15:52-53*

God's way is perfect.

ALL THE

LORD'S

PROMISES PROVE TRUE.

He is a shield
for all who
look to him
for protection.

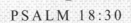

PSALM 18:30

A Certain Hope

Christ died for us so that, whether we are dead or alive when he returns, we can live with him forever.

—*1 Thessalonians 5:10*

The Thessalonian believers had some insecurities about Christ's return. Either they were worried that they might not be prepared or they were concerned about their loved ones who had died. Paul reassured them that the day of Christ's return would be their day of salvation. They did not need to fear it because they were children of light and their eternal salvation was secure.

Many believers struggle with insecurity and doubt just like the Thessalonians. It might not be over the end times specifically, but we sometimes wonder if we are interpreting the Bible right—or even if the Bible is true. This verse brings us back to the essentials of our faith.

First, it reminds us that our faith rests on Christ's work, not ours. He died for us. That is what we need to cling to each day of our lives—nothing more, nothing less. Second, it reminds us that our future hope is guaranteed by the finished work of Christ. We may not get all our theology quite right, we may be confused by some things, but if we believe that Christ died for us, we will live with Him forever. Don't let yourself get so caught up in advanced doctrine that you lose sight of the great, overarching promise of God—He died so we can live with Him forever. Such a simple truth, such a big hope.

Christ died and rose again for this very purpose— to be Lord both of the living and of the dead.

—*Romans 14:9*

Called to Holiness

God will make this happen, for he who calls you is faithful.
—*1 Thessalonians 5:24*

After some final instructions Paul ends the letter to the Thessalonians, as he often did, with a prayer: "May the God of peace make you holy in every way, and may your whole spirit and soul and body be kept blameless until our Lord Jesus Christ comes again" (1 Thessalonians 5:23). He didn't just ask that they would make progress in their Christian walk, he asked in faith that they would be completely sanctified, holy in every way, blameless in soul and spirit and body. I don't know about you, but my prayers are not usually quite that impossible-sounding. In fact, many of my prayers don't require much of God at all.

Paul was able to pray boldly because of the promise of this verse—God would do the work because God had called them and God is faithful. In the end, that is where all of our prayers rest. We can ask God for big things, especially for big spiritual things, because anything we pray that is in line with God's purposes, He will do. And His purpose is for us to be holy in every way.

Let's start praying for more than a little bit of God or a little bit of holiness. Let's pray that God would make our areas of struggle into areas of strength. That He would complete the work He has begun. That He would sanctify every part of the people we're praying for—beginning with us. God will make it happen, for He is faithful.

God will do this, for he is faithful to do what he says, and he has invited you into partnership with his Son, Jesus Christ our Lord.
—*1 Corinthians 1:9*

Kept Safe

But the Lord is faithful; he will strengthen you and guard you from the evil one.
—2 Thessalonians 3:3

What makes you feel vulnerable? Is it when you fall into the sin you promised yourself you would never again succumb to? Is it when physical limitations force you to face your human frailty? Is it when you realize how fragile life is, how thin the line between life and death? Or perhaps it's when you sense that you are under attack from Satan.

This promise is for moments like that. God always comes through. He will give you strength when you are weak and protection from the evil one. Whether the problem is your frailty or dangers from the outside, there is nothing to fear because the Lord is faithful.

Our task, then, is to believe it and live it. Step out and do the next thing, trusting that God will give you the strength. Face down spiritual attacks like someone who sees the armies of heaven encamped around them. Trust that when you fall, the everlasting arms of God are underneath to lift you up. The Lord is faithful—He will give you the strength you need to face today and the protection you need to face all your tomorrows until you see Him face-to-face.

Yes, and the Lord will deliver me from every evil attack
and will bring me safely into his heavenly Kingdom.
All glory to God forever and ever! Amen.
—2 Timothy 4:18

Peace for All Times

Now may the Lord of peace himself give you his peace at
all times and in every situation. The Lord be with you all.
—2 Thessalonians 3:16

God is a God of peace. That's not something we always keep in the forefront of our minds. We think of Him as loving, as just, as holy—and He is. But He is also the God of peace. He is the God of "it is well with my soul," the God of reconciliation, the God of "do not be afraid."

Paul makes the application for us—because God is a God of peace, we can have peace in every situation. There are no exceptions. It is not "peace most of the time, when you are well rested and able to think logically." It is not "peace in every situation except when the doctor tells you there are no more options and to prepare for the end." This is peace at all times and in every situation. Even the one you are in right now.

God is able to make this promise based on two bedrock truths. First, He is the God of peace. When He promises us peace it is "not as the world gives," it is the supernatural peace that is only possible because God is who He is. God is in control and God loves you—therefore you can have peace in every situation. Second, peace is possible because God is with us. When you are feeling anxious, when you get bad news, when the worst possible thing happens, the God of peace is with you, ready to trade you His peace for your fear.

I am leaving you with a gift—peace of mind and heart.
And the peace I give is a gift the world cannot give.
So don't be troubled or afraid.
—John 14:27

Training for Godliness

Physical training is good, but training for godliness is much better, promising benefits in this life and in the life to come.

—*1 Timothy 4:8*

Scientists tell us that physical exercise provides many benefits and enriches our lives. In the short term it gives us endorphins to improve our mood and energy to get more done in a day. In the long term it staves off disease and helps us live longer.

God promises that godliness is even better than physical exercise because it is of value not just for this life, but also for the life to come. The time you spend reading God's Word, mulling it over, praying, and preparing yourself for good works is never wasted. It helps you face each day from now to eternity with courage, joy, and peace.

It's good to spend thirty minutes exercising, but it's far better to spend thirty minutes growing in godliness. Do your daily habits reflect this priority? Are you spending as much time thinking about, planning for, and executing your God goals as you are your health goals? If you never miss a day at the gym, do you also never miss a day in God's Word? The promise that training for godliness has benefits in this life and the next is only of benefit to you if you put in the time and effort to exercise your spiritual muscles. Put your best energy into the kind of training that lasts forever.

Seek the Kingdom of God above all else, and live righteously, and he will give you everything you need.

—*Matthew 6:33*

True Joy

Teach those who are rich in this world not to be proud and not to trust in their money, which is so unreliable. Their trust should be in God, who richly gives us all we need for our enjoyment.

—1 Timothy 6:17

It starts on the playground when we are toddlers—I want what he has, just because he has it. As we grow, so do our desires. I want those shoes, that car, a kitchen as big as hers. When we don't have what we think we deserve we may become bitter, thinking God is holding out on us.

Here is the twofold promise, one part which we know from experience and one part which we must believe by faith. Even when we are jealous of what someone else has, we know in our heart of hearts that earthly wealth is fleeting. Money is unreliable, here one day and gone the next. What we must believe by faith is that God gives us all we need for our enjoyment. He cares about our happiness. He delights in our delight over the good gifts He has given us. God is not a cosmic killjoy, He is the ultimate pleasure-giver. In the final analysis, what God declares good and beautiful are the only things that give us true enjoyment.

The practical application is that we should hold loosely the things of this world and hold tightly the things of God. Enjoy the gifts God has given you, thank Him for providing all you need, share what you have with others, and find your true joy in God Himself.

The thief's purpose is to steal and kill and destroy. My purpose is to give them a rich and satisfying life.

—John 10:10

Power That Overcomes

*For God has not given us a spirit of fear and
timidity, but of power, love, and self-discipline.*

—*2 Timothy 1:7*

How's your spirit today? Is it crushed? Anxious? Burdened? All of the above with a little bit of doubt thrown in? We all have those days when we feel fragile and fearful, but God promises that He has given us a different spirit, one of power, love, and self-discipline.

So much of the Christian life is about assuming our new identity. We became a new creature because of God's work in us, and each day we can get up and put on that new identity and walk in it. This is another one of those truths that we have to live out by faith. Because you are in Christ, your true self is characterized by power, love, and self-discipline. The broken spirit, the fear and worry and habitual sins—those are part of your old nature. They don't fit anymore, now that Christ has transformed you into His likeness.

If you're feeling down, embrace this promise. Throw off the old spirit of fear and timidity. Say no to the thought patterns that drag you down. Put on God's power that overcomes. Put on His love that enables you to love the unlovely and undeserving. Put on the self-discipline to say no to fear and temptation. God has given you this new spirit, now choose to walk in it.

*But you will receive power when the Holy Spirit comes upon you.
And you will be my witnesses, telling people about me everywhere.*

—*Acts 1:8*

Called for a Purpose

For God saved us and called us to live a holy life.
He did this, not because we deserved it, but
because that was his plan from before the beginning
of time—to show us his grace through Christ Jesus.

—2 Timothy 1:9

Do you sometimes wonder why God has brought you to this moment? Why are you alive—what's your purpose? We all wonder that sometimes, whether it's because of a midlife crisis or the awareness of the fragility of life or because we are facing a job loss. It's healthy to take stock every now and then and ask ourselves what life is all about.

This verse offers the answer. You were saved and called by God to live a holy life. That's it. The specifics of what job you have or what ministries you should serve in are secondary; the primary goal is for you to live a holy life. This is God's plan from the beginning of time.

Note that the subject here is God. He does the saving, He does the calling, He made the plan, He shows us grace. All it says about us is that we didn't deserve it, which is kind of comforting if you think about it. We didn't have to do anything to receive God's gracious call. He planned it from before the beginning of time because He loves undeserving creatures like us. What can we do in the face of this amazing grace but respond by living out God's call to holy living?

You are a chosen people. You are royal priests, a holy nation,
God's very own possession. As a result, you can show others the goodness
of God, for he called you out of the darkness into his wonderful light.

—1 Peter 2:9

Undeniably Faithful

If we are unfaithful, he remains faithful,
for he cannot deny who he is.

—*2 Timothy 2:13*

"This is a trustworthy saying," Paul told his young protégé Timothy. You can count on this promise: If you die with Christ, you will live forever. If you endure suffering, you will reign with Him in glory. If you are unfaithful, He will still be faithful (2 Timothy 2:11-13). How can we know this? Why should we trust it? Because God can't be less than He is. He is faithful, therefore every promise is sure. These covenant promises are so amazing, we should linger here in worship every minute of our lives.

Look at the trade-offs God offers us: life in place of death; glory in place of suffering; faithfulness despite our unfaithfulness. And this is all a free gift, offered out of love by a holy God in spite of the fact that we can do nothing to deserve it. We were wretched, putrid sinners when God offered us eternal life in His glorious presence.

There is one trustworthy saying in the list that I haven't mentioned yet: If we deny Him, He will deny us (2 Timothy 2:12). What Paul has in mind here is apostasy—a final denial of Christ. God forgives the temporary doubts and lapses in the faith of a believer, but if we make a final renunciation of Christ we will face eternal judgment. This, too, is part of who God is, the holy Judge. Take heed of the warning as well as the promise. Receive the life God offers and be as faithful to Him as He is to you.

The faithful love of the LORD never ends! His mercies never cease.
Great is his faithfulness; his mercies begin afresh each morning.

—*Lamentations 3:22-23*

Sufficient for the Task

*All Scripture is inspired by God and is useful to teach us what
is true and to make us realize what is wrong in our lives. It
corrects us when we are wrong and teaches us to do what is right.
God uses it to prepare and equip his people to do every good work.*
—2 Timothy 3:16-17

These verses are often quoted to prove the sufficiency of Scripture: It teaches us, rebukes us, and trains us. They are also used to understand the origin of Scripture: It is breathed out by God, His very words. It is for good reason that this is one of the most commonly memorized verses.

There are two promises here. First, *all* Scripture is inspired and useful. Even Leviticus, even the genealogies, even the prophecies we can't understand. We must not neglect any part of the Bible in our personal devotions and our formal studies. Not one word of holy Scripture is extra—we need all of it to fully understand God and His ways.

Second, we are promised that if we study the Bible we will have everything we need to do the good works God has for us. We don't need the Bible plus some self-help guru or the Bible plus a really good preacher. Everything we need to understand what we should do and be empowered to carry it out is found on the pages of Scripture. With all of these good reasons to read God's Word, why would we ever go a day without it? Devote yourself to these words of God that will teach you and equip you in every way for everything God wants you to do.

*It is the same with my word. I send it out, and it
always produces fruit. It will accomplish all I want
it to, and it will prosper everywhere I send it.*
—Isaiah 55:11

Twofold Protection

*The Lord will deliver me from every evil attack
and will bring me safely into his heavenly Kingdom.
All glory to God forever and ever! Amen.*

—*2 Timothy 4:18*

A few verses earlier (2 Timothy 4:8) Paul wrote about the prize that awaits everyone who eagerly anticipates the return of Christ. When He comes back to claim us as His own, we will each receive a crown of righteousness. That is really the key to how we are brought safely into God's heavenly Kingdom—we gain entrance to it because Jesus has made us righteous . . . holy . . . blameless by His death and resurrection.

The promise of this verse is twofold protection. First, we are delivered from evil attacks. This includes persecution at the hands of men and the fiery arrows of Satan. Though evil is done to us, we can be sure that no ultimate harm will come to our souls as long as we are in Christ. Second, we are promised entrance into God's heavenly Kingdom. There is no sin so great that God will not forgive it. Once we have embarked on the journey of faith, God guarantees that we will make it to the end.

If you are feeling discouraged and under attack today, claim this promise for your own. God will in the end rescue you from every evil attack and ensure your safe entry into heaven. Today may be crushingly difficult, but there is a bright future ahead of you when God fulfills His promises.

The LORD keeps you from all harm and watches over your life.

—*Psalm 121:7*

Looking Forward with Hope

We look forward with hope to that wonderful day when the
glory of our great God and Savior, Jesus Christ, will be revealed.

—*Titus 2:13*

Some days the clouds arrange themselves in just such a way that the sun bursts forth in glorious beams of light. There is a golden edge to the clouds, and one can easily imagine Christ rending the heavens and returning to claim those who are His. If you listen closely you can almost imagine that you are hearing the echo of trumpets.

A glorious skyscape like that is a reminder of what's in store for us. We look forward with hope—the biblical kind of hope that is a settled reality—to the wonderful day when we will see Jesus as He is. The full radiance of His glory will be on display for all to see, and every knee will bow before Him and every tongue confess that He is Lord.

Are you living in light of that future hope? If you've recently had to bury a loved one, or if you are facing a terminal diagnosis, or if you are just weighed down by all the injustice in the world—here is your promise for today. Jesus is coming on the clouds. Your faith is not in vain, it is the surest thing in this world. Don't let your temporary circumstances impede your vision of eternity.

As for me, I know that my Redeemer lives, and he will stand
upon the earth at last. And after my body has decayed, yet
in my body I will see God! I will see him for myself. Yes, I will
see him with my own eyes. I am overwhelmed at the thought!

—*Job 19:25-27*

Able to Help

*Since he himself has gone through suffering and
testing, he is able to help us when we are being tested.*

—*Hebrews 2:18*

We often gloss over the incarnation of Christ. Yes, He was born as a baby, we know all about it. But the theology of incarnation means so much for our daily walk with Him. Jesus truly understands everything we're going through. He understands not just as a detached bystander, but as One who went through it Himself. Whatever temptation we face, whatever suffering, whatever discouragement or despair—Jesus gets it.

That is why He is able to help us. The Greek word here means more than just "assist." It includes the concepts of comfort, of support, of running to respond to the cries of someone who is in distress. It was often used to describe the way a parent lovingly soothes a crying child. The help Jesus offers is real and deep and meaningful. He knows exactly what we need, and He is able to provide it.

Are you feeling tested today? Are you suffering? Jesus understands, and He is running to help you. He cares about your pain and is coming to your aid with genuine help and comfort. Will you direct your cries toward the only One who truly understands and who is truly able to help you? Will you let Him help you as only He can?

The father instantly cried out, "I do believe, but help me overcome my unbelief!"

—*Mark 9:24*

How to Know God's Will

For the word of God is alive and powerful. It is sharper than the sharpest two-edged sword, cutting between soul and spirit, between joint and marrow. It exposes our innermost thoughts and desires.
—Hebrews 4:12

Have you ever had one of those moments when the preacher seems to be preaching straight to you? It's as if he knows what went on in your house this week and is calling you out right there in front of everyone—except he isn't really. What is actually happening is that the Word of God is doing its job.

The Bible is unique among all books because it is inspired, illuminated, and empowered by God Himself. The words are alive in a way no other book's words are because God is breathing it out afresh each time we read it. That's why it is able to lay us bare and expose us, cutting down our excuses and our doubts. It does surgery on our hearts so that we can live the abundant life of joy and peace found in Jesus.

It is instructive to note the context of this verse. Just before this verse, we have been exhorted to obey God so that we can find eternal life. Just after, we are reminded of the judgment and comforted by the fact that Jesus understands our weaknesses and has made a way for us to enter heaven. The Bible is the key to how we can know what God's will is and learn how to escape from judgment. Take these words of life and let them do their work in you—God has promised that not one moment spent in His Word will be wasted time.

The teaching of your word gives light, so even the simple can understand.
—Psalm 119:130

Paid in Full

This High Priest of ours understands our weaknesses, for he faced all of the same testings we do, yet he did not sin.

—Hebrews 4:15

Here is the same truth we looked at a few days ago—Jesus understands our weaknesses. He truly "gets us," because He took on human flesh with all of its weaknesses, temptations, and limitations. There is nothing we face that He did not also face, and that is why He is able to minister to our souls in a way that no detached, impersonal god ever could.

But there is a key difference between the way we deal with our weaknesses and testing and the way Jesus did: He did not sin. This is the foundation of our salvation. He was able to make the once-for-all sacrifice that paid the penalty for our sin because He was the perfect sacrifice. He didn't deserve the death penalty, and so the fact that He willingly took it in our place made it a sufficient sacrifice. The price has been paid. We are no longer under the curse and destined for judgment. Now we are forgiven and free—and it's all because when Jesus was tested, He did not sin.

What a glorious gift this is, that we get the righteousness of Christ imputed to our account, and yet also what a challenge. The temptations we face can be overcome—we know that because Jesus overcame them and He is the One who is helping us. We are without excuse. Next time you are tempted, lean into your Savior who understands and has overcome, and let Him help you also overcome.

It was our weaknesses he carried; it was our sorrows that weighed him down. And we thought his troubles were a punishment from God, a punishment for his own sins! But he was pierced for our rebellion, crushed for our sins. He was beaten so we could be whole. He was whipped so we could be healed.

—Isaiah 53:4-5

A Royal Invitation

So let us come boldly to the throne of our
gracious God. There we will receive his mercy, and we
will find grace to help us when we need it most.

—Hebrews 4:16

"The King requests the honor of your presence in the throne room. He wants to bless you with a gift." Who would ever turn down an invitation to meet the King, especially one who promises to meet us with mercy and grace?

Yet how often we do spurn His invitation. We know God would like to meet with us as we read our Bible and pray, but we're too busy. Our social media feed distracts us. Our calendar is full. There is a good show on TV and we're just too tired to do anything else. We are working too hard to give ourselves the luxury of resting with God—and the irony is that so many of us are pushing Him out because we are busy working for Him, doing ministry He's called us to.

The invitation stands. You can boldly walk right up to the throne of God anytime you want. You don't need to make yourself ready, He wants you just as you are. You don't need to abide by certain rituals, He is offering you mercy and grace. God wants to listen to you, speak to you, and minister to your heart. It's such a great offer—grace to help you when you need it most. Won't you respond to this invitation from the King of kings?

Because of Christ and our faith in him, we can now
come boldly and confidently into God's presence.

—Ephesians 3:12

An Anchor for Our Souls

*Therefore, we who have fled to him for refuge can have
great confidence as we hold to the hope that lies before us.
This hope is a strong and trustworthy anchor for our souls.
It leads us through the curtain into God's inner sanctuary.*

—Hebrews 6:18-19

Huge ships are moored in rough waters with an anchor. They are tethered to safety, held fast by a simple weight no matter how angry the storms become. That is the image the writer of Hebrews uses to urge readers to cling to our salvation hope with great confidence. God has given a promise and an oath, so we know that He will not—He cannot!—lie or change His mind about the promises He has made. This is why we flee to Him for refuge; we know that He will never let us down.

There is another image here, that of being led by our hope behind the curtain into the inner sanctuary. Here the reference is to the Most Holy Place, the inner sanctuary of the Temple where God dwelt. There were all kinds of rules about who could go there (only the high priest) and how often (only once a year). Yet now, through Jesus, we can go behind the curtain into the inner sanctuary anytime we want. All we have to do is let our hope lead us to engage with God in worship and prayer, and we will find ourselves right at His feet.

Is your soul steadfastly anchored to Jesus? Do you let your hope lead you to the throne room of God? Let your confidence grow as you meditate on the great hope that is yours in Christ.

*God's truth stands firm like a foundation stone with
this inscription: "The Lord knows those who are his."*

—2 Timothy 2:19

Help for Weakness

*Therefore he is able, once and forever, to
save those who come to God through him. He lives
forever to intercede with God on their behalf.*

—Hebrews 7:25

Jesus is praying for you. This very minute, He is asking the Father to show you His goodness. He is asking the Father to apply His redemption over your sin. He is asking for God's will to prevail over all the things that concern you. He is even praying things you can't understand or imagine—they are too precious and mysterious for the human intellect. And He promises to continue this supernatural intercession forever.

I don't know about you, but when I consider Christ's mediation on my behalf it gives me renewed energy to add my own prayers. If Jesus Himself is praying for us, then surely this is what we should be about as well.

If your prayer life has been a bit dry lately, let this promise spur you on to renew it. Set up a time to pray. Get yourself a system. Find a prayer partner. Do whatever it takes to begin the habit of intercession. Don't let Jesus' words to the disciples in the garden of Gethsemane be said of you: "Are you asleep? Couldn't you watch with me even one hour? Keep watch and pray, so that you will not give in to temptation. For the spirit is willing, but the body is weak" (Mark 14:37-38).

*Now all glory to God, who is able, through his
mighty power at work within us, to accomplish
infinitely more than we might ask or think.*

—Ephesians 3:20

Better Promises

*Jesus, our High Priest, has been given a ministry that is far
superior to the old priesthood, for he is the one who mediates
for us a far better covenant with God, based on better promises.*

—Hebrews 8:6

The theme throughout Hebrews is that the old covenant—the system by which God promised to make a people for Himself and live among them in the land He would lead them to as long as the people obeyed His commands—has been replaced by a new covenant in Christ's blood. The repeated refrain is that the new covenant is better, and here we have the summary statement of why it is superior. Whereas the old covenant was mediated by priests from among the people, now we have Christ as our High Priest, and He is better in every way. He made a onetime sacrifice to end all sacrifices, and the effectiveness of His sacrifice ensures His promise of eternal life.

From our position after the death and resurrection of Christ it's hard for us to comprehend just how much better the new covenant is than the old. The old promises were all about life on earth and therefore had an end date. The rituals of atonement had to be made each day because the forgiveness didn't last. And they relied on a level of obedience we can never attain.

But now we have promises for an eternal homeland, a forever relationship with God, once-for-all-time forgiveness, perfected bodies, and eternal peace. Best of all, these promises are assured because they depend on Christ's perfect sacrifice, and He is even now standing in the gap and mediating the covenant for us before the Father.

*Because of his glory and excellence, he has given us great and precious
promises. These are the promises that enable you to share his
divine nature and escape the world's corruption caused by human desires.*

—2 Peter 1:4

Our Future Hope

Just as each person is destined to die once and after that comes judgment, so also Christ was offered once for all time as a sacrifice to take away the sins of many people. He will come again, not to deal with our sins, but to bring salvation to all who are eagerly waiting for him.

—Hebrews 9:27-28

Here is the gospel in succinct terms. Each one of us will die, and when we do, we will face the righteous Judge to make an accounting for our sins. Every one of us has fallen short of God's holy standard and rebelled against His commands, and therefore every one of us deserves eternal death. That is our status before Christ.

But thanks be to God, Christ was offered once for all time as a sacrifice to take away our sins. He lived a perfect human life and then took the judgment for our sins on Himself and died in our place. Therefore, at the judgment we will not face punishment and condemnation, but salvation.

This is why we so eagerly wait for Christ's return. We know what's coming, and it is salvation rather than judgment. Forgiveness rather than shame. Righteousness rather than rebellion. Are you living in light of these realities? Do you eagerly await that moment when you will see Jesus face-to-face? Whatever is going on in your life right now, whatever urgent tasks are waiting for you or heartaches are weighing you down, this is the future hope you have to look forward to. Let it give you comfort and joy.

Christ suffered for our sins once for all time. He never sinned, but he died for sinners to bring you safely home to God. He suffered physical death, but he was raised to life in the Spirit.

—1 Peter 3:18

Works in Progress

For by that one offering he forever made perfect those who are being made holy.
—*Hebrews 10:14*

At first glance this verse seems to say that Christians are perfect people, but we all know that isn't true. We still sin, suffer the wasting away of our bodies, and make mistakes. So what is being promised here?

The word *perfect* in Scripture denotes completion, the accomplishing of a task. Here the word is in the past tense—Jesus by His death on the cross has already made us perfect. Our salvation is complete. Meanwhile, the next phrase, "being made holy," is in the present tense. We are in the process of becoming holy. This is another instance in Scripture of the already and not yet, of the now and later.

We are already completely saved because we are in the process of being sanctified. We stand before God as perfectly holy. He looks at us and sees the righteousness of Christ. But this finished status is ours because we are a work in progress, submitting to the process of sanctification. In other words, we are in the midst of a daily process of sanctification that has a guaranteed end result: We will be sanctified because Jesus has already made the perfect offering. This truth ought to make us all the more determined to make progress in our Christian walk. Our faith is attainable and realistic. We are weak sinners in need of a Savior, and the Savior has come to help us in our pursuit of holiness.

*I am certain that God, who began the good work
within you, will continue his work until it is
finally finished on the day when Christ Jesus returns.*
—*Philippians 1:6*

Unwavering

Let us hold tightly without wavering to the hope we
affirm, for God can be trusted to keep his promise.

—*Hebrews 10:23*

We've spent a lot of time over the past eleven months looking at why we can trust God to keep His promises. It is part of His character to do so—He cannot do anything other than be true to what He has said. We have the evidence of all of human history that He is faithful to His Word. Based on all the objective evidence, it is far more sensible to take God at His word than to doubt Him. In our heads we know that He can be trusted.

Yet how often we fail to trust Him in our hearts. We somehow think that our problem is too big or that even though He is faithful to everyone else, He won't be to us. We think of ourselves as the exception to all the rules of human history. We lose sight of God because the mountain in front of us blocks the view.

That is why the writer of Hebrews urges us, "Hold tightly without wavering!" The Greek word for "hold tightly" means to keep someone or something from leaving. It is as if our hope is trying to fly away and we need to hang on to it. So here is the challenge: Don't lose your grip on the hope of the gospel. Cling tightly to the things you know to be true about God even when your circumstances loom large before your sight. Don't forget in the nighttime what you learned in the day.

God has given both his promise and his oath. These two
things are unchangeable because it is impossible for God
to lie. Therefore, we who have fled to him for refuge can have
great confidence as we hold to the hope that lies before us.

—*Hebrews 6:18*

Patient Endurance

Faith shows the reality of what we hope for; it is the evidence of things we cannot see. . . . And it is impossible to please God without faith. Anyone who wants to come to him must believe that God exists and that he rewards those who sincerely seek him.

—Hebrews 11:1, 6

The writer of Hebrews has just shown readers what faith looks like: "When all you owned was taken from you, you accepted it with joy. You knew there were better things waiting for you that will last forever" (Hebrews 10:34). Here we are given a succinct definition of faith. People are able to have the kind of radical obedience that is willing to give up everything for the gospel because they are more sure that God's promises are true than they are about anything else. This is the kind of faith that pleases God—faith that joyfully accepts whatever happens in life because of what is promised in the life to come.

Faith changes our vision. It is by faith that we see the things around us as evidence of God's existence and care for us. Others may see the same things, but when we see with eyes of faith we are able to see that the realities of this life point to a greater, deeper reality.

This kind of faith is only possible if we know the promises of God and believe them. We have to taste the reality. We can't give up the comforts of this life in favor of the promise of heaven if we do not know what God has said about eternity and have not experienced the One who made the promises. Faith, then, is the glorious reward of seeking God.

Do not throw away this confident trust in the Lord. Remember the great reward it brings you! Patient endurance is what you need now, so that you will continue to do God's will. Then you will receive all that he has promised.

—Hebrews 10:35-36

An Unshakable Kingdom

*Since we are receiving a Kingdom that is unshakable, let us be
thankful and please God by worshiping him with holy fear and awe.*
—*Hebrews 12:28*

God often calls us to action, but it is in response to a promise He has made. He commands based on relationship, and the rewards of obedience always far outweigh the costs. Here the promise is an unshakable Kingdom and the command is to worship God with thankful and reverent hearts.

So much in this life is about change and disruption. We face changing seasons, changes in our circumstances, even changes in our bodies as we age. Every relationship goes through change as well, whether it is the natural result of new circumstances or the violent schism of a betrayal. There just isn't anything we can count on in this life except that things will be shaken up from time to time.

What a relief it is that the Kingdom we are inheriting is unshakable. God's promises are sure. The life to come will be one of total peace and joy and wholeness forever. The only right and proper response to these glorious promises that we are eternally secure in God's love is to worship Him with a thankful heart and reverent awe that He is so good to us. If life is feeling uncertain and shaky right now, rejoice in the assurance that an unshakable Kingdom is coming and let that promise drive you to worship the unshakable King.

*Then the King will say to those on his right, "Come, you
who are blessed by my Father, inherit the Kingdom
prepared for you from the creation of the world."*
—*Matthew 25:34*

No Fear

God has said, "I will never fail you. I will never abandon you." So we can say with confidence, "The Lord is my helper, so I will have no fear. What can mere people do to me?"

—Hebrews 13:5-6

It might sound a little bit arrogant to say "God is my helper." He is the Creator, and we are the creatures who have rebelled against His rightful authority. Who are we to say "God is my helper," as if our welfare is His priority?

It would be arrogant, except that God has promised, "I will never fail you. I will never abandon you." That is why we can face any trial or temptation with confidence, why we are able to be content in any and every circumstance, and why we are able to say that God is our helper. We are merely repeating what He has promised.

What do you need God's help with today? What is making you fearful? Whatever it is, you can confidently assert that it's all going to turn out okay. It may not turn out the way you had hoped, but you can know without a doubt that it will turn out according to God's plan. He is by your side, and He is helping you. Therefore, do not fear. Don't fear the assaults of Satan or the schemes of man. Don't fear even if the thing you were worried about happens—or worse. God is with you. What can man do to you? Even Satan cannot prevail, for he was defeated once and for all at the cross of Christ.

The LORD is for me, so I will have no fear. What can mere people do to me?

—Psalm 118:6

Unchanging

Jesus Christ is the same yesterday, today, and forever.

—Hebrews 13:8

When I think of the things that make me anxious, in the end they all come down to the fact that there is nothing in this life that can be counted on to last forever. Our health may fail. Our loved ones may die. We may lose our job. The balance in our bank account may not be enough to see us through. The institutions and relationships we depend on may not last. If you think about it for too long you can easily become worried about what is coming around the bend.

But here's the good news: The frailty and uncertainty of this life leads us to the One who will never change. We can depend on Jesus because He is forever the same. In all the yesterdays of humanity He was loving, good, and just. Today He is loving, good, and just. And into eternity He will be loving, good, and just. We can count on everything we learn about God in Scripture and everything we experience in relationship with Him being true forever.

If the changes of life are making you fearful or discouraged, take heart. Jesus is the same. He has led you through the ups and downs of life thus far, and He will keep on leading you and loving you until He brings you safely to eternal life. Keep on learning about Him, keep on experiencing Him, and keep on trusting Him. He is the same yesterday, today, and forever.

Long ago you laid the foundation of the earth and made
the heavens with your hands. They will perish, but you
remain forever; they will wear out like old clothing.
You will change them like a garment and discard them.
But you are always the same; you will live forever.

—Psalm 102:25-27

Tested

*For you know that when your faith is tested, your endurance
has a chance to grow. So let it grow, for when your endurance is
fully developed, you will be perfect and complete, needing nothing.*
—James 1:3-4

No one likes to be tested. We wish we could live each day in perpetual vacation mode, doing what we want, when we want, with no obstacles to meeting our goals. But Scripture tells us that testing is good—so good we should even be happy about it.

Testing is kind of like exercise. Without it our faith muscles atrophy through disuse. We become spiritually out of shape and gradually lose our ability to persevere and overcome. But when we are tested, we are forced to rely on God, and we discover that He is more than able to carry us through. Just like a runner trains their body to run farther and faster each day, testing teaches us to endure.

Even so, we are hardwired to resist difficulties. That's why we need to heed the advice of the previous verse: "consider it an opportunity for joy" (James 1:2). The word *consider* literally means to "to command, rule." In other words, we must by an act of the will choose to be joyful about our trials. We have to become the boss of our attitudes. This week when problems come your way, think of it as exercise for your faith muscles. Thank God for sending difficulties that will help you grow in spiritual maturity and endurance. Over time you appreciate what it does for your soul and maybe even come to enjoy it, just like the feeling of being a little sore after a good workout.

*We can rejoice, too, when we run into problems and trials,
for we know that they help us develop endurance. And
endurance develops strength of character, and character
strengthens our confident hope of salvation.*
—Romans 5:3-4

The Source of Wisdom

If you need wisdom, ask our generous God, and he
will give it to you. He will not rebuke you for asking.

—James 1:5

We all have questions, things we wonder about, even doubts. It is part of God's image imprinted on us as humans that we are curious and want to discover things about ourselves and the world and the God who made it all. But sometimes we hesitate to voice our questions, especially if they are about God or about what He wants us to do.

Here is God's word to you: If you need wisdom, ask. Whatever the need, whatever the question, God is generous with His answers. He gives wisdom in abundance, more than we can ask or imagine. When we come to Him with our questions He never tells us they are silly, never acts like we should have already figured this out, never judges us for our past failures. If we ask for wisdom, God is pleased to give it without reproach.

The key to finding answers to life's questions, then, is recognizing God as the source of wisdom and then seeking out His wisdom through prayer and studying the Bible. It's not God's wisdom plus the answers of prevailing cultural trends. If you need wisdom, go to God first, and He will give you exactly the answer you need at the moment you need it. Ask Him your questions and you will find that He is generous and kind to answer.

Fear of the LORD is the foundation of wisdom.
Knowledge of the Holy One results in good judgment.

—Proverbs 9:10

The Crown of Life

God blesses those who patiently endure testing and
temptation. Afterward they will receive the crown of
life that God has promised to those who love him.

—James 1:12

So many of God's promises boil down to this basic truth: The reward that awaits those who trust in Christ far outweighs the troubles of this life. There is no doubt that life can be hard. Even Jesus, the Son of God, staggered in grief when He looked at the suffering of the Cross. He wasn't sure He could go through with it and begged God to find another way. It shouldn't surprise us when we also shudder at the suffering God asks us to endure.

But after the testing, after the temptation, after the enduring—then comes the crown of life. It's all going to be worth it. The grief we face now is mere shadow when compared with the rock-solid reality of heavenly joy. The suffering we endure is earning for us an eternal weight of glory that far outweighs anything we have experienced or imagined in this life.

Go after that blessing. Live with the long view. Trust that God's promise of eternal joy is every bit as assured as all of His other promises that He has already kept. Patiently endure testing and temptation because you know that if God has said it's going to be worth it, then it definitely will be.

Consider the joy of those corrected by God!
Do not despise the discipline of the Almighty when
you sin. For though he wounds, he also bandages.
He strikes, but his hands also heal.

—Job 5:17-18

Out of the Shadows

*Whatever is good and perfect is a gift coming down to us
from God our Father, who created all the lights in the
heavens. He never changes or casts a shifting shadow.*

—James 1:17

It's an encouraging exercise to occasionally pause and count our blessings. Whether it's a daily list of three things you're thankful for or an annual sharing time of God's goodness over the last year, it is helpful to raise up stones of remembrance, markers of God's faithfulness that help you endure times of suffering.

This verse reminds us that anything good in our lives is a gift from God. Even the lights in the sky, the sun and moon and stars, which are for the benefit and enjoyment of believers and nonbelievers alike, are part of God's goodness. We should get in the habit of noticing and appreciating all the beautiful things God does for us, the blessings that descend to us each day we are alive. The delicate loveliness of a flower, the cry of a newborn baby, the laughter of loved ones— these are all good gifts from God.

Yet even those good gifts fade away, and that's why the second half of this verse is such a great promise. God never changes. He doesn't shift His disposition toward us. He is always there, always good, always showering us with good and perfect gifts. So today, look for the good things. Thank God for His tender mercies that are new every morning. And let them move your heart to praise the God who never changes or casts a shifting shadow.

*The Lord God is our sun and our shield. He gives
us grace and glory. The Lord will withhold
no good thing from those who do what is right.*

—Psalm 84:11

Surely your

GOODNESS

and unfailing love

WILL PURSUE ME
ALL THE DAYS OF MY LIFE,

and I will live

in the house

of the LORD forever.

PSALM 23:6

True Wisdom

*But the wisdom from above is first of all pure.
It is also peace loving, gentle at all times, and willing
to yield to others. It is full of mercy and the fruit of
good deeds. It shows no favoritism and is always sincere.*

—James 3:17

It's easy to get confused by the messages of culture. Arguments are shrouded in terms that sound good—even biblical—and are difficult to debate against. But not every message that sounds good is true, and we have to learn to discern truth from error. These verses give us a checklist of what true wisdom consists of.

True wisdom is first of all pure. There is no hint of deception or sin. It is peace-loving and gentle, looking out for the long-term welfare of others. It is willing to yield when it is wrong, willing to listen to other viewpoints rather than asserting its own way. It is merciful and full of good deeds, looking to serve rather than be served. It does not show favoritism or prejudice, choosing instead to view every person as a bearer of God's image and equally in need of redemption. It is always sincere, not hypocritical or deceitful.

Think of the last argument you took part in, whether on social media or in the public arena or even with your coworker or spouse. Were you seeking this kind of wisdom and sharing it with others? Were your interactions pure, peaceable, gentle, willing to yield, full of mercy and goodness, sincere, and without bias or discrimination? The true test of having wisdom is whether or not you can put your name in place of "wisdom" in the verse above.

The fear of the LORD is true wisdom; to forsake evil is real understanding.

—Job 28:28

Godly Resistance

So humble yourselves before God. Resist the devil, and he will flee from you.
—James 4:7

Many Christians live with a perpetual sense of defeat. We want to do what is right, but we think we are subject to the whims of emotion or the attacks of Satan. We find ourselves falling into the same sin over and over, and eventually we stop fighting it. We think, *I'll never be able to get over this habit; I might as well just live with it.*

Scripture promises that if we resist Satan, he will flee. He has to, because Jesus won the victory and He is living inside us. We can overcome. We do have the willpower to fight temptation. We don't need to give up, because we have God's power on our side.

Our job in the battle is twofold. First, we have to humble ourselves before God. In context that means that we must admit that we are weak and that we need God's help. We can't fight the battle alone—we need God to fight in and through us in order to win. Second, we have to resist the devil. We can't be apathetic about the sin in our lives, we must root it out. We need to be so serious about living a holy life that we are willing to gouge out our eye if it is the cause of our sin and remove all access to the temptation (Mark 9:43-49).

You can stop living a defeated life. Humble yourself before God and resist the devil. If you do, God promises that Satan will flee.

Put on all of God's armor so that you will be able to stand firm
against all strategies of the devil. For we are not fighting against
flesh-and-blood enemies, but against evil rulers and
authorities of the unseen world, against mighty powers in
this dark world, and against evil spirits in the heavenly places.
—Ephesians 6:11-12

Undivided Loyalty

Come close to God, and God will come close to you.
Wash your hands, you sinners; purify your hearts,
for your loyalty is divided between God and the world.

—*James 4:8*

Yesterday's verse told us that if we resist Satan he will flee. Today's verse tells us the next step—draw close to God and He will come close to us. Once we have run away from Satan we have to choose to then run toward God. We have to change our loyalty, choosing the treasure of God Himself over all the so-called treasures the world offers.

All too often our loyalty is divided. We want the things of the world alongside the things of God. We want to have as much pleasure as we can and still call ourselves Christians. The thing is, those treasures of the world tend to take up more and more of our time. They lure us in, and before we know it, we are spending less and less time with God. We can't make it to church because we were out with friends late on Saturday night. We intended to go to small group but we had to work late. We planned to read our Bible but we're too tired.

Don't let your loyalty be divided. Come close to God, to a quiet place away from the voices of the world, and let Him draw close to you. Hear His voice above the din of culture and find out what He wants for your life.

The LORD is close to all who call on him, yes, to all who call on him in truth.
—*Psalm 145:18*

Unexpected Joy

*Now we live with great expectation, and we have a priceless
inheritance—an inheritance that is kept in heaven for you,
pure and undefiled, beyond the reach of change and decay.*

—1 Peter 1:3-4

Most of us, when we wake up in the morning, have certain expectations for the day. Maybe we make a to-do list or review our calendar. We know that there will be interruptions and surprises, but for the most part we know what to expect in the day ahead.

What we often fail to do is look ahead with great expectation to the final page in the story of our lives. This verse reminds us to live with eagerness, looking forward to the inheritance that is kept in heaven for us. It is pure and perfect and unable to change or decay. In other words, we are guaranteed that all the promises of Scripture about eternal life will come true. We will not be disappointed.

In a world where we have learned to keep our expectations low so we won't be disappointed by life, it is wonderful to know that our expectations about heaven can't be too high. In fact, it will be better than we can ever imagine. Today, while you make your plans, do the things you expect, and maneuver through the unexpected things that come up, lift your gaze to the horizon of heaven. Let yourself eagerly anticipate the final day when you will see Jesus and discover that He is better than your wildest dreams.

*And now the prize awaits me—the crown of righteousness,
which the Lord, the righteous Judge, will give me on
the day of his return. And the prize is not just for me
but for all who eagerly look forward to his appearing.*

—2 Timothy 4:8

Rebirth

For you have been born again, but not to a life that
will quickly end. Your new life will last forever
because it comes from the eternal, living word of God.

—*1 Peter 1:23*

While it is truly amazing to witness the birth of a baby, Scripture tells us that it is even more amazing to take part in spiritual rebirth. That's because physical birth isn't the beginning of true life. Ephesians 2:1 tells us we are born dead, with no spiritual heartbeat and destined for eternal death. Our physical life will quickly end and is characterized by futility and heartache. But spiritual birth, that process by which we are "born again," leads to eternal life. When we trust in Jesus for salvation, we embark on a trajectory that leads to new life that lasts forever. Perishable seed gives birth to imperishable, and mortality puts on immortality.

The source of this rebirth—the only true birth—is God's Word. We place a lot of emphasis on the Holy Spirit's work in conversion, and Jesus Himself said, "The Holy Spirit gives birth to spiritual life" (John 3:6). But here Peter only mentions the "eternal, living word of God." The Bible is a living document, and the words written there are capable of bringing rebirth to eternal life. Therefore we should set ourselves to the task of reading Scripture. As you meditate on the promise of eternal life, devote yourself to the task of reading the eternal words of God in the Bible so that you can grow in this miraculous life you have been given. Then share what you discover with others so they can find new life too.

Jesus replied, "I tell you the truth, unless you are
born again, you cannot see the Kingdom of God."

—*John 3:3*

True Identity

But you are not like that, for you are a chosen people.
You are royal priests, a holy nation, God's very own possession.
As a result, you can show others the goodness of God,
for he called you out of the darkness into his wonderful light.

—*1 Peter 2:9*

There is a stark contrast between the people who reject God and stumble (1 Peter 2:8) versus those who are chosen and set apart by God. The original readers of this verse would have immediately associated the imagery with Israel, God's chosen people down through history. Since Jesus' death and resurrection it was clear that God's people were not an ethnic race but a spiritual one. Jews and Gentiles alike who trusted in Jesus were labeled as chosen people, royal priests, a holy nation, God's very own possession.

That means that the titles in this verse are the names God calls you by, if you trust in Him. He has taken ownership of you. Yes, you chose to trust in Him by an act of your own free will, but He has made you belong. He chose you. And more than that, He has given you a job to do—tell others about His goodness and about the way He called you out of darkness into light. In other words, since you are thus beloved and honored by God, tell others how to come to Him also. Don't keep it to yourself; show off God's goodness, which is available to all peoples from all nations.

In the same way, let your good deeds shine out for all
to see, so that everyone will praise your heavenly Father.

—*Matthew 5:16*

He Bore Our Sins

*He personally carried our sins in his body on
the cross so that we can be dead to sin and live
for what is right. By his wounds you are healed.*

—*1 Peter 2:24*

Jesus willingly endured the suffering and shame of the cross—suffering so great that it caused Him to sweat drops of blood as He anticipated what He had to do—as our substitute. He took all of our sins, all of our disgrace, all the things we are ashamed of and helpless to fix, and He carried them to the cross. That word "personally" is so intimate. We can imagine Jesus lifting up the burden of our sin and taking it to the cross so that we can let all those things go. We don't have to carry them anymore because He took them for us.

Why did Jesus do this for us? First, so that we could be healed from our sin sickness and live for Him. God cares about your healing. He cares that you are stuck in sin and unable to fix what is wrong in your heart. He is concerned about your spiritual wounds and wants to bind them up as only He can.

The other reason Jesus took our sins to the cross is so that we can live for Him. And who wouldn't want to in light of this loving thing He did for us? Today, as you pick up the cross of your daily living for Jesus, do it with a grateful heart. You have the ability to pick up that joyful burden of serving God because He took the burden of your sin and healed you.

*For since our friendship with God was restored by the
death of his Son while we were still his enemies, we
will certainly be saved through the life of his Son.*

—*Romans 5:10*

Safely Home to God

Christ suffered for our sins once for all time. He never sinned,
but he died for sinners to bring you safely home to God.
He suffered physical death, but he was raised to life in the Spirit.

—*1 Peter 3:18*

The theological truth presented here is one that is probably well worn for you. Because Jesus lived a sinless life, He was able to be the once-for-all sacrifice for our sins. We no longer have to offer sacrifices each day; we can be saved once and forever because Jesus took our place at the cross. The price of our sins—physical death—is now paid so we can be raised to new life in the Spirit, just like Jesus was.

But this is more than theological fact, it is personal. We see that in the phrase "safely home to God." Do you hear God's love in those words? Your home is with God. That is where you belong, and He wants you there. Like a loving parent who misses their child when they are away and longs for them to return and sleep under the same roof, God is waiting for you.

More than that, God has taken on the responsibility to get you home. He will bring you safely to His side. What a comfort that is for the prodigals who stray from God or those who experience the failing of their physical body. God has everything under control. He died to bring us safely home, and He won't rest until it's done.

There is more than enough room in my Father's home. If this
were not so, would I have told you that I am going to
prepare a place for you? When everything is ready, I will come
and get you, so that you will always be with me where I am.

—*John 14:2-3*

Cared For

Give all your worries and cares to God, for he cares about you.

—1 Peter 5:7

On any given day, we carry around a lot of burdens. We are worried about our health, our future, our finances. We have concerns for our children, our aging parents, and our dear friends. Sometimes we don't even know what is weighing us down, only that our hearts are heavy. There's a lot of background noise in our heads and hearts, things that weigh us down even if we aren't consciously thinking about them.

Here is the promise: You have a place you can go with those worries and cares—you can take them to God. He cares about you, and that means He cares about the burdens you're carrying. The things that bother you bother Him simply because He loves you. And best of all, He has the power to do something about all the things you're worried about and the wisdom to have a perfect plan. You can take the burdens from your heart and lay them at the cross with the knowledge that He will take care of them—and you.

So turn your worries and cares over to God instead of turning them over in your mind. Let Him handle the things you can't. He is ready to take over the heavy lifting for you and replace the overwhelming burdens you're carrying around with His light ones. Let Him care for you.

Jesus said, "Come to me, all of you who are weary and carry heavy burdens, and I will give you rest. Take my yoke upon you. Let me teach you, because I am humble and gentle at heart, and you will find rest for your souls. For my yoke is easy to bear, and the burden I give you is light."

—Matthew 11:28-30

Lifted Up

*In his kindness God called you to share in his eternal
glory by means of Christ Jesus. So after you have suffered
a little while, he will restore, support, and strengthen you,
and he will place you on a firm foundation.*

—*1 Peter 5:10*

When life is hard, our suffering can so obscure our view of God that we think He is out to get us. We start to believe the lies of Satan that God doesn't really love us, doesn't care about our suffering, or is powerless over evil. This verse reminds us that God is kind all the time, even when we are suffering.

God is first of all kind because He has called us to share in His eternal glory. When the suffering of this life is over, we will be with Him. Through Jesus we have an eternal hope that can get us through the hard times. But even in the midst of our suffering God is kind, and that is the second part of the verse. God restores, supports, and strengthens us. He lifts us up and gives us a firm foundation. In other words, God helps us to stay standing even when the tragedies of life try to push us down.

If you're feeling beaten down by life lately, let this verse give you hope. God is kind, even in this. He has given you an eternal hope, and even now, in the middle of the mess, He is at work. Look for the restoration, for the support that so often comes through the help of those around you, for the supernatural strength that God gives by His Spirit, and for the firm foundation of God's promises that are sure and secure no matter what happens in this life.

*We know that God causes everything to work
together for the good of those who love God and are
called according to his purpose for them.*

—*Romans 8:28*

Great and Precious Promises

*By his divine power, God has given us everything we need
for living a godly life. . . . He has given us great and precious
promises . . . that enable you to share his divine nature and
escape the world's corruption caused by human desires.*

—*2 Peter 1:3-4*

Perhaps the beginning of this verse is familiar to you. It is often used as a rallying cry to a life of obedience because it promises us that God has given us everything we need to obey Him, everything we need to withstand temptation and do the right thing. We have all the knowledge and all the power we need to live a godly life, and therefore we are culpable for the areas in which we fall short.

But here's the part you may not have considered before: God has, through His promises, enabled us to share in His divine nature. We are not left alone in this task of living a godly life—we have the promises of God to motivate us and the power of God to move us. We can escape the corruption of the world and our own evil desires because God's power lives within us to overcome.

Whatever sin you are battling today, whatever the struggles of your heart, know that God is empowering you to conquer them. He has given you His own divine nature that provides a way of escape. So go ahead and fight the good fight with all that is within you, but know that you are not fighting alone—God Himself is wielding the sword of truth and the Holy Spirit is standing guard.

*Put on your new nature, and be renewed as you
learn to know your Creator and become like him.*

—*Colossians 3:10*

Responding to the Promises

In view of all this, make every effort to respond to God's promises.
—2 Peter 1:5

If you've been following this devotional, you have been thinking about God's promises every day for almost a year. But while meditating on the promises is helpful, each of us must by faith appropriate them for ourselves. We must hold them close to our hearts and live by them or they won't do us any good. God offers the invitation, but we must respond.

The practical result of responding to God's promises is found in the previous verses, the ones we looked at yesterday. When we respond to God's promises we take hold of His power to live a godly life. The Christian life isn't about pulling ourselves up by the bootstraps and trying to live the way God wants us to; it's about appropriating God's nature—His power and His desires. We live a godly life by putting our trust in God's promises and letting them change the way we view the world and live in it.

But while God has initiated the process by making the promises and enabling us to share His divine nature (2 Peter 1:4), we must put forth every effort. Responding to God's promises involves 1) knowing what they are by studying the Bible; 2) believing that they are true; and 3) living in such a way that we are aligning our thoughts, attitudes, and actions with God's desires for us. In other words, we must respond to God's covenant love by obeying the commands of Scripture that precede and follow from God's promises.

I pray that your hearts will be flooded with light so that you can understand the confident hope he has given to those he called—his holy people who are his rich and glorious inheritance.
—Ephesians 1:18

Confession

*But if we confess our sins to him, he is faithful and just to
forgive us our sins and to cleanse us from all wickedness.*

—1 John 1:9

Confession is such a holy moment. It is when we open up and are totally honest about who we are and what we have done. Afterwards we experience a sense of peace because we have been known and accepted despite our shortcomings. Yet it is our nature to avoid confession. We are proud creatures, and we don't like to dwell on our failures. We would much rather bask in our successes and ignore the parts of our character that make us feel inferior.

The Bible tells us that confession is our access point to forgiveness and new life. Without it we can't even begin the life of faith, let alone move forward in it. Here we are promised that when we confess, God responds with faithfulness and justice. It is part of His nature and character to always listen and respond in the same way, with fairness. We don't have to wonder if this time we've messed up too badly for Him to forgive us.

The result of God's faithfulness and justice is that He not only forgives, He also cleanses us. Our record is wiped clean and we are supernaturally transformed. The Greek word used is the word from which we get "catharsis," and it is often used in Scripture to refer to healing from disease. When we confess, making an honest appraisal of the ways we have fallen short of God's standard, God always responds with forgiveness, restoration, and full healing of our sin disease.

*Because we have these promises, dear friends, let us cleanse
ourselves from everything that can defile our body or spirit.
And let us work toward complete holiness because we fear God.*

—2 Corinthians 7:1

Our Advocate

*My dear children, I am writing this to you so that you will not sin.
But if anyone does sin, we have an advocate who pleads our case
before the Father. He is Jesus Christ, the one who is truly
righteous. He himself is the sacrifice that atones for our sins—
and not only our sins but the sins of all the world.*

—1 John 2:1-2

A few verses after the promise that God is faithful and just to forgive us and cleanse us if we confess our sins, we read this promise about the mechanics of how that happens. When we sin, Jesus pleads our case before the Father. He stands in the gap for us, acting as our legal advocate to remind God the Father that we have been washed clean and therefore need not suffer the consequences of our sin. Mercy is continually granted to us based on the advocacy of Jesus.

How can Jesus make this promise? Because He Himself is the sacrifice for our sins. He was there, He paid it, and now it is done. Jesus is not arguing our case based on our own merits (praise God!), but on His. We sinned, but He did not, and He asks the Father to impute His righteousness to our account. The truly righteous One is pleading on our behalf before the Father, saying that His perfect life was given for ours and so it is as if we have not sinned.

When you think of Jesus pleading your case before the Father, the only logical response is to do what is commanded in the first part of the verse—don't sin. Strive for the holy life that Jesus bought for you with His precious blood. But when you sin, know that you have an advocate with the Father, and therefore you have boundless forgiveness.

*Who then will condemn us? No one—for Christ Jesus
died for us and was raised to life for us, and he is sitting
in the place of honor at God's right hand, pleading for us.*

—Romans 8:34

Cravings

*And this world is fading away, along with everything that people
crave. But anyone who does what pleases God will live forever.*

—1 John 2:17

Cravings are a funny thing. They usually start out with a taste of something, and before you know it you feel like you have no power over your desire for it. The word used here is also translated "lust, desire, or passion," and it usually refers to the desire for something that is forbidden. Sometimes our desire is for something good, such as food, but when the desire gets to the level of a craving it becomes an idol. John lists physical pleasure, lust for possessions, and pride in achievements as the cravings that rule in people's hearts.

Here is God's promise: The world is fading away, and it will take with it everything that people crave. Whether your desire is for food or sex or fun or success—all of it is fading away. But there is one thing that will last forever, and that is our relationship with God. Seek after what lasts forever. Set your affections there. In the words of John, "Do not love this world nor the things it offers you" (1 John 2:15). Instead, love God Himself.

Our cravings are set by our habits. When we eat healthy foods we start to crave healthy foods. When we study God's Word we start to desire more and more of it. Recalibrate your habits toward the things of God and you will begin to crave more of Him rather than more of this fast-disintegrating world.

*Whom have I in heaven but you? I desire you more than anything
on earth. My health may fail, and my spirit may grow weak,
but God remains the strength of my heart; he is mine forever.*

—Psalm 73:25-26

Loved Much

*See how very much our Father loves us, for he
calls us his children, and that is what we are!*

—*1 John 3:1*

There is such tenderness in these words. "See how very much our Father loves us!" He loves us enough to make us His children and lavish on us all the love of a father for his child. You have been adopted by Father God. You belong. And you are loved so very much.

The contrast set forth in 1 John is between those who are God's children and those who are not. In earthly families we might say, "In the Smith family we don't do that" or "You belong to the Johnson family, and that means you have these responsibilities and privileges." Likewise, the family of God has certain characteristics that mark them. Not everyone belongs to God, and John offers various criteria by which we can distinguish who is part of His family and who is not.

The key comes in 1 John 5:1, where it says, "Everyone who believes that Jesus is the Christ has become a child of God. And everyone who loves the Father loves his children, too." Belief leads to adoption, and adoption leads to love for others. God doesn't ask us to obey first, He asks us to come into the family and then act as befits a member of the family. It is an invitation to love borne out of an invitation to be loved. Taste and see God's great love for you, let Him lavish Fatherly affection on you, and then show that love to others. That is what it means to be called God's child.

*To all who believed him and accepted him, he gave
the right to become children of God. They are reborn—
not with a physical birth resulting from human
passion or plan, but a birth that comes from God.*

—*John 1:12-13*

More than Our Feelings

*Dear friends, if we don't feel guilty, we can come to God
with bold confidence. And we will receive from him whatever
we ask because we obey him and do the things that please him.*

—1 John 3:21-22

There is reassurance in the verses just before this that if there is spiritual fruit in our lives—if we are growing in love for others—we have assurance of God's forgiveness and our position before Him. If at times we feel guilty for our sin, we need not linger there. We are forgiven, and "even if we feel guilty, God is greater than our feelings" (1 John 3:20).

The logical conclusion of this assurance is that we will come to God with bold confidence. This is the confidence of a child who knows that their Father always wants to listen to them. It is the confidence of knowing we belong to God and that He will keep us to the end. And this confidence causes us to pray differently. For one thing, we pray with confidence that because God loves us, He is listening and responding. For another thing, we pray with the heart of one who is living in obedience. It is not that our obedience earns favor with God, but rather our obedience means that we are asking things in line with God's will. The more we know Him, the more we obey Him, and the more we obey, the more we know what kinds of things to pray for.

Spend time in prayer today, imagining yourself in the throne room of your dear Father. Ask Him for what's on your heart, and know with confidence that you will receive whatever you ask when you ask for the things that please Him.

*If you remain in me and my words remain in you, you
may ask for anything you want, and it will be granted!*

—John 15:7

Victorious

*But you belong to God, my dear children. You have already
won a victory over those people, because the Spirit who
lives in you is greater than the spirit who lives in the world.*

—1 John 4:4

John has just told his readers about the Antichrist and false prophets. We are living in scary days when it's not always clear who is telling the truth and who is not. In these uncertain times, we have three promises to assure us.

There is first the comfort of identity. We are God's dear children, under His fatherly care. We are protected and secure in our relationship with Him. In addition, we have victory over the evil in the world. Jesus' completed act of redemption is our assurance of final victory. At the last day, we will stand before the throne of God fully absolved. Finally, the Holy Spirit who lives in us is more powerful than any evil spirit. Satan can attack us, but we have a greater power within that will overcome—the power of God Himself that raises the dead and calms the storm and moves mountains.

The presence of evil in the world is very real, and it can seem overwhelming at times. Praise God for these foundational promises that help us face down evil and untruth with courage. We don't need to fear evil; we can battle it with all the courage of someone who knows that they will win.

*For we are not fighting against flesh-and-blood enemies, but against
evil rulers and authorities of the unseen world, against mighty powers
in this dark world, and against evil spirits in the heavenly places.*

—Ephesians 6:12

The Higher Way

*And we are confident that he hears us whenever
we ask for anything that pleases him. And since we
know he hears us when we make our requests, we
also know that he will give us what we ask for.*

—1 John 5:14-15

There is a tightly woven logical argument in these verses. It goes like this: If we ask for things that are in line with God's character and purposes—things that God would give His stamp of approval to—then we know that He hears us. And if He hears us, then we know that He will give us what we ask for. This is the same promise and condition that Jesus gave in John 14:13 and 15:7.

There is great freedom in these verses. It should certainly motivate us to make ourselves students of God's Word and His ways so that we know what kinds of things please Him. But if we get it wrong (and we often will), God will still do whatever is in His holy will. He will do what is best. If we ask for the wrong thing, He will still do the right thing.

There is such love here. God hears us. He cares. And He answers according to what is best for us. Let these promises inform and energize your prayers today. Be confident in your requests for the things that please God, for prayers of restoration and repentance and Kingdom advancement. Know that if you ask God for wisdom and power to do what is right, He will gladly answer. And when your prayers come with answers you didn't hope for, humbly submit to God's will, knowing that His ways are higher than yours and His love for you is immeasurable.

*We know that God doesn't listen to sinners, but he
is ready to hear those who worship him and do his will.*

—John 9:31

From Failure to Forgiveness

We know that God's children do not make a practice of sinning, for God's Son holds them securely, and the evil one cannot touch them.

—1 John 5:18

It's common for Christians, even those who have followed Jesus for many years, to occasionally have doubts. We wonder, *If I am truly saved, why do I keep sinning? What about the Christian leaders I know who have fallen away from the faith—if it can happen to them, will it happen to me?* This verse offers the promise to assuage all such doubts.

God's children will, over time, see increasing victory over sin. We know this is true because Jesus holds us securely. Even if it feels like we are subject to the powers of evil, even if it feels like we are in a constant state of failure, even if it feels like God cannot possibly still love us . . . the truth is, Jesus is holding us in His grasp and will never let us go. We are safe in His hand. The world is under Satan's control (1 John 5:19), but we are not.

Take heart, then, when you struggle with doubt or sin. Your failures cannot change your identity as a child of God. You belong to Him as part of His family, and He will not let you go. More than that, He will help you grow more and more into His likeness so that you can overcome sin. The progress may be slow, but it is there.

I give them eternal life, and they will never perish. No one can snatch them away from me, for my Father has given them to me, and he is more powerful than anyone else. No one can snatch them from the Father's hand.

—John 10:28-29

Hope for the Prodigals

Now all glory to God, who is able to keep you from falling away and will bring you with great joy into his glorious presence without a single fault.

—Jude 1:24

Here is another promise about where we are heading, and it is really a whole bundle of promises wrapped up into one. First, God will keep us from falling away. We may try our best to run away from God, but if we have truly trusted in Him for salvation then He will keep us. What comfort this is for those who have spiritual prodigals in their lives. God keeps those who are His.

In the original Greek the next thing we are promised is faultlessness. It could also be translated "unblamable." In ourselves we are hopelessly flawed, but in Christ we will stand before God totally free from all blemishes, unable to be rebuked for anything. We are, in other words, clothed with the righteousness of Christ. The Day of Judgment will be for us a day of triumph.

Finally, we are promised great joy in God's presence. There is the joy of being without fault, but this goes deeper than that—it is the joy of knowing and being known, the joy of finally being where we have always belonged. This side of heaven standing before God is a little terrifying, but when we actually see Him we will feel nothing but joy because we will be at home with the lover of our souls forever.

Await the mercy of our Lord Jesus Christ, who will bring you eternal life. In this way, you will keep yourselves safe in God's love.

—Jude 1:21

From Beginning to End

"I am the Alpha and the Omega—the beginning and the end,"
says the Lord God. "I am the one who is, who always was,
and who is still to come—the Almighty One."

—*Revelation 1:8*

This is the promise that gives ultimate comfort. When life is hard, God is the Alpha and Omega. When things don't make sense, He is the One who always was, and who is still to come. When everything seems to be falling apart, He is there. And so everything is still okay, even if it doesn't look like it right now.

Really this verse is a promise that God is enough to build a life on. He is A to Z and everything in between. He was before the world began and will be after it ends, from eternity past to eternity future. He is the beginning and end of all things—of wisdom and love and justice and goodness and mercy. He is everything. Best of all, He is coming back! God hasn't left us in our pain and hopelessness, He has promised to return so He can dwell among us. And He is the Almighty King, so everything He says will come to pass.

This is the God you love and serve if you are a Christian. He is more than enough for all your questions, for all your yesterdays and tomorrows, for every tear and every joy. He is enough for today and He will be enough for tomorrow— in fact, He is already in the tomorrow just as He was in the yesterday. Therefore, you can trust Him with everything.

He existed before anything else, and he holds all creation together.

—*Colossians 1:17*

The Keys of Death

I am the living one. I died, but look—I am alive forever
and ever! And I hold the keys of death and the grave.

—*Revelation 1:18*

This verse takes us back to Jesus' death on the cross. Remember that at the time, Jesus' followers were dejected. Their dreams had been crushed when Jesus—the One they hoped was the promised Messiah—had been crucified like a common criminal. Everything they had put their hope in had turned out to be a lie. If only they could have looked ahead a few days to Jesus' triumphant resurrection, they would have seen that His death was not defeat but victory. He had gained for them, and for us, far more than an earthly kingdom.

Jesus died in His body, but He rose to eternal life because He paid the price for our sin. Now instead of Satan holding power over us, like he did between the Fall and the Resurrection, Jesus has obtained the keys of death and the grave, and that means He is the One with all the power. What immense comfort this is in the face of death.

Because Jesus lives, you also shall live. Put your faith in the risen Christ, trust in Him for your salvation, and you, too, will have victory over sin and death. Your physical death will be the beginning of eternal life as you rise to meet Jesus in the air and share in His eternal glory.

Since we have been united with him in his
death, we will also be raised to life as he was.

—*Romans 6:5*

Holding Out for a Crown

I am coming soon. Hold on to what you have,
so that no one will take away your crown.

—*Revelation 3:11*

When parents leave their young children for a time, they reassure them that they will be back soon, and urge them to behave for the babysitter who is taking care of them in the meantime. This verse is sort of the spiritual equivalent of that. Jesus is reminding the church in the ancient city of Philadelphia, and us as well, that His return is imminent and will come suddenly. In light of that, we must hold fast to our faith even in the midst of suffering.

The church in Philadelphia was in desperate need of this exhortation. They were oppressed and under great pressure to give up the faith, yet they did not deny Jesus. Because of their perseverance, God promised to protect them. Even so, they would have to hold fast. The promises—"I will protect you" (Revelation 3:10) and "I am coming soon"—are balanced with a command to hold on. Don't give up. Keep clinging to hope even when it's hard.

It is challenging to persevere in the face of suffering, but we have the promise of eternal life to help us stay strong. Ours is not a blind faith or a baseless hope, it is secured by the promise that God is with us and is returning soon to make everything right. So today, if you're feeling pressured and discouraged, take heart. You just need to hang on a little longer, because Jesus is coming soon. And in the meantime, He is right there with you, holding you fast.

And now the prize awaits me—the crown of righteousness,
which the Lord, the righteous Judge, will give me on the
day of his return. And the prize is not just for me but
for all who eagerly look forward to his appearing.

—*2 Timothy 4:8*

A Meal between Friends

*Look! I stand at the door and knock. If you hear my voice and open
the door, I will come in, and we will share a meal together as friends.*
—*Revelation 3:20*

At its heart, the Christian faith is an invitation to a relationship with the Almighty. That's why Jesus came to dwell among us. These words of Jesus to the church in Laodicea remind us of the relationship Jesus desires to have with us. The church had become lukewarm, not really standing for anything or recognizing their need for God. They were apathetic and indifferent toward their faith.

These words, then, are an invitation to anyone whose faith has grown cold and distant. Jesus wants relationship with you. He is standing at the door of your heart, not forcing His way in but asking to share a meal as friends. The word here for *stand* is a prolonged form of the word, often used in conjunction with covenants. In other words, God isn't going anywhere. He will keep on waiting until you let Him in. And when you do open the door to Him, He promises to come in and live in relationship with you.

Perhaps you want to know God, but He still seems distant. Hear these words of invitation as a cry of love—God wants to share a meal with you. Perhaps you are going through the motions, acting like a Christian out of habit, but if you're honest you're feeling a little apathetic. If that is you, hear these words as a call to renew your first love for God. Let Him come in to all the closed-off places in your heart and love you.

*Jesus replied, "All who love me will do what I say. My Father will
love them, and we will come and make our home with each of them."*
—*John 14:23*

Eternal Song

[Jesus'] blood has ransomed people for God from every tribe and language and people and nation.

—*Revelation 5:9*

These words are part of the new song that is sung by the elders when Jesus opens the final seal on the scroll. They have always been worshiping, but at the moment described here they sing a new song because Jesus has been found worthy to open the scroll that outlines God's plan for the world. They worship Him because He suffered for our sake and through His suffering has redeemed a people for God.

God's redeemed people are described here in terms of their magnificent diversity. Every ethnicity and people group is represented; none is left out. Christ's sacrifice is for all, and His will is that there are representatives from every nation on earth worshiping at God's throne. Ethnic diversity is part of the eternal worship of God, the very purpose for which we were created.

This is the heart-song of missions. The reason we go out into all the world and preach to all nations the name of Jesus is because we know that throughout eternity we will be worshiping at the throne of God with a whole rainbow of ethnicities, and we need to make sure they know they are invited. This is why Jesus came to earth, why He lived among us and demonstrated how to love one another, why He suffered and died and rose again—so that throughout eternity there will be a beautifully diverse choir of worshipers declaring God's worthiness.

After this I saw a vast crowd, too great to count, from every nation and tribe and people and language, standing in front of the throne and before the Lamb. They were clothed in white robes and held palm branches in their hands.

—*Revelation 7:9*

Final Reign

*Then the seventh angel blew his trumpet, and there were loud voices
shouting in heaven: "The world has now become the Kingdom
of our Lord and of his Christ,and he will reign forever and ever."*
—*Revelation 11:15*

We can't quite imagine how glorious this event will be. A loud trumpet blast followed by spontaneous praise as all of heaven erupts in worship. The affirmation that God has taken possession of the world. And the promise that His reign will never end. This is our hope, the moment we are waiting for, and it will be more glorious than our imagining.

Right now this world is the kingdom of Satan. Even though Christ has won the victory and nothing happens outside of God's permission, the truth is that much of our life is characterized by sin, death, and futility. Things are not as they should be, and we feel the sting of that often.

That's why this promise is so important for us to keep in front of our minds and hearts. Worship is the activity we will be about for eternity, and therefore is what we should be about now. The core of worship is affirming what is true about God, and this is what is true: He will return to make this world His own, and He will reign forever and ever. His rule will have no end. Meditate on this glorious moment of triumph, worship God for it, and then live in the joyful assurance that this day will be here soon.

*Then I heard again what sounded like the shout of a vast crowd
or the roar of mighty ocean waves or the crash of loud thunder:
"Praise the LORD! For the Lord our God, the Almighty, reigns.
Let us be glad and rejoice, and let us give honor to him."*
—*Revelation 19:6-7*

An End to Sorrow

He will wipe every tear from their eyes, and there will be no more
death or sorrow or crying or pain. All these things are gone forever.
—*Revelation 21:4*

This might be the most quoted verse in times of sorrow, and rightly so. Human history, with all of its suffering, is hurtling toward that day when all crying and pain will cease—what a comfort for those times when we wonder if we'll ever stop crying.

There is a tender intimacy in these verses. Jesus Himself wipes every tear from our eyes. He first takes away—forever—all sources of grief, and then He reaches out with His nail-scarred hand and wipes away every trace that such sorrow even existed.

This is the Christian's hope. One day there will be no more death, no more goodbyes, no more broken relationships, no more abuse, no more sickness, no more pain. As you live the earthly journey that includes so many of those things, look with hope to that day when they will cease to exist. Endure them now as one who knows that the reign of Satan is coming to an end, and with it everything that makes us cry. And in the meantime, entrust yourself to the Savior who has died to make a way for you to experience the pure joy of the new heavens and the new earth.

You keep track of all my sorrows. You have collected all my
tears in your bottle. You have recorded each one in your book.
—*Psalm 56:8*

Everything New

The one sitting on the throne said, "Look, I am making everything new!"
—Revelation 21:5

At the end of the calendar year we often take stock of our lives. What habits do we want to break, and which do we want to begin? What things have worn out their purpose and need to be set aside in favor of something new?

That is sort of what Jesus is doing in this verse. The world is so tarnished by sin, so destroyed by evil, that it needs to be renovated. In the last day, the things we have wrecked with sin will be remade in perfection. Everything is made new and restored to God's original intention so that He can dwell with His people.

When God remakes the world it will be glorious and perfect, and of course the remaking we might do in our own lives will never be perfect. But that doesn't mean we shouldn't try. In fact, when we work toward redemption and restoration in our lives we are reflecting God's image and working with His purposes. So go ahead and make your resolutions this year. Don't give up on the holy task of remaking your life more and more in the image of God. But as you do so, rest in the hope that one day Jesus Himself will do it once and for all. Where you fall short, He will not. Where you are disappointed and where you disappoint others, He will make up the lack. Life now will never be quite what it should be, but one day it will.

I am about to do something new. See, I have already begun!
Do you not see it? I will make a pathway through
the wilderness. I will create rivers in the dry wasteland.
—Isaiah 43:19

Alpha and Omega

And he also said, "It is finished! I am the Alpha and the Omega—
the Beginning and the End. To all who are thirsty I will give freely
from the springs of the water of life. All who are victorious will inherit
all these blessings, and I will be their God, and they will be my children."
—Revelation 21:6-7

"It is finished!" These are the same words Jesus uttered from the cross (John 19:30), and they remind us that all of history is built around Creator God making a way for us to be with Him. When Jesus paid the penalty for our sins to make that possible, the task was finished. But of course then He went back to heaven for a time, leaving us with more time to build the eternal church—people from every tongue and tribe and nation who will be with Him forever.

At the end of time, when God is finished making everything new, there will be a final "It is finished." This is the fulfillment of the covenant promise made throughout Scripture: He will be our God and we will be His people, the inheritors of His blessing.

There is more here than just the promise that redemption will be complete and all of God's promises will be fulfilled. God also promises the water of life—unhindered access to Jesus, the living water who satisfies our every longing. Jesus is all the refreshment and life that we are seeking, and when we satisfy ourselves in Him we have springs of living water bubbling up inside of us so that others can find life in Him too. We are offered free and ready access to complete satisfaction, utter joy, and eternal life. These are indeed wonderful blessings!

Those who drink the water I give will never be thirsty again. It
becomes a fresh, bubbling spring within them, giving them eternal life.
—John 4:14

The Lamb on the Throne

No longer will there be a curse upon anything. For the throne of God and of the Lamb will be there, and his servants will worship him. And they will see his face, and his name will be written on their foreheads. And there will be no night there—no need for lamps or sun—for the Lord God will shine on them. And they will reign forever and ever.

—Revelation 22:3-5

Here at last is the promise to end all promises. The curse uttered against Adam and passed on to all of humanity has been lifted. God is on His throne, and we have been given the right to worship Him there, gazing at His beauty full-on, with no barrier between us. His name is written on our foreheads, declaring that we belong to Him. The relationship that began when we put our faith in Christ has reached its end—we are standing before the throne of God clothed in white. What a glorious hope this is.

God is so glorious, so brilliant in His purity, that there is no other light needed. We will live in perpetual sunshine, like the best day of summer vacation only even better, because we will be in the presence of God.

This is the eternal destiny of those who love God, who have His name written on their hearts. This is the experience even now of those who have died in Christ. This is the promise of God, and it is beautiful and glorious and awesome. Let this future hope fill your vision and occupy your thoughts as you live for Jesus.

The Lamb on the throne will be their Shepherd. He will lead them to springs of life-giving water. And God will wipe every tear from their eyes.

—Revelation 7:17

About the Authors

Nancy Taylor has spent the past 18 years raising her brood of five children while maintaining an active freelance writing and editing schedule. Born and raised in Wheaton, Illinois, she is a graduate of Wheaton College with a degree in English and Christian Education.

When she isn't writing or driving the kids to music lessons and activities, she enjoys traveling (especially with her husband, Jeremy), playing board games, and creating jewelry.

Chris Johnsen has been involved in the Christian Publishing Industry for more than 45 years.

During his career he has been the dynamic driving force behind the creation and distribution of countless best-selling Christian books, Bibles and innovative gift products. He received the CBA Lifetime International Achievement Award in 2017 in recognition of his outstanding service in the Christian book industry and unwavering commitment to further the Gospel around the world.